SCHOOL LEADERSHIP
for Results

SCHOOL LEADERSHIP
for *Results*

Shifting the Focus of Leader Evaluation

Beverly G. Carbaugh
Robert J. Marzano
Michael D. Toth

With:
Kathy Houpt
Tzeporaw Sahadeo-Turner

Learning SciencesInternational

1400 Centrepark Blvd, Suite 1000
West Palm Beach, FL 33401
717.845.6300

email: pub@learningsciences.com
learningsciences.com

Printed in the United States of America

20   19   18   17   16   15   3   4   5

Publisher's Cataloging-in-Publication Data

Carbaugh, Beverly G.
    School leadership for results : shifting the focus of leader evaluation / Beverly G. Carbaugh, Robert J. Marzano, [and] Michael D. Toth.
        pages cm
    ISBN: 978-1-941112-10-6 (pbk.)
    1. School administrators—Handbooks, manuals, etc.   2. Educational leadership.   3. School personnel management.   I. Marzano, Robert J.   II. Toth, Michael D.   III. Title.
LB2805 .C266 2014
    371.2'011—dc23
                                                                                                    [2014958393]

This book is dedicated to the many courageous, passionate school leaders we have met and worked with, and to the next generation of teachers and leaders who continue the work of creating schools of excellence.

Table of Contents

Acknowledgments

Learning Sciences International would like to thank the following:

John E. Ash
Principal
Central Magnet School
Murfreesboro, Tennessee

Paul R. Gausman
Superintendent of Schools
Sioux City Community School District
Sioux City, Iowa

Diane Hampel
Staff Developer
Marzano Center
West Palm Beach, Florida

Michael J. Hobin
Principal
Coventry High School
Coventry, Rhode Island

David D. McDonald
Principal
Northwest Middle School
Greenville, South Carolina

Tracy L. Ocasio
Staff Developer
Marzano Center
West Palm Beach, Florida

David Pennington
Superintendent
Ponca City Public Schools
Ponca City, Oklahoma

Ria A. Schmidt
Staff Developer
Marzano Center
West Palm Beach, Florida

Shirley Simmons
Assistant Superintendent
Norman Public Schools
Norman, Oklahoma

Jared C. Wastler
Assistant Principal
Liberty High School
Eldersburg, Maryland

About the Authors

Dr. Beverly G. Carbaugh, Senior Adviser and Vice President, Learning Sciences Marzano Center

Beverly Carbaugh, EdD, specializes in school- and district-level leadership. She is coauthor of white papers and the district leadership model with Dr. Robert Marzano. Before joining Learning Sciences International, she was Deputy Superintendent of Florida's Osceola County School district. She began her career in 1979 as a teacher and served as a principal in Tampa, Florida, of Mintz Elementary; charter principal of the National Blue Ribbon School, Colleen Bevis Elementary in Lithia, Florida; and principal of Tomlin Middle School in Plant City, Florida.

Dr. Carbaugh's expertise includes executive leadership in school administration, human resources, and business/finance. She also has extensive experience in professional development and presenting at state and national forums. She earned her Doctorate of Education in Education Leadership at the University of South Florida and her BS in Elementary Education from the University of Arizona.

Dr. Robert J. Marzano, Executive Director, Learning Sciences Marzano Center

Robert Marzano, PhD, is a nationally recognized education researcher, speaker, trainer, and author of more than 30 books and 150 articles on topics such as instruction, assessment, writing and implementing standards, cognition, effective leadership, and school intervention. His practical translations of the most current research and theory into classroom strategies are widely practiced internationally by both teachers and administrators. Dr. Marzano serves as an adviser for Learning Sciences Marzano Center research and pilot projects.

Dr. Marzano has partnered with Learning Sciences International to offer the Marzano Teacher Evaluation Model, the Marzano School Leadership Evaluation Model, and the Marzano Center Instructional Support Personnel and District Leader Evaluation Models. Dr. Marzano received his doctorate from the University of Washington.

Michael D. Toth, Chief Executive Officer, Learning Sciences International

Michael Toth, nationally acclaimed e-learning and performance-management pioneer for K–12 education professionals, leads the efforts of Learning Sciences International to continually pioneer adult learning methodologies for online acquisition, application, and retention of knowledge. His team has created standards using cognitive load theory for instructional designers and graphic designers. Mr. Toth was a faculty member at Indiana University of Pennsylvania, where he was a leader of the university's research and development teams, as well as a grant director. He also led the National Center for the Profession of Teaching, where he presided over nearly 140,000 education professionals and increased grant funding by 2,600 percent. Mr. Toth is a national presenter and frequent coauthor with Dr. Robert Marzano.

Kathy Houpt

Kathy Houpt, EdD, has been deeply involved in multiple aspects of K–12 education for more than forty years, beginning as a substitute teacher and bilingual teaching assistant, then a middle school teacher, and subsequently a principal at Northeast Elementary School in Danville, Illinois. She received her Doctorate in Educational Administration.

Tzeporaw Sahadeo-Turner

Tzeporaw Sahadeo-Turner, MSEd, has made effective pedagogy and student achievement the primary focuses of her career. She has held roles as a high school science teacher, an eighth-grade comprehensive science teacher, and an administrator. She received a Master's degree in Educational Leadership and in Public Health.

Preface

The more crucial role of the principal is as head learner, engaging in the most important enterprise of the schoolhouse—experiencing, displaying, modeling, and celebrating what it is hoped and expected that teachers and pupils will do.
—Roland Barth (1990)

This book takes as its foundation a straightforward premise: school leaders are crucial to the success of schools. That doesn't mean, in any sense, that school leaders can or should go it alone. In fact, although educators often take it for granted, it's worth repeating a truism: *We are all—emphatically—in this together.*

More than ever, research and practice in K–12 education is showing that no one individual, department, or job function is responsible for the success of our students. Instead, schooling is a complex web of interdependencies that crosses from the teacher's classroom to the school leader's office, from legislative session to district building to school board meeting, and into the homes and lives of students and their parents. This understanding, that no one person or idea or reform effort—no matter how brilliant—can "fix" what's wrong with American education, should challenge school administrators to examine our role as school leaders.

Many K–12 educators recognize the relationship between school leader practice and student learning, the link between the daily decisions the school leader makes and the success of each and every student in the classroom. While school leaders' direct interactions with students in or out of the classroom may be motivating, inspiring, instructive, or otherwise influential, most of the school leader's impact is indirect—that is, mediated through teachers and others. However, school leaders do influence teachers directly, and teachers, in turn, impact student learning.

What *has* been difficult to achieve is charting a clear course *to ensure that school leaders have the support, training, vision, and tools to facilitate performing at the highest levels of effectiveness.*

The recent state and national reform efforts that have overhauled teacher and school leader evaluation systems have revealed the flaws in our old ways of thinking about school improvement, especially the cherished belief that excellence can be mandated from the top down, or one dynamic individual with the right blend of personal characteristics can single-handedly transform a district. What we are learning from our new evaluation systems, as district after district struggles with rapid implementation and all the bumps and slides that installing new systems entails, is that first of all, change is *hard*. In fact, without the cooperation and committed collaboration of the majority of stakeholders in the system, and without a shared focus, common goals, and agreement about best practices, change is not just hard; it's impossible.

Why the School Leader?

The school leader has always stood as the man or woman with a foot in both worlds—the person with direct personal connections to teachers, students, and parents, on the one hand, and who is accountable to district leaders and board members, on the other. The school leader is buffer and fulcrum, translator and adviser—the transformationalist who takes the dreams and challenges of policy and makes them practicable in real, working classrooms. Years of reliable K–12 research reflects the importance of this vital position—three decades of studies have confirmed not only the critical nature of the school leader's role but also his or her measurable impact on increasing student achievement.

The Wallace Foundation, in its 2007 report *Education Leadership: A Bridge to School Reform* (DeVita, Colvin, Darling-Hammond, & Haycock, 2007), supports the conclusions of many previous researchers in affirming the direct and indirect links between school leader practices and student achievement (Goldring, Porter, Murphy, Elliott, & Cravens, 2007; Leithwood, Seashore-Louis, Anderson, & Wahlstrom, 2004; Marzano, Waters, & McNulty, 2005; Waters, Marzano, & McNulty, 2003). The influence of the school leader on student learning is felt through a host of interrelated practices that include focusing school culture on high performance, demonstrating instructional leadership, hiring and retaining effective teachers, and establishing clear school-wide goals for increasing student achievement. The effect on student achievement appears to be particularly pronounced in the most challenging schools (Branch, Hanushek, & Rivkin, 2009; Branch, Hanushek, & Rivkin, 2012; Clark, Martorell, & Rockoff, 2009; Loeb, Kalogrides, & Horng, 2010).

A McKinsey education survey, reported in *Closing the Talent Gap* (Auguste, Kihn, & Miller, 2010, p. 33), found that effective principals are a crucial factor in both attracting and retaining talented teachers.

The test of any school leader's effectiveness is his or her ability to create a climate of continuous improvement, where both teacher proficiency and student learning measurably increase from year to year.

We believe we can provide the guidance to move past areas of confusion or misalignment. This book lays out a clear plan of action to use school leader evaluation as a model to measurably improve the performance of principals and assistant principals. The model described here does much more than just improve school leader performance, however. It also aligns the vision, mission, and goals of school leaders and connects the practices of school leaders to their impact on instruction and learning. Because district leaders observe and evaluate school leaders, evaluation should be and must become a collaborative, shared process of focused improvement. This dynamic model aligns school leader practices, and the evidence of those practices, to best support the growth and improvement of the school leader, teachers, and students.

School Leadership for Results: Shifting the Focus of Leader Evaluation

In *School Leadership for Results*, we outline the theory and practice of implementing a school leader evaluation and growth system that foregrounds instructional leadership, from planning, to action, to monitoring for the desired results. We believe that developing the capacity for visionary instructional leadership can turn a school around. Such visionary leadership will inspire the trust and support of teachers and foster schools that become what Phillip Schlechty (2009) characterizes as dynamic "learning organizations"—organizations that allow school leaders, teachers, and students to reach their highest potential.

But this book is also intended as a practical, hands-on guide to meeting the challenges of fair and accurate evaluation of instructional leaders. Along with the Marzano School Leader Evaluation Model, it is meant to provide a developmental road map for leaders who desire continuous self-improvement. Based on our conversations with school and district leaders, it appears that too many educators are being asked to implement evaluation or growth systems without either the training or mentorship to create truly effective, collaborative evaluation systems that foster growth and measure proficiency. Our goal in writing this book is to clear the path for successful implementation of evaluation systems, so educators can focus on what's important: the success of schools and the people in them.

The Effective School Leader

We know much more today about the school leader's role in creating successful schools than we did two or three decades ago. It's safe to say that research into leadership in general, and school leadership in particular, has been relentless since the *Interstate School Leaders Licensure Consortium* (ISLLC) published their original, visionary Standards for School Leaders in 1996, subsequently updated those standards in 2008, and substantially reformulated them in 2014 as knowledge about best practices in school leadership has continued to accumulate. The ISLLC standards have created a clear structure for instructional leadership. The Educational Leadership Constituencies Council (ELCC) followed with related standards in 2002. Those documents drew on and consolidated the lessons of previous decades. They brought to the forefront the importance of instructional leadership as a skill, and necessary focus, for all school leaders. They set out not only clear evidence for the rationale behind this emphasis but also a preliminary map to guide school leaders as they moved toward that destination. Further, recent research has also attempted to codify a definition of both school leader effectiveness and instructional leadership for the purposes of fair, accurate, and reliable evaluations called for by reformers.

Unfortunately, the majority of K–12 schools in the United States are still failing to realize the promise of the ISLLC and ELCC standards. The problem, however, is not with the standards, nor is it with the teachers and school leaders, who value instructional expertise and would like to see it have a primary place in their schools. Instead, the difficulty lies with the large shifts required of the organizational culture. This culture must absorb and integrate a host of national and state reforms that include standards-based systems, high accountability, measurable yearly achievement growth, and research-based teacher and leader evaluations. It is also a culture that is notoriously slow to realize the effects of such reforms.

In his paper "Three Stories of Education Reform," Michael Fullan (2000) notes that it takes about three years to achieve successful change in student performance in an elementary school and six years in a secondary school. But even where change happens, it may not last. "Put in terms of the change process, there has been strong adoption and implementation, but not strong institutionalization" (p. 581).

Further, the Southern Regional Education Board (SREB, 2010) finds that "districts and states are failing to create the conditions that make it possible for school leaders to lead school improvement effectively" (p. ii).

The Marzano School Leader Evaluation Model was developed as a tool to integrate the vigorous educational reform efforts of recent years and to actualize the recommendations of extensive research recommending instructional leadership—all aimed at giving American students the best possible chances of success. The Marzano School Leader Evaluation Model is a practical, cohesive model to give school leaders, and the district leaders who evaluate them, effective tools to lead comprehensive school improvement. Even if not used for evaluation, the model can be used for the professional growth and development of current and future school leaders.

Conceptual Framework and Recent Research

The conceptual framework for this book and the Marzano School Leader Evaluation Model discussed here is based on historical and contemporary research.

We also draw on recent public policy initiatives to formulate and refine our theoretical perspective and recommendations. The research, which we discuss in detail in Resource B, draws from four primary documents:

1. The multi-year Wallace Study conducted and published jointly by the Center for Applied Research and Educational Improvement (CAREI) at the University of Minnesota and the Ontario Institute for Studies in Education at the University of Toronto (Louis, Leithwood, Wahlstrom, & Anderson, 2010)

2. The study of *What Works in Oklahoma Schools* conducted by Marzano Research Laboratory (2011) with the Oklahoma State Department of Education over the 2009–2010 and the 2010–2011 school years

3. The Marzano, Waters, and McNulty meta-analysis of school leadership published in 2005 in *School Leadership That Works*

4. The Marzano study of school effectiveness published in *What Works in Schools* in 2003

Additionally, we have drawn on the large body of research published in the past decade on instructional leadership and school leader effectiveness. The discussion of these studies in Resource B serves as both a summary of current best practices for new school leaders beginning their careers and as a refresher for experienced leaders as they continue to hone their practice and build expertise.

How This Book Is Organized

The Introduction addresses three essential questions: What defines an effective school leader? How do we measure effectiveness? What outcomes do we expect to see? The Marzano School Leader Evaluation Model was developed in the context of pressures to reconceptualize school leadership as measurably effective *instructional* leadership.

The Introduction discusses the policy decisions and social pressures that have influenced the definitions of effective school leadership, and how the Marzano School Leader Evaluation Model addresses challenges identified by current research. This introductory chapter also describes the design of the model's domains, performance scales, and evidences; the research base for these interrelated elements; and the role of the evaluator in helping facilitate professional development for school leaders within the evaluation model.

It is one thing to understand and select a research-based school leader evaluation and growth system; it is quite another to implement that system successfully—to *institutionalize* the changes and *sustain* them.

Chapters 1 through 5 take a close look at each of the five domains of the Marzano School Leader Evaluation Model, the responsibilities entailed within each domain, and an analysis of the elements. We pay particular attention to how both school leaders and their evaluators monitor for evidence of success within these primary responsibilities.

Each chapter includes the scales and evidences for each domain and a set of key questions for school leaders to ask themselves as they prepare for evaluation or as they recognize areas for growth. We also include sample scenarios of authentic situations compiled from stories we have heard in the field. These can be used as conversation starters; they are not intended to be all-inclusive, but they begin the process of how to give and receive feedback using the scales discussed in the Introduction.

We share stories about principals, assistant principals, and district leaders who are applying the model in their individual districts and schools, and learn from their challenges and successes. These discussions provide a groundwork for research-based practices for both school and district leaders so school leaders have clear direction in how to prepare for evaluations and district leaders are similarly prepared to offer fair, unbiased evaluations and the kind of feedback most useful to drive improvement.

Chapter 6 is devoted to implementation. It describes the three phases that take your school or district from introduction in Year 1 through fidelity in Year 2 and full efficacy in Year 3. In this chapter, we dive into the specific, daily decision making in introducing an evaluation model—from developing an implementation plan to setting targets and goals and using data to determine the best goals for your school and district. We also touch on self-assessment—productive methods for districts to implement professional development for school leaders. The Marzano School Leader Evaluation Model is a growth model, one component of the comprehensive hierarchical evaluation system discussed in Chapter 6. While it certainly can and does measure performance, the overarching goal of this model is to develop leaders who can direct and mentor their schools to excellence.

Using This Book

School Leadership for Results is an entry point to help educators understand how best to get desired results from expert school leadership. It is also a practical guide for understanding and implementing the Marzano School Leader Evaluation Model, which may be used successfully with any state or national teacher evaluation model or as part of an aligned system with the Marzano teacher, district leader, and instructional support staff models. *School Leadership for Results* is designed to be a valuable resource both for districts exploring evaluation frameworks and for districts in search of fully aligned evaluation systems. Specifically, the following stakeholders will find of value the information, recommendations, and case histories detailed here:

- District leaders tasked with evaluating school leaders and assistant principals
- School leader induction programs and academic programs centered on school leadership
- Central office staff, including human resource officers, directors of special education, and others
- Principals and assistant principals who expect to be evaluated either with the Marzano model or state models aligned with this model
- Teacher coaches and staff developers desiring to understand aligned evaluation and growth systems
- Teacher leaders who plan to move into leadership positions
- Policy makers and state departments of education requiring evaluation resources to guide decisions related to state and district programs

It's an exciting—if challenging—time to be an educator. We believe that K–12 education has made crucial shifts over the past decade toward a brighter future—one where American students will successfully compete on a global level and thrive in demanding 21st-century careers. Our goal in writing this book is to provide practical, researched strategies to help make these global demands a reality.

SCHOOL
LEADERSHIP
for Results

INTRODUCTION

Why Evaluate School Leaders? The Policy Push

> *The contribution of effective leadership is largest when it is needed the most; there are virtually no documented instances of troubled schools being turned around in the absence of intervention by talented leaders . . . leadership is the catalyst.*
> —Leithwood, Seashore-Louis, Anderson, and Wahlstrom (2004)

We have entered the age of school leader accountability. Never have principals and assistant principals been under such pressure to be "effective," to produce measurable results that include increases in student achievement, declines in high school dropout rates, and data showing a steadily narrowing achievement gap between student subpopulations. The 2009 economic stimulus bill that included the $4.35 billion Race to the Top (RTTT) federal grants raised the stakes for all educators, but this accountability movement put a special onus on school leaders—the buck stopped on the principal's desk. As Davis, Kearney, Sanders, Thomas, and Leon note in their 2011 paper, *The Policies and Practices of Principal Evaluation*, we now find ourselves at a point where "a principal's job security rests squarely upon his or her success in promoting and sustaining acceptable levels of student achievement" (p. 1).

States receiving RTTT funding agreed to put in place rigorous teacher and principal evaluation systems and to weight those systems with value-added student test scores. Simultaneously, under Title 1 of the Elementary and Secondary Education Act (1965), interim final requirements were issued for School Improvement Grants (SIGS) that made evaluations for teachers and school leaders mandatory. In 2012, Race to the Top district grants, a competition "to support bold, locally directed improvements in learning" (Clifford & Ross, 2012, p. 7), made principal, superintendent, and teacher evaluation a nonnegotiable standard for applicants. Moreover, such systems are required to be in place by the 2014–2015 school year.

In 2013, waivers from No Child Left Behind further compelled states, if they hadn't already done so, to implement teacher and principal evaluation to measure educator effectiveness and boost student achievement.

The change was intense and rapid, and districts scrambled to meet the new requirements. Not surprisingly, given the pace of these reforms, it was sometimes difficult for states and school systems to properly vet, test, measure, and pilot new models in time to meet deadlines. Clifford and Ross (2012, p. 5), for example, elaborate on the widening gap between what was *required* by these initiatives and what was actually being *done*: "Two independent reviews of research on principal evaluations concluded that evaluation systems have not been designed or enacted in ways that promote accurate judgments of principal effectiveness (Clifford & Ross, 2011; Davis, Kearney, Sanders, Thomas, & Leon, 2011)."

Specifically, research studies indicate that

- Principals view performance evaluation as having limited value for feedback, professional development, or accountability to school improvement (Portin, Feldman, & Knapp, 2006).
- Principal evaluations are inconsistently administered; therefore, performance is inconsistently measured (Thomas, Holdaway, & Ward, 2000).
- Performance evaluations may not align with existing state or national professional standards for practice (Heck & Marcoulides, 1996; Reeves, 2009) or personnel evaluation (Goldring, Cravens, Murphy, Elliot, & Carson, 2009).
- Few widely available principal evaluation instruments display psychometric rigor or make testing results public so that validity and reliability can be examined (Clifford, Menon, Gangi, Condon, & Hornung, 2012; Condon & Clifford, 2010; Goldring et al., 2009; Heck & Marcoulides, 1996). (Clifford & Ross, 2012, p. 5)

Limited feedback. Inconsistency. Lack of alignment with standards. Lack of rigor. These same failings had been noted by previous researchers looking into school leader evaluation long before Race to the Top. But by 2013, both the carrot and the stick had been liberally applied: any school or district either *not* implementing new principal evaluation systems or at the very least substantially tweaking existing ones was an anomaly rather than a norm. And unfortunately, although a great deal of research had been compiled on school leader effectiveness over the past several decades, the research on school leader *evaluation* was surprisingly sparse. Since 2009, researchers have taken a growing interest in not only what fosters and constitutes principal effectiveness but also what constitutes best design and implementation of effective principal evaluation systems.

Defining School Leader Effectiveness

We begin our discussion of school leader evaluation with perhaps a deceptively simple definition of school leader effectiveness: *An effective school leader achieves desired results*. To identify and measure desired results, a robust, well-defined school leader evaluation model based on research is essential. *(Note: In this book, we use the terms* desired results, desired effects, *and* desired outcomes *synonymously.)*

A robust school leader evaluation model, we believe, does three things:

1. Identify the *desired results*
2. Identify the *actions* or *behaviors* most likely to achieve the desired results
3. Accurately and fairly *measure* the results achieved

To elaborate these ideas still further, an evaluation model that works to increase school leader effectiveness will help principals and assistant principals produce the *measurable expected results* that have been defined and articulated within the model. For example, one of the desired outcomes for school leader effectiveness is *a school-wide understanding of clear, measurable goals for student achievement*. In this case, then, the evaluation model must (1) clearly identify the desired results so that both the school leader and evaluator have an agreed-upon measure; (2) provide sample evidences that observers/evaluators may look for; (3) provide scales specific enough to measure the level of performance the school leader has achieved. The result of such an evaluation system is to empower school leaders to take charge of their own performance and professional development in a manner that allows them to reach specific goals agreed upon with their supervisors.

The Challenges of School Leader Evaluation

In 2011, Davis, Kearney, Sanders, Thomas, and Leon published a comprehensive review of the existing literature on school leader evaluation that identified many of the key challenges inherent in successfully implementing new principal evaluation systems across the country—and also the many good reasons for doing so. Among the challenges identified by their review, for instance, are:

- Most district-developed evaluation systems lack validity and reliability.
- Alignment between district evaluation systems and professional standards is mixed among districts.
- Methods and tools used to evaluate principals vary widely.
- Principals often perceived their evaluations as driven by politics or subjective opinions.
- Superintendents and principals did not always see eye to eye on either performance domains or on how important the evaluation was at all (the superintendents tended to give evaluation more weight) (p. 13).

Further, evaluation instruments that were *valid, reliable, and focused on principal behaviors* were few and far between (p. 16).

Because research was sparse, principal evaluation systems were often built on wobbly theoretical foundations. The systems had not been tested in any reliable way and, as a consequence, failed to accurately assess principal behaviors or provide useful feedback. It was difficult to gather precise data on whether the evaluations produced real or lasting change. And many districts took a checklist approach that wasn't granular enough to provide the kind of analysis of principals' strengths and weaknesses to generate effective professional development objectives. Finally, a significant number of districts still viewed principals as building managers, failing to align their evaluation systems to a focus on instructional leadership (p. 27).

It was the rare school district, in other words, that had effected a coherent implementation of a research-based school leader evaluation framework, one designed either to develop capable leaders or produce measurable results in student achievement.

The Fix

Davis et al. (2011) didn't stop at just describing past evaluation systems, however. They went on to identify the most common recommendations and suggestions for reforming principal evaluation. Among their findings were the following:

- Evaluation should guide professional development.
- Evaluation criteria and standards should be clear and align with school and district goals and student outcomes.
- Principals should collaborate in their evaluation goals, planning, and assessment.
- The tools should be reliable and valid.
- The evaluation system should be built on a foundation of research on effective school leadership and organizations.
- A balance of formative and summative functions will best ensure school leader buy-in and collaboration.
- Evaluations conducted by multiple stakeholders, and drawing on multiple measures, appear to be most effective (pp. 33–35).

The Marzano School Leader Evaluation Model

It was in the context of the existing research on school leader effectiveness and principal evaluation that Robert Marzano and the executive team at Learning Sciences Marzano Center, led by Dr. Beverly Carbaugh, developed the Marzano School Leader Evaluation Model. The model, which was developed, field tested, and refined over a period of several years, was designed to accomplish the following objectives:

1. *To create a systematic approach to school leader evaluation*

   The model is one component of what we propose as a larger, fully aligned, hierarchical evaluation system (see Chapter 6) that includes teachers, district leaders, and nonclassroom instructional support members. The school leader model supports a "common language of evaluation" that helps all the stakeholders in the system share a vision of research-based practices. It aligns the agreed-upon critical needs of the school within the context of the entire system for a focus on driving student achievement.

2. *To support school leader growth and development, reward demonstrated instructional leadership, and foster collaboration between district supervisors and school leaders*

   Although the model does measure principal performance with high accuracy and inter-rater reliability, the purpose of this model is much broader than evaluation models that merely measure performance. Specifically, we built the Marzano School Leader Evaluation Model to empower school leaders to take ownership of improving their professional expertise. Additionally, the system fosters collaboration and mutual support between school and district leaders and between school leaders in the same district.

   Evaluation systems that are *developmental* (as opposed to focused solely on measurement of performance) have three primary characteristics: they are comprehensive and specific, they include a developmental scale, and they recognize and reward growth (Marzano, 2012). All the Marzano evaluation models are developmental and facilitate continuous improvement through specific elements, derived from research, that have been shown to have the highest correlation to improvement in the classroom and in the school as a whole.

3. *To focus on obtaining desired effects*

   The model was developed with sample evidences of desired effects to help supervisors and evaluators provide specific feedback targeted at helping school leaders grow. The proficiency scales embedded in the model make it possible for evaluators to measure specific desired results for each of the model's twenty-four elements. These twenty-four elements are "leading indicators" of effective leader behavior. The phrase comes from the study of economics, where an "indicator" may act as a prediction of future performance.

4. *To foster inter-rater reliability*

Because the model is evidence based, observers and evaluators are discouraged from making subjective decisions. This high level of inter-rater reliability ensures that more than one evaluator may observe and score a school leader's performance and that the measurement of performance is both accurate and fair. This measurement component functions as an important base for school leaders and their evaluators to work from as they formulate professional development plans.

To summarize: The model is comprised of focused domains and elements and employs a performance scale designed to facilitate the school leader's professional growth. The evaluation of performance is *evidence based*. The model supports a common language of instruction so that teacher and school leader definitions of effective pedagogy are aligned. And finally, the evaluation model is designed to fully support teacher improvement—in other words, the school leader is evaluated on how well he supports and facilitates teacher growth. The successful school leader is one who most effectively helps teachers develop expertise, even as the leader also continues to develop.

The Model's Domains and Elements

To understand the specificity and impact of this evaluation model, consider its components. The model is comprised of five domains of professional influence. These domains constitute what research, policy, and the testimony of teachers, school leaders, and district leaders have determined to be critical areas of expertise for school leaders (Marzano, 2003):

1. A data-driven focus on student achievement
2. Continuous improvement of instruction
3. A guaranteed and viable curriculum
4. Cooperation and collaboration
5. A positive school climate

Within those domains, twenty-four elements identify specific leader actions or behaviors correlated with their demonstrable impact on student learning. It is useful to think of the elements as action statements or questions that school leaders will continually ask themselves as they monitor their own performance. These elements also form the questions evaluators of school leaders will ask as they measure leaders' behaviors and skills. Each of the twenty-four elements is paired with a corresponding performance scale upon which the outcome of each element can be measured. Each element is also accompanied by a list of sample evidences to which the observer/evaluator may refer to inform her decision about the school leader's proficiency in regard to that element (action or behavior). Figure I.1 illustrates the relationship of domains to elements, scales, and evidences.

Figure I.1. Relationship of domains to elements, scales, and sample evidences in the Marzano School Leader Evaluation Model

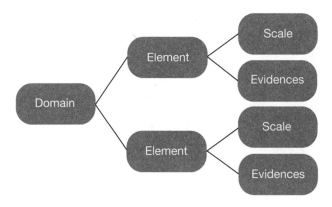

The five domains of school leader influence were identified based on the extant research (see Resource B for a fully detailed review of the research base for the Marzano School Leader Evaluation Model). The twenty-four elements were similarly based on actions and behaviors identified by research as having the most powerful impact on student learning. Figure I.2 illustrates the five domains and the twenty-four elements.

So, for example, in *Domain 1, A Data-Driven Focus on Student Achievement*, Element 1 describes the desired action or behavior: "The school leader ensures clear and measurable goals are established and focused on critical needs regarding improving overall student achievement at the school level."

Understanding the Constructs of Each Element

It's important to note that each element is made up of a number of important constructs, or components. In order for the school leader to show that he is meeting the necessary criteria for each element, the leader must be providing evidence of meeting *all* the constructs in the element.

The three constructs of Element 1 are italicized here:

The school leader ensures clear and measurable goals are established and focuses on critical needs regarding improving overall student achievement at the school level.

Note that the school leader's responsibility is to *ensure* the behavior, not necessarily *perform* it (this will be truer for some elements than others). The *desired effect* of this action would then be measured on the individual performance scale for that specific element at the level *Applying* (see Figure I.3), which is the desired level of performance.

Figure I.2. Learning Map: The Marzano School Leader Evaluation Model

Domain 1

A Data-Driven Focus on Student Achievement

Element 1:
The school leader ensures clear and measurable goals are established and focused on critical needs regarding improving overall student achievement at the school level.

Element 2:
The school leader ensures clear and measurable goals are established and focused on critical needs regarding improving achievement of individual students within the school.

Element 3:
The school leader ensures that data are analyzed, interpreted, and used to regularly monitor progress toward school achievement goals.

Element 4:
The school leader ensures that data are analyzed, interpreted, and used to regularly monitor progress toward achievement goals for individual students.

Element 5:
The school leader ensures that appropriate school-level and class-room-level programs and practices are in place to help all students meet individual achievement goals when data indicate interventions are needed.

Domain 2

Continuous Improvement of Instruction

Element 1:
The school leader provides a clear vision as to how instruction should be addressed in the school.

Element 2:
The school leader effectively supports and retains teachers who continually enhance their pedagogical skills through reflection and professional growth plans.

Element 3:
The school leader is aware of predominant instructional practices throughout the school.

Element 4:
The school leader ensures that teachers are provided with clear, ongoing evaluations of their pedagogical strengths and weaknesses that are based on multiple sources of data and are consistent with student achievement data.

Element 5:
The school leader ensures that teachers are provided with job-embedded professional development that is directly related to their instructional growth goals.

Domain 3

A Guaranteed and Viable Curriculum

Element 1:
The school leader ensures that the school curriculum and accompanying assessments adhere to state and district standards.

Element 2:
The school leader ensures that the school curriculum is focused enough that it can be adequately addressed in the time available to teachers.

Element 3:
The school leader ensures that all students have the opportunity to learn the critical content of the curriculum.

Domain 4

Cooperation and Collaboration

Element 1:
The school leader ensures that teachers have opportunities to observe and discuss effective teaching.

Element 2:
The school leader ensures that teachers have formal roles in the decision-making process regarding school initiatives.

Element 3:
The school leader ensures that teacher teams and collaborative groups regularly interact to address common issues regarding curriculum, assessment, instruction, and the achievement of all students.

Element 4:
The school leader ensures that teachers and staff have formal ways to provide input regarding the optimal functioning of the school and delegates responsibilities appropriately.

Element 5:
The school leader ensures that students, parents, and community have formal ways to provide input regarding the optimal functioning of the school.

Domain 5

School Climate

Element 1:
The school leader is recognized as the leader of the school who continually improves his or her professional practice.

Element 2:
The school leader has the trust of the faculty and staff that his or her actions are guided by what is best for all student populations.

Element 3:
The school leader ensures that faculty and staff perceive the school environment as safe and orderly.

Element 4:
The school leader ensures that students, parents, and the community perceive the school environment as safe and orderly.

Element 5:
The school leader manages the fiscal, operational, and technological resources of the school in a way that focuses on effective instruction and the achievement of all students.

Element 6:
The school leader acknowledges the success of the whole school, as well as individuals within the school.

Go to www.learningsciences.com/bookresources to download this page.
School Leadership for Results © 2015 Learning Sciences International

Figure I.3 demonstrates the performance scale for Domain 1, Element 1. Note that at the *Applying* level, "The school leader ensures clear, measurable goals with specific timelines focused on critical needs regarding improving student achievement are established at the school level AND regularly monitors that everyone has understanding of the goals."

Figure I.3. Scale for Domain 1, Element 1

Scale Value	Description
Innovating (4)	The school leader ensures adjustments are made or new methods are utilized so that all stakeholders sufficiently understand the goals.
Applying (3)	The school leader ensures clear, measurable goals with specific timelines focused on critical needs regarding improving student achievement are established at the school level AND regularly monitors that everyone has understanding of the goals.
Developing (2)	The school leader ensures clear, measurable goals with specific timelines focused on critical needs regarding improving student achievement are established at the school level.
Beginning (1)	The school leader attempts to ensure clear, measurable goals with specific timelines focused on critical needs regarding improving student achievement are established at the school level but does not complete the task or does so partially.
Not Using (0)	The school leader does not attempt to ensure clear, measurable goals with specific timelines focused on critical needs regarding improving student achievement are established at the school level.

In this instance, the school leader is responsible for ensuring that appropriate learning goals are posted and embedded in the instruction; she is not going from room to room creating or posting the goals herself. But she is certainly *monitoring* that everyone understands the goals—perhaps by asking individual teachers or students, distributing a survey, or gathering data.

The Role of the Evaluator

A district leader evaluating a school leader on Domain 1, Element 1 behaviors would turn to the sample evidences for that element (or additional evidences devised by the district) to gauge the success of the initiative (see Figure I.4). The evaluator might ask, for example, Are school-wide achievement goals posted and discussed regularly at faculty meetings? Are student performance scales in place to chart student and school progress toward meeting the standards?

Go to www.learningsciences.com/bookresources to download figures and tables.

Figure I.4. Sample evidences for Domain 1, Element 1

Sample Evidences for Domain 1, Element 1
• Written goals are established as a percentage of students who will score at a proficient or higher level on state assessments or benchmark assessments.
• School-wide achievement goals are posted and discussed regularly at faculty and staff gatherings.
• Written goals are established for eliminating the achievement gap for all students.
• Written goals address the most critical and severe achievement deficiencies.
• Written timelines contain specific benchmarks for each goal, including individual(s) responsible for the goal.
• Scales are in place to chart student and school progress toward meeting the standards.
• When asked, faculty and staff can explain how goals eliminate differences in achievement for students of differing ethnicities.
• When asked, faculty and staff can explain how goals eliminate differences in achievement for students at different socioeconomic levels, English language learners, and students with disabilities.
• When asked, faculty and staff can describe the school-wide achievement goals.
• When asked, faculty and staff can identify the school's most critical needs goals.

For now, it is enough to understand that the components of the system have been designed based on recent research into school leader effectiveness, with the specificity (in domains, elements, scales, and evidences) to meet three overarching objectives:

1. To develop school leader capacity
2. To ensure fair, accurate, and reliable evaluation of school leaders
3. To improve student achievement

Understanding the Developmental Performance Scales and Evidences

Evaluation implies measurement. Indeed, without an accurate and detailed measure of performance in all desired actions or behaviors, school leaders and their evaluators simply don't have the groundwork or data to construct a targeted and effective professional growth plan.

Therefore, it's critical to understand the measurement component of the Marzano School Leader Evaluation Model, as it provides the path to move forward with growth. The measurement component is the developmental performance scale for each element or category of leader behavior. These scales guide both the school leader and his evaluating supervisor. The school leader uses the scale as a way to self-assess and as a guide to develop expertise in precise, targeted behaviors. The evaluator uses the scale to assess the leader's behavior and provide the specific feedback necessary for mentorship and growth.

The scales represent a continuum of behaviors for each of the model's twenty-four elements, yet the statistical measure of each scale is identical, from *Not Using* to *Innovating*, as we saw in Figure I.3. For seamless alignment, the three other Marzano evaluation models employ the same scale.

The Developmental Performance Scale

By way of example, we now turn to an examination of the scale for Domain 1, Element 3 *(The school leader ensures that data are analyzed, interpreted, and used to regularly monitor progress toward school achievement goals)*.

Not Using (Score: 0)

The school leader does *not attempt* to use the strategy or demonstrate the behavior called for in the element.

Beginning (Score: 1)

The school leader *attempts to use the strategy* or tries to demonstrate the behaviors indicated in the element but does so only partially or with errors. For example, the school leader may have begun putting together a team to collect and post data on student achievement (see Figure I.5), and she may have notified her teachers that they should use this data to set achievement goals for their classes. But she may not yet have done any systematic monitoring of how her teachers are using the data.

Figure I.5. Scale for Domain 1, Element 3

Scale Value	Description
Innovating (4)	The school leader ensures that data are analyzed in a variety of ways to provide the most useful information and refines achievement goals or the tracking process as achievement data accrue.
Applying (3)	The school leader ensures that data are available for tracking overall student achievement AND monitors the extent to which student data are used to track progress toward goal.
Developing (2)	The school leader ensures that data are available for tracking overall student achievement.
Beginning (1)	The school leader attempts to ensure that data are available for tracking overall student achievement but does not complete the task or does so partially.
Not Using (0)	The school leader does not attempt to ensure that data are available for tracking overall student achievement.

Go to www.learningsciences.com/bookresources to download figures and tables.

From the preceding example, it's clear that a *Beginning* school leader is not necessarily a school leader who is falling short or failing. If the evaluator does a first observation early in the year and notes this behavior as *Beginning*, the school leader may well have put all the pieces in place to achieve a score of *Applying* by year's end. A conference at the beginning of the year will be a good place for the evaluator and school leader to assess where the school leader is in the process and develop a plan of action to ensure that she can accomplish her goals and reach *Applying* before summer break.

Developing (Score: 2)

The school leader *accurately displays all the behaviors* called for in the element. This rating often represents the compliance stage, where the leader is consciously completing all the constructs required in the element but is so focused on doing it correctly, completely, and accurately that action stops. Again, it will be important for the evaluator to help the school leader develop a plan of action to move beyond this level and grow to the next stage.

Applying (Score: 3)

The school leader has reached the target or proficiency level. This is the most critical level in the scale progression. A school leader at *Applying* incorporates all of the behaviors of the *Developing* level, with an important addition. At *Applying*, the school leader begins the process of analyzing whether the strategy is achieving the element's desired effect. So, for example, in Figure I.5, the *Applying* leader is not only ensuring that data are available for tracking overall student achievement, but, crucially, is also regularly monitoring how the data are used to track student progress toward the goal.

Innovating (Score: 4)

The school leader achieves the desired effect with *all* of those impacted by the element. To move from *Applying* to *Innovating*, a school leader may need to change, modify, or adapt the current strategy. In the school leader model, there is a unique descriptor for each element at the innovating level that actually serves as a potential guide for the leader who desires to achieve results with all members. If we look back at Figure I.5, for example, we see that "the school leader ensures that data are analyzed in a variety of ways to provide the most useful information and refines achievement goals or the tracking process as achievement data accrue."

The important descriptor words here are "a variety of ways" and "refines achievement goals." These two behaviors describe flexible, creative behavior that responds to unique demands posed by the staff, students, and school culture. The *Innovating* school leader would also be monitoring to make sure that every instructor in the school is able to work with the data and make good use of it to inform his own practice. We explore all twenty-four elements, and the desired effects of each, in detail in future chapters.

The scale can serve as a self-assessment for the school leader as well as an evaluative measure for the evaluator. It establishes a common language of evaluation and straightforward description of behaviors, actions, and goals that allows everyone within the system to understand exactly what is meant at each level of the scale.

Using Evidence for Scoring

The scoring of the school leader model is based on evidence, making it an objective model and facilitating inter-rater reliability if the school leader has multiple evaluators giving input to inform the evaluation. Evidence may be obtained from multiple sources including observation, conferencing, or artifacts. Artifactual evidence is another critical component of this model, as it facilitates the school leader's ongoing use of survey data, formative student data, and other evidence to substantiate that the leader's actions are achieving the desired effect.

Collecting Evidence and Providing Artifacts

In order to move from leadership focused on compliance to leadership focused on desired results within an evidence-based evaluation model, both the school leader and her supervisor must be clear about the kinds of evidence and artifacts that demonstrate the school leader is meeting desired results for each element.

As part of the school leader's preparation for evaluation, she will want to start planning what kinds of evidence or artifacts to present for each of the five elements in Domain 1. The school leader and supervisor may collaborate to obtain general agreement on what kinds of evidence determine each level of performance, from *Not Using* to *Innovating*. The Marzano model does offer sample evidences for each element. But these sample evidences may not be all-inclusive; individual schools and districts may use them whole-scale or adapt them. Most importantly, evidences should be designed to help a leader focus on achieving desired results.

Planning Exercise for Evaluators of School Leaders

As a beginning planning exercise, a supervisor might ask the following questions:

- Has the leader met all the constructs (or parts) described in the element?
- What is the desired effect/outcome for this element?
- What evidence/documentation supports my conclusion?
- What does it mean for the school leader to ensure?

Conclusion

In summary, the Marzano School Leader Evaluation Model is designed to support, develop, and measure the behaviors of school leaders that have been identified as leading to substantive whole-school improvement and increased student achievement, based on the extant scholarly research. The model's five domains and twenty-four elements offer school leaders and their supervisors a clear guide, along with performance scales and suggested evidences, with which to accurately and fairly measure school leader growth. In the next chapter, we turn to Domain 1, which focuses on collecting and analyzing the right data to help school leaders determine nonnegotiable goals and track the success of those goals using formative and summative measures.

CHAPTER 1

A Data-Driven Focus on Student Achievement (Domain 1)

Effective leaders at the district and/or building level "ensure that the collaborative goal-setting process results in non-negotiable goals (i.e., goals that all staff members must act upon) in at least two areas: student achievement and classroom instruction."
—Waters and Marzano (2006)

School leaders, as we know, are already overburdened. Both district supervisors and principals may rightly wonder how, in light of the demands already placed on the system, it will be possible to faithfully implement a complex new evaluation system focused not only on professional development for the school leader, but school-wide improvement.

In other words, how do we move from "juggling as fast as we can" toward focused, systematic implementation of targeted programs? How do we ensure that every student has a fair chance of success? How do we focus for results?

Domain 1 of the Marzano School Leader Evaluation Model streamlines many complex components around three main areas of focus for school leadership:

1. Identification of school-wide and individual student achievement goals
2. Data analysis, including school-wide, subgroup, and individual student data
3. Analysis of intervention programs at the school level and classroom level for specific students or subgroups

The actions and behaviors in this domain are intended to help ensure that the school as a whole, as well as individual teachers, have a clear focus on student achievement guided by relevant and timely data.

An Emphasis on Leadership Formative Assessment

As noted in our Introduction, in each domain of the Marzano school leader model, the elements of the model function as *leading indicators* of expected leadership behavior, and the desired outcomes for each element as *lagging indicators*. In

Domain 1, the actions of the school leader in setting school-wide goals and using data to monitor progress toward those goals are leading indicators for ensuring the *desired outcome* for the lagging indicator of school improvement. The model is designed to move the entire school away from a "compliance mentality" toward an approach that values and monitors measurable results—in other words, an approach that identifies and produces desired effects. The model is designed to help school leaders and supervisors make effective decisions based on results.

The Marzano model helps school leaders and their evaluators draw on timely, effective data analysis to make decisions. A component of a results-oriented process should incorporate data gathered during *formative assessment* of leadership skills and practices. The formative assessment component of the model is a departure from evaluation-as-usual. Rather than administering one summative annual evaluation, the school leader's supervisor regularly checks in to see how goals established early on in the year are progressing, and works with the school leader to reevaluate, if necessary, or take action to ensure that goals are met.

In this chapter, we examine the process school leaders use to identify and establish school-wide goals for improving student achievement and how school leaders will use data most effectively to track progress toward overarching school-wide goals. A unique aspect of Domain 1 is the additional focus on establishing goals, not just for the school as a whole, but for *individual students*, and on monitoring their growth within the school.

Domain 1 is a highly aligned process, as the behaviors represented in the elements (the action statements, guides, or questions we explored in our Introduction) work together to create a focus on student achievement.

Determining and Monitoring the "Right" Goals

We emphasize that Domain 1 has three major criteria: establishing the right goals, using data to monitor progress toward those goals, and designing intervention programs to meet the needs of individual students. In this evaluation model, school leaders and their supervisors keep their eyes on the nonnegotiable goal—steady growth in student achievement.

Determining the "right" goals is crucial. In *School Leadership That Works* (2005), Marzano, Waters, and McNulty discuss the opinions expressed by researchers and theorists that American schools evidence a "pathology" around change: "They know how to change promiscuously and at the drop of a hat" (Elmore, 2003, p. 11) but without attaining any real improvement. Fullan (1993) notes that the problem is not resistance to change so much as too many mandated innovations accepted uncritically. Given this atmosphere of relentless innovation, "an effective school leader ensures that change efforts are aimed at clear, concrete goals" (Marzano et al., 2005, p. 50). As Leithwood and Riehl put it, "Leadership involves purposes and direction. Leaders know the ends toward which they are striving. They pursue goals with clarity and tenacity and are accountable for their accomplishments" (2003, p. 7).

In this model, how does this focus on setting and monitoring goals differ from past practices?

There are probably few school leaders in the United States who have not set annual goals. Most principals set school-wide goals, but the issue is not just setting goals, or even meeting goals, but the kinds and the number of goals that are being set. As we have said, effective school leaders and their supervisors move beyond mere compliance, to set goals based on critical needs for increasing student achievement and optimizing school improvement.

The school leader needs to ask

- Who decides on school-wide goals, and which goals are most critical?
- Are the goals focused on student achievement?
- Is the appropriate level of data analysis completed to ensure the goals are the right ones?
- How many goals are reasonable to set in a given year?
- Are the goals nonnegotiable, or do they depend on the success or failure of other initiatives (i.e., are they supporting goals)?

Districts often require schools to submit yearly goals, sometimes in the form of a school improvement document with arbitrary requirements for the number of goals and arbitrary deadlines for monitoring and demonstrating progress. States often provide elaborate templates and require numerous goals to address student achievement in any subject tested by the state. Some school leaders question whether the school improvement document is ever approved at a higher level within the organization—or even, for that matter, read at all.

In a brief submitted by the California Collaboration on District Reform, for example, fourteen superintendents and public school administrators note that

> the compliance mentality and over-specification of required practices contribute to teacher and administrator burn-out and disengagement, thus undermining professional responsibility and commitment. Current checklist approaches to program monitoring reinforce these negative conditions and do little to build the capacity of district and school personnel to improve practice and student learning. Moreover, program evaluations that identify these problems often fall on deaf ears and produce little substantive change. (Alonzo et al., 2007, p. 7)

This is not a problem unique to California. In our travels around the country, we often hear similar laments from school and district leaders who view the paper trail for strategic planning as primarily busy work. Furthermore, discussions between school leaders and their supervisors about whether the established goals have produced desired outcomes may be infrequent.

Regular, scheduled conversations about progress toward goals and their outcomes must also take place between school leaders and teachers—in fact, they're vital to the success of the school leader and school.

In a recent informal survey of more than twenty-five schools in a large urban district representing elementary, middle school, and high school buildings, we found that few teachers were aware of the process for establishing their school-wide goals. Further probing revealed that the principal or a small select committee of teachers had established the goals without input from the majority of teachers.

The Marzano model emphasizes in Domain 1, Element 1 that the school leader is responsible for ensuring *all* teachers are aware of school-wide goals and that teachers have a stake in seeing goals are met. Why is this a critical behavior? One cannot aim at an invisible target. When the school leader ensures that teachers are aware of school-wide goals, teachers are more likely to implement the strategies for meeting them. Ownership of goals begins with knowledge of the goals.

Unpacking the Elements

We turn now to a discussion of the five elements in Domain 1. Figure 1.1 lays out the relationship between Domain 1 and the goals for each of these five elements.

The five elements of Domain 1 are as follows:

1(1): The school leader ensures clear and measurable goals are established and focused on critical needs regarding improving overall student achievement at the school level.

1(2): The school leader ensures clear and measurable goals are established and focused on critical needs regarding improving achievement of individual students in the school.

1(3): The school leader ensures that data are analyzed, interpreted, and used to regularly monitor progress toward school achievement goals.

1(4): The school leader ensures that data are analyzed, interpreted, and used to regularly monitor progress toward achievement goals for individual students.

1(5): The school leader ensures that appropriate school-level and classroom-level programs and practices are in place to help all students meet individual achievement goals when data indicate interventions are needed.

Figure 1.1. Domain 1 is comprised of five elements, all of which help identify specific goals for school, individual students, data systems, and classroom interventions.

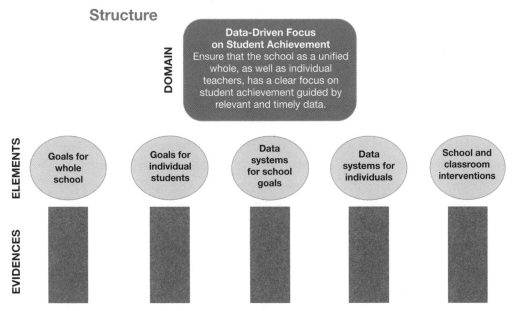

What Do We Mean When We Say *Ensure*?

As evaluators and school leaders begin to familiarize themselves with the five elements of Domain 1, it will be helpful to note important recurring words and phrases and formulate definitions for clear understanding. For example, all five elements ask the school leader to "ensure" that certain practices, methods, strategies, and actions are in place—he does not need, necessarily, to perform the actions.

At first glance, the number of elements and constructs within the elements may seem overwhelming, but understanding what we mean by *ensure* actually allows the school leader to distribute leadership and develop leadership talent in others. The word *ensure* implies that the school leader has ultimate responsibility for outcomes. Yet, when appropriate, the school leader directs other school personnel to perform the tasks necessary to create the desired results. For instance, one look at the body of possible evidences quickly reveals the need for shared leadership responsibilities so that others are enlisted to perform many of the expected tasks.

Rarely does the school leader work in isolation, but the buck stops at his desk. The school leader is ultimately responsible for the outcome of all measures taken, making it critical to constantly monitor progress and measure results. Because the school leader has the final responsibility to ensure that the actions of Domain 1 are completed, she should develop the data system to monitor that the desired results are achieved.

Setting Measurable School-Wide Goals (Domain 1, Element 1)

The school leader ensures clear and measurable goals are established and focused on critical needs regarding improving overall student achievement at the school level.

Most school leaders have an understanding that the collective goal of all educators—from teachers to superintendents—is, as Stiggins (1996) notes, "to help the largest possible percentage of our students get 'there.' . . . Any energy a school leader . . . invests in becoming clear about targets will pay big dividends" (p. 304). Element 1 is about defining, first of all, where "there" is.

This cornerstone element asks the school leader to establish goals that are clear—which means the goals are specific enough to be clearly understood. The goal must be measurable, not just a broad-based statement of improvement. And its focus must be on the critical achievement needs of the school as a whole.

Determining Nonnegotiable Goals

Successful leaders begin by determining nonnegotiable goals aligned with critical needs at the student level; they identify what must happen in their buildings regarding student achievement. In most cases, a guiding team or school improvement team uses school-wide data to set nonnegotiable goals. This data might include student achievement tests, school surveys, or student/parent surveys, for example. Typically, the process involves data disaggregation—or analysis of data by broad demographic descriptors such as student subpopulations, gender, and socioeconomic status, and by proficiency levels for tested disciplines (e.g., reading or mathematics)—so that school leaders may determine areas of critical need for the school as a whole.

The process described in Element 1 requires the school leader to ensure the development of school-wide goals that are S.M.A.R.T.—that is, goals that are (1) strategically aligned with school and/or district goals, (2) measurable, (3) attainable, (4) results oriented (requiring evidence of higher levels of student learning in order to be achieved), and (5) time-bound (DuFour & Marzano, 2011, p. 24).

Once the school leader has identified critical goals, the next step is to identify the who, what, when, where, and how—the factors necessary to determine how the goals will be accomplished.

Expectations for goal setting should meet the following criteria:

- Principals accept responsibility for the success of their school.
- Principals know and work within the unique context of their school.
- Principals lead with flexibility within the boundaries of district goals.

Key Questions

1. What is the process you use to decide the critical and nonnegotiable goals for your school?

2. What data are used to help you decide the most critical achievement needs?

3. What process do you use to determine the critical needs for improving student achievement at your school?

4. How do you determine which persons, tools, or strategies are necessary to see these goals realized?

5. Are the established goals strategic, measurable, attainable, results-oriented, and time-bound?

6. How will you monitor whether everyone knows the critical goals within the school?

The Scale for Domain 1, Element 1

Figure 1.2 details the performance scale for Domain 1, Element 1: The school leader ensures clear and measurable goals are established and focused on critical needs regarding improving overall student achievement at the school level.

Figure 1.2. Scale for Domain 1, Element 1

Scale Value	Description
Innovating (4)	The school leader ensures adjustments are made or new methods are utilized so that all stakeholders sufficiently understand the goals.
Applying (3)	The school leader ensures clear, measurable goals with specific timelines focused on critical needs regarding improving student achievement are established at the school level AND regularly monitors that everyone has understanding of the goals.
Developing (2)	The school leader ensures clear, measurable goals with specific timelines focused on critical needs regarding improving student achievement are established at the school level.
Beginning (1)	The school leader attempts to ensure clear, measurable goals with specific timelines focused on critical needs regarding improving student achievement are established at the school level but does not complete the task or does so partially.
Not Using (0)	The school leader does not attempt to ensure clear, measurable goals with specific timelines focused on critical needs regarding improving student achievement are established at the school level.

Figure 1.3 details sample evidences for Domain 1, Element 1.

Go to www.learningsciences.com/bookresources to download figures and tables.

Figure 1.3. Sample evidences for Domain 1, Element 1

Sample Evidences for Domain 1, Element 1
• Written goals are established as a percentage of students who will score at a proficient or higher level on state assessments or benchmark assessments.
• School-wide achievement goals are posted and discussed regularly at faculty and staff gatherings.
• Written goals are established for eliminating the achievement gap for all students.
• Written goals address the most critical and severe achievement deficiencies.
• Written timelines contain specific benchmarks for each goal including individual(s) responsible for the goal.
• Scales are in place to chart student and school progress toward meeting the standards.
• When asked, faculty and staff can explain how goals eliminate differences in achievement for students of differing ethnicities.
• When asked, faculty and staff can explain how goals eliminate differences in achievement for students at different socioeconomic levels, English language learners, and students with disabilities.
• When asked, faculty and staff can describe the school-wide achievement goals.
• When asked, faculty and staff can identify the school's most critical needs goals.

Scenario

Mr. Jameson, school principal, established a school improvement team during the summer to initially examine all state assessment student achievement data and identify primary areas in which student achievement was lagging behind expected proficiency levels. After careful analysis, the team identified the specific achievement areas needing the most improvement and introduced school-wide goals to the entire faculty and later to the school's community parent group. During the course of the year, the goals were published in the school newsletter and posted strategically throughout the schools.

At a faculty meeting, Mr. Jameson asked each teacher to identify which school-wide goals were most relevant to the students in his or her class. After reviewing the input from all teachers, the principal and initial school improvement team members met several times to refine the goal statements to ensure they were measureable, included timelines, and identified individuals responsible for communicating the goals.

Feedback and Explanation

In this scenario, we would give the school leader feedback at the *Innovating* level. Using the scale, he clearly evidenced all constructs of the element statement. Had he stopped at that point, he would have scored at *Developing*. However, Mr. Jameson *monitored for the desired effect*, which is that everyone knows the goals

(*Applying*). He then made adjustments after obtaining feedback (*Innovating*). This scenario would probably span several months of a school year, and it models the developmental progression of the leader's behavior from *Developing* to *Applying* and, finally, to *Innovating*.

Setting Measurable Goals for Individual Students (Domain 1, Element 2)

The school leader ensures clear and measurable goals are established and focused on critical needs regarding improving achievement of individual students within the school.

Our discussion of Domain 1, Element 1 focused on creating and monitoring school-wide goals. Element 2 focuses on establishing goals to meet the critical needs of individual students to improve their achievement.

Note the constructs of Element 2. As with Element 1, the goals must be *clear and measurable*. They must focus on *critical needs*. And finally, they must focus on *improving achievement of individual students*.

With Element 2, teachers and students all need to be aware of individual student achievement goals. The school leader must also ensure that teachers have a deliberate plan to monitor progress toward these goals. To this end, teachers will disaggregate class data to determine which students may be highly proficient or proficient, and conversely, where there may be achievement gaps. Having access to disaggregated data, as we will see in our discussion of Element 4, allows the teacher to adjust instruction to the appropriate level of rigor for individual students and set appropriate goals for each child in the class. We argue that such specific interventions are a long way from the "one size fits all" or "factory model" of instruction historically practiced at many schools (Baglieri & Knopf, 2004).

As indicated in Figure 1.4, the school leader's job is to ensure that teachers know the critical needs of their students and that, in turn, students know their own critical achievement goals. And to go one step further, the test of Element 2 will be whether the desired results have been achieved. *The desired outcome for Element 2 is that every teacher knows the critical achievement goals for every student in her classroom.*

To formulate goals for individual students, teachers must have a solid knowledge of grade-level expectations or standards. Here the school leader can help teachers understand and focus on ways to plan for discrepancies in student performance in relationship to grade-level expectations, a likely subset of overall goals for student achievement. The Common Core State Standards and other college and career readiness standards were designed as grade-level expectations. To monitor critical achievement goals, a teacher must first consider the expectations for the grade level and set the right goals for individual students.

Figure 1.4. Scale for Domain 1, Element 2

Scale Value	Description
Innovating (4)	The school leader ensures adjustments are made or new methods are utilized so that all faculty and students sufficiently understand the goals.
Applying (3)	The school leader ensures each student has written achievement goals that are clear, measurable, and focused on appropriate needs AND regularly monitors that teachers and students have understanding of individual student goals.
Developing (2)	The school leader ensures each student has written achievement goals that are clear, measurable, and focused on appropriate needs.
Beginning (1)	The school leader attempts to ensure that written achievement goals that are clear, measurable, and focused are established for each student but does not complete the task or does so partially.
Not Using (0)	The school leader does not attempt to ensure that written achievement goals that are clear, measurable, and focused are established for each student.

Figure 1.5 details sample evidences for Domain 1, Element 2.

Figure 1.5. Sample evidences for Domain 1, Element 2

Sample Evidences for Domain 1, Element 2
• Written goals are established for each student in terms of his/her performance on state/district assessments, benchmark assessments, or common assessments.
• Written goals accompanied by proficiency scales are established for each student in terms of his/her knowledge gain.
• Students keep data notebooks regarding their individual goals.
• Student-led conferences focus on the individual student's goals.
• Parent-teacher conferences focus on the individual student's goals.
• When asked, teachers can explain the learning goals of their students.
• When asked, students perceive that their individual goals are academically challenging.
• When asked, students are aware of their status on the achievement goals specific to them.
• When asked, parents are aware of their child's achievement goals.

Student Participation in Goal Setting and Tracking

Students, of course, should participate in the process and know their own goals for individual achievement; they should also track their own progress toward the goals. Student participation not only helps students "buy in" to the goals, but ideally helps them stay focused on the end goal—to improve achievement and meet their grade-level expectations.

Go to www.learningsciences.com/bookresources to download figures and tables.

A principal we know recently shared a school-wide process that she implemented during the first two weeks of school as a first step to students knowing their individual proficiency targets. Every student was presented with his or her achievement data from the prior year. Teachers then made students aware of the school/state proficiency targets in each tested subject. Each student set goals to meet his or her proficiency targets. Students recorded the process in their daily homework or agenda notebooks, then teachers and school leaders used this information to informally monitor and track progress toward students' individual goals.

This process could be the beginning phase of working with students not only to know their long-term achievement targets but also their goals for units, or even courses.

Key Questions

1. How will you know teachers have established goals focused on the most critical needs of their students?

2. How will you help students become aware of their own achievement goals?

3. Will the goals established by individual teachers help the school close any achievement gaps?

4. Do you have a systematic process for establishing goals at the classroom level?

5. How will you monitor that teachers update and refine the achievement goals of their students throughout the course of the year?

6. What data do students use to determine their individual achievement goals?

7. Who ensures and monitors this process?

Scenario

At the beginning of the school year, Principal Alba schedules a meeting with the leadership team. The leadership team consists of the administrative staff, instructional coaches, and teachers representing grade levels and content areas. The intent of the meeting is to focus on ways to help teachers establish goals for their individual students. The team recognizes there are achievement gaps in a subgroup population and wants to ensure that teachers establish goals to move these students toward established proficiency targets.

The team discusses what data teachers will need, makes a timeline for when the goals should be established, and announces the plan at a faculty meeting. During the course of the year, the leadership team continues to meet at regular intervals. One of their agenda items is always to update the status of individual student goals.

However, in discussing the meetings with Principal Alba and reviewing meeting outcomes, Principal Alba's supervisor notes that meetings have resulted in the creation of school-wide discipline procedures, awards ceremonies, and professional development focused on new statewide graduation and testing requirements. In a conversation with her supervisor, Principal Alba has expressed concern about finding the right data for teachers to use to establish goals for their individual students.

Feedback and Explanation

In the preceding scenario, Principal Alba has established meetings to discuss and monitor individual student goals. But she is unable to present evidence that teachers have established goals for their students, or students themselves know their learning goals. In this example, Principal Alba would receive feedback at the *Beginning* level. The major constructs of Element 2 require clear and measureable goals for individual students. Teachers should know the individual achievement goals for their students, and individual students should be able to articulate their own goals.

A *Beginning* rating means that the school leader *attempts to ensure* that written achievement goals are clear, measurable, and focused, and that goals have been established for each student, but the school leader either does not complete the task or does so only partially. For this principal to move to the *Developing* level, there must be evidence that teachers have established learning goals for their students, and students know those learning goals.

Why is Element 2 a critical step in the process of creating a data-driven focus on student achievement? Element 2 sets the foundation for success with Element 4. In the absence of individual student achievement goals, it will be impossible for teachers and school leaders to *track progress toward achievement* of individual goals, as required in Element 4. Throughout the book, we will continue to elaborate on the close relationships between elements. Effective leadership is not achieved through an element-by-element checklist but rather through a complex set of intertwined skills that can be disaggregated into individual elements.

Analyzing Data for School-Wide Goals (Domain 1, Element 3)

The school leader ensures that data are analyzed, interpreted, and used to regularly monitor progress toward school achievement goals.

Accurate and Timely Measurement

Domain 1 is a highly aligned process that uses data to design specific interventions to drive student achievement. Elements 3 and 4 are critical to the monitoring of progress in Elements 1 and 2 and provide the data to facilitate the actions in Element 5. Therefore, accurate and timely measurement is key to success in this domain. Without such measures, it's impossible for school leaders to monitor the success of goals, monitor the achievement of individual students, or plan appropriate interventions.

Element 3 ensures that appropriate data are available to allow the school leader to *monitor* the progress the school is making toward meeting established school-wide achievement goals (Element 1). The actions in Element 3 require the leader to aggregate formative data rather than merely focus on summative data sources. To monitor progress toward goals, school leaders need data that are not only accurate, but actually measure the right factors. The aggregated data provides the school leader with measures that will facilitate tracking progress toward achieving school-wide goals.

We have found that if school-wide goals are typically written to meet state proficiency targets using summative measures such as state assessment tests, the school leader will need to find ongoing assessment measures, or appropriate *formative* assessments, to track student progress toward school-wide goals.

We recognize that it may be problematic for school leaders to find appropriate measures aligned to state achievement tests. Leaders often share examples of how they have monitored data throughout the school year, but when the results of the state test arrive, the scores are significantly different from data derived from benchmark and formative measures. In other words, it seems that schools sometimes write global goals so broadly that it is difficult to track progress, because the formative measures do not accurately predict the summative measures. Therefore, when setting goals in Element 1, the school leader needs to be aware of what formative measures will be available to ensure that data is actually tracking progress toward the goal.

The Uses and Challenges of Formative Data

The challenge of obtaining ongoing formative measures continues to plague school leaders, who often rely on end-of-year summative measures to chart school progress (lagging indicators). It is precisely such formative assessment data that allow school leaders to identify and work to close achievement gaps.

As Marzano and Toth explain in *Teacher Evaluation That Makes a Difference*, large-scale summative assessments are not a particularly useful measure for early identification of intervention needs:

> This is because large-scale summative assessments are not designed with individual students in mind. As Abrams (2007) explains, NCLB "only prescribes how schools—not students—should be held accountable" (p. 82). In spite of this, many schools assemble teachers in "data teams" to analyze status assessments on a diagnostic level regarding the needs of individual students. Cizek (2007) cautions that many state-level status assessments are not precise enough to provide data about students' strengths and weaknesses in specific topics within a given subject area. (as quoted in Marzano & Toth, 2013, p. 18)

Marzano and Toth go on to note that Cizek found that the total score reliability across forty items on a mathematics test in a large Midwestern state was .87

(an acceptable level of precision). But the subscores on specific topics such as algebra, measurement, or data analysis were far less reliable (from .33 to .57). "Even more disturbing is the reliability of difference scores between the reporting categories in the mathematics test. It is .015" (2013, p. 18).

Cizek notes:

> In many cases, a teacher who flipped a coin to decide whether to provide the pupil with focused interventions in algebra (heads) or measurement (tails) would be making that decision about as accurately as the teacher who relied on the examination of sub differences in the two areas. (2007, p. 104)

Figure 1.6 illustrates the scale for Domain 1, Element 3.

Figure 1.6. Scale for Domain 1, Element 3

Scale Value	Description
Innovating (4)	The school leader ensures that data are analyzed in a variety of ways to provide the most useful information and refines achievement goals or the tracking process as achievement data accrue.
Applying (3)	The school leader ensures that data are available for tracking overall student achievement AND monitors the extent to which student data are used to track progress toward the goal.
Developing (2)	The school leader ensures that data are available for tracking overall student achievement.
Beginning (1)	The school leader attempts to ensure that data are available for tracking overall student achievement but does not complete the task or does so partially.
Not Using (0)	The school leader does not attempt to ensure that data are available for tracking overall student achievement.

Figure 1.7 details sample evidences for Domain 1, Element 3.

Figure 1.7. Sample evidences for Domain 1, Element 3

Sample Evidences for Domain 1, Element 3
• Reports, graphs, and charts are available for overall student achievement.
• Student achievement is examined from the perspective of value-added results.
• Results from multiple types of assessments are regularly reported and used (e.g., benchmark, common assessments).
• Reports, graphs, and charts are regularly updated to track growth in student achievement.
• Achievement data for student subgroups within the school are routinely analyzed.
• School leadership teams regularly analyze school growth data.
• Data briefings are conducted at faculty meetings.

(Continued)

Go to www.learningsciences.com/bookresources to download figures and tables.

> • When asked, faculty and staff can describe the different types of reports available to them.
>
> • When asked, faculty and staff can explain how data are used to track growth in student achievement.

Key Questions

1. What data do you use to track overall student progress?
2. What data analysis processes do you use to analyze data?
3. How do you regularly monitor the progress the school as a whole is making toward reaching its goal?
4. Do you have evidence of making adjustments to the school's goals based on ongoing data analysis?
5. How do you ensure monitoring of progress is for diagnostic purpose versus compliance?

Analyzing Data for Individual Students (Domain 1, Element 4)

The school leader ensures that data are analyzed, interpreted, and used to regularly monitor progress toward achievement goals for individual students.

In Elements 2 and 4, we see the focus drilling down to include setting, maintaining, and monitoring goals for individual students.

Effective leaders know that it takes more than just setting individual student goals (Element 2) in order to drive improvement. There is a ripple effect in play here between Elements 2 and 4. For a school to reach its overall goal, the school leader must pay careful, ongoing attention to individual student data. As noted, the elements in Domain 1 are deeply interconnected.

About Data Analysis

For example, Elements 3 and 4 set the expectation for the leader to collect, organize, analyze, and interpret data. Leaders are often overwhelmed with sources of data, including state assessments in multiple disciplines, district-generated end-of-course and benchmark tests, and formative assessments created by teachers. To analyze data, school leaders will find it helpful to have a systematic process.

We suggest thinking in terms of "levels of data analysis," or steps in a protocol to analyze data (Preuss, 2003). These steps for analyzing data are meant for practitioners in the field to go into *deeper levels of analysis* on their data sets. If we want to get to the root cause of an issue, these levels constitute a process to identify it (see page 31). Equipped with this understanding, the leader and school teams may then take steps toward a solution.

Level One Data Analysis

School leaders will often begin the process with *level one data analysis*; in other words, quantifying by category to describe the data set. Paul Preuss defines level one data as the initial aggregated data set: most often "prior to disaggregation or further analysis." Level one data is used to identify "red flag issues" (p. 201).

Level one data analysis can be important for specific purposes. For example, in analyzing a summative assessment or even a student survey, the school leader will look at percentages of students who answered the same way. The school leader would consider the percentage of the total survey population and compare those numbers with the percentages in subgroups.

The data examined in level one analysis answer basic questions such as, How many students were proficient or meet benchmarks? Is attendance improving, or are there changes in behavioral data? This data is typically *descriptive* in terms of the quantities in any given category.

Examples include disaggregating the number of graduates by demographic subgroups; the percentage of proficient students by grade level on an assessment; and the number of students attending an intervention and their rate of attendance. This is probably the level of data analysis with which we are most familiar, and often it is the level of analysis at which we make important decisions—perhaps shortsightedly. Although level one data analysis provides much demographic and broad achievement information, and it is useful in setting school-wide goals, it may not help a leader interpret data at a level that will inform instruction or assist in making intervention decisions.

Level Two Data Analysis

Level two data analysis is a process that questions and examines the strengths and weaknesses in the data in terms of their intended use. Preuss (2003) defines level two data as data that have been disaggregated from an initial set of aggregated data, for a deeper understanding of the issue. Analysis of level two data may also include looking at "the who" and "on what" in terms of a data set. For example, we may want to examine the names of students who have failed one or more classes during the first quarter and whether they are enrolled in an intervention program. Or, we might examine the students participating in a specific intervention in relationship to their performance on a current assessment. This level of analysis could include identifying students who have not been proficient on the state assessment and have low value-added scores—but as we discussed earlier in this chapter, state assessment results alone would not be the most relevant data to determine specific interventions for specific students. A diagnostic assessment would be a better source of data for placing a student in a specific intervention.

The questions at level two data analysis focus on whether the data we are analyzing provide us with enough specific information to plan for appropriate interventions, or make changes in core programs or instructional strategies. It is the responsibility of the school leader to identify the appropriate level of data analysis and ensure that staff examine the data as thoroughly as necessary for the task at hand.

To illustrate: If staff are attempting to monitor whether the school is closing the achievement gap, it will be appropriate to use *level one analysis* to look at the percentage of proficient students on an assessment over time. However, if staff are trying to determine who may need additional opportunities to learn a particular area of content, they would be remiss if they did not engage in *level two analysis* to identify *which* students, and *what* specific content, and *how much* additional instructional time should be provided.

Level Three (Root Cause) Data Analysis

A process of level three data analysis, which often draws on multiple sources of data, is recommended for a school leader to discover *root causes*. The root cause, according to Preuss, is "the deepest underlying cause or causes of positive or negative symptoms within any process, which, if dissolved, would result in elimination, or substantial reduction, of the symptom" (2003, p. 204). It is important to distinguish between symptoms (the *results* of a problem) and the root cause of the problem. For example, poor attendance is a *symptom* of a root cause—the root cause itself could turn out to be a high incidence of bullying, widespread drug use, lack of engagement, and so on.

This synthesis process, using multiple sources of data to determine root cause, is probably the least used level of data analysis. But in reality, level three analysis will allow school leaders to address, and even remedy, specific root causes of negative symptoms. As noted, this level of analysis usually involves using information from multiple data sources to answer specific questions.

For example, a data team reviews the names of students, by teacher, who have not shown any percentile increases on the benchmark assessment from the first to second quarter. They analyze proficiency levels for specific items related to a skill or standard. Finally, they identify the items, by level of complexity, where students show proficiency or are below proficiency. They consider this information in relationship to prior assessments, the curriculum, and perhaps even other sources of data.

Using this type of analysis, the data team can zero in on instructional or curriculum changes that should be implemented. The root cause in the earlier case would be identified as a problem with the curriculum or implementation of the curriculum. Perhaps the implemented curriculum did not reach the same level of complexity as items on the benchmark test. Once root cause has been identified, the team, or even a specific teacher, can use specific feedback. It advances the process from merely having data to using the data to determine how to adapt presentation of classroom content to the required level of complexity.

To illustrate: A secondary school principal shared an example of level three data analysis. At the end of the first quarter, more than 50 percent of the students taking algebra were failing the course. A data-team meeting was convened to analyze why the school was experiencing such a high failure rate. The team began by reviewing the absence rates, number of tardies, and behavior incidences for each failing student. The team also analyzed and compared the periods and teachers with the most failing students, and the formative assessment data for each student (i.e., multiple data sources). With an eye on discovering the root cause, the team began asking questions to determine why students were failing.

The team discovered a group of first-period students who rode a bus that routinely arrived late. When reviewing the students' formative assessments, it was apparent interventions should have been implemented but had not been put in place. In the process, the data team also discovered most algebra classes were scheduled during the first period of the school day, and the failing students had high tardy rates. When they interviewed the students, most students said they did not find algebra relevant or engaging, so they avoided coming to first period. Once the data team discovered the root causes, changes were made to the master schedule so that algebra classes met later in the day, and teachers in the department worked on engagement strategies to make algebra relevant to their students.

With level three or root cause data analysis, a leader can make intervention decisions that focus on root causes (late buses, lack of engagement) rather than symptoms (low algebra scores). Deeper levels of data analysis are what help school leaders make better decisions. These systematic processes will ensure the school leader has the appropriate data to monitor disaggregated student data and also to aggregate data to monitor school-wide progress. Figures 1.8 and 1.9 illustrate the scale and evidences for Domain 1, Element 4.

Key Questions

1. What data do you use to track individual student progress?

2. What process do you use to analyze individual student progress?

3. Do you focus on root cause analysis?

4. How do you regularly monitor that you are achieving the desired effect?

5. Do you have evidence of teachers making goal adjustments for individual students when data show lack of progress or that students are not achieving their goals?

6. Do data reveal you are closing any achievement gaps?

Figure 1.8. Scale for Domain 1, Element 4

Scale Value	Description
Innovating (4)	The school leader ensures that data are analyzed in a variety of ways to provide the most useful information and refines individual achievement goals or the tracking process as achievement data accrue.
Applying (3)	The school leader ensures that data are available for individual student achievement AND monitors the extent to which data are used to track progress toward individual student goals.
Developing (2)	The school leader ensures that data are available for individual student achievement.
Beginning (1)	The school leader attempts to ensure that data are available for individual student achievement but does not complete the task or does so partially.
Not Using (0)	The school leader does not attempt to ensure that data are available for individual student achievement.

Figure 1.9 details sample evidences for Domain 1, Element 4.

Figure 1.9. Sample evidences for Domain 1, Element 4

Sample Evidences for Domain 1, Element 4
• Reports, charts, and graphs are available for individual students depicting their status and growth.
• Individual student achievement is examined from the perspective of value-added results.
• Individual student results from multiple types of assessments are regularly reported and used (e.g., benchmark, common assessments).
• Individual student reports, graphs, and charts are regularly updated to track growth in student achievement.
• Teachers regularly analyze school growth data for individual students.
• School leadership teams regularly analyze individual student performance.
• When asked, individual students and their parents can describe the student's achievement status and growth.
• When asked, faculty can describe the different types of individual student reports available to them.
• When asked, faculty and staff can analyze data of their individual students, including all subgroups.

Developing Interventions (Domain 1, Element 5)

The school leader ensures that appropriate school-level and classroom-level programs and practices are in place to help all students meet individual achievement goals when data indicate interventions are needed.

In the context of school leader evaluation, both school leaders and their supervisors must understand how and why they use data. It's important to emphasize that the collection and monitoring of data is not an exercise designed to exert some big-brotherly control over students, teachers, or school leaders. Rather, effective leaders view data as a means not only to pinpoint problems but also understand their nature and causes. *Data collection serves one primary purpose: to allow school leaders and teachers to track progress toward goals and design interventions when necessary to get struggling students back on track.*

For example, appropriate use of data helps identify struggling learners in order to design early interventions; monitor *response to interventions* (RTI); and provide multi-tiered systems of support (MTSS), integrated systems of instruction, assessment, and specific interventions to support student needs. These specific strategies allow us to design programs focused on academic goals and narrow achievement gaps.

Once the school leader has a process for monitoring individual data and recognizes its impact on overall school data, the leader must ensure that appropriate school-level intervention programs are in place.

Such interventions are typically a first step, but the most critical component of any intervention is how the leader knows whether the intervention is *yielding results*. For every intervention established—whether school wide or for individual students—she should determine early both the desired results and criteria for success. Such a determination allows the school leader a definite way to measure results.

The school leader might, for example, implement a program to improve students' organizational skills to facilitate a readiness to learn. If the leader puts in place such a school-wide intervention, requiring that all students use organizational notebooks, the leader ought to know both the desired result (e.g., all students use notebooks) and also how to measure the desired result (e.g., a teacher survey indicates that students are better prepared for class). In other words, for every element, the leader should begin with the end in mind and a plan for monitoring progress toward that end. Figures 1.10 and 1.11 illustrate the scale and evidences for Element 5.

Figure 1.10. **Scale for Domain 1, Element 5**

Scale Value	Description
Innovating (4)	The school leader continually examines and expands the options for individual students to make adequate progress.
Applying (3)	The school leader ensures that programs and practices are in place for individual students who are not making adequate progress AND monitors whether interventions are helping students meet their achievement goals.
Developing (2)	The school leader ensures that programs and practices are in place for individual students who are not making adequate progress.
Beginning (1)	The school leader attempts to ensure that programs and practices are in place for individual students who are not making adequate progress but does not complete the task or does so partially.
Not Using (0)	The school leader does not attempt to ensure that programs and practices are in place for individual students who are not making adequate progress.

Figure 1.11 details sample evidences for Domain 1, Element 5.

Figure 1.11. **Sample evidences for Domain 1, Element 5**

Sample Evidences for Domain 1, Element 5
• Extended school-day, -week, or -year programs are in place.
• Tutorial programs are in place (during the school day and/or after school).
• Individual student completion of programs designed to enhance their academic achievement is monitored (e.g., gifted and talented, advanced placement, STEM, etc.).
• Response to intervention measures is in place.
• Enrichment programs are in place.
• Data are collected and available to monitor student progress and achievement as a result of enrollment in intervention or enrichment programs.
• When asked, teachers can explain how interventions in place help individual students meet their goals.
• When asked, student and/or parents can identify interventions in place to meet the student's goals.
• When asked, students report their school has programs in place to help them meet their achievement goals.

Determining Individual Student Interventions

So far, we have discussed school-wide interventions. But how does a leader determine appropriate and necessary *individual student* interventions? Such interventions are dependent upon the data analyzed and interpreted as part of Element 4. Interventions for individual students may include small group or

Go to www.learningsciences.com/bookresources to download figures and tables.

one-on-one interventions, but the key is that they must be based on data and aligned to narrow students' individual achievement gaps.

The real problem is that schools sometimes plan a "menu" of intervention options and then try to plug students into the available options. We would suggest an approach that uses multiples sources of data analyzed for root causes and then planning interventions to address individual root causes. This is where data analysis should be at a level that helps a school leader and teachers drill down to root causes.

Let's look at a hypothetical example involving Student A. The school leader has examined data showing that Student A has not made progress toward a specific reading goal. In a worst-case scenario, the teacher might assign the student to participate in a tiered reading group that does not focus on the student's specific reading proficiency. But perhaps when doing root cause analysis, the school leader and teacher discover Student A needs targeted help in analyzing story elements and text features. If the student has been homogenously grouped with Students B, C, and D, who have different proficiency needs, the group has not been differentiated for Student A's critical needs. Student A needs targeted instruction that will address specific deficits. Remember, the purpose of the intervention is to increase proficiency in the targeted skill. The teacher will use formative assessments to track Student A's progress toward achieving specific goals.

Again, when planning individual student interventions, the school leader must begin with the end in mind and have specific measures identified to clearly determine if the desired outcomes have been met.

Key Questions

1. How do you determine appropriate interventions at the school level?
2. How do you determine appropriate interventions for individual students?
3. How do you know if a specific intervention is achieving the desired results?
4. How often do you make adaptations to interventions based on data?
5. What evidence shows interventions are working or not working?
6. How do you involve school personnel in establishing and monitoring the results of interventions?

Scenario

Parker East Middle School has implemented a school-wide intervention developed after the team realized that almost 50 percent of students were entering ninth grade at less than proficient levels in reading. To address this concern, the English language arts (ELA) teachers worked with the assistant principal, reading coach, and principal to implement a new comprehensive reading intervention program. The program had a quick identification system through electronic assessment that yielded a Lexile level for each student. The same system offered progress monitoring data. ELA teachers tested students at each grade level and developed a schedule for implementation of the interventions. Throughout the first part of the year, dramatic increases in formative achievement measures were noted for many students, increases not seen with other interventions. The reading coach suggested that teachers have the opportunity for professional development on the instructional techniques in the program so they could replicate them in their classrooms.

During the second part of the year student achievement continued to show gains when the team analyzed data provided by the intervention assessment tool and in their own benchmarks, which led them to believe that not only was the intervention successful, but when it was coupled with changes to the instructional strategies, they would see gains on the summative assessment.

For students who were not identified to participate in the intervention program, the team developed a reading enrichment program where they gave students more complex texts. The instructional techniques seemed to be useful with these students, and while they didn't see the same dramatic improvements, students did continue to show increases in their bench-mark data. Teachers also noted other qualitative changes: students were showing more resiliency and self-efficacy. This intervention was working with all students.

Explanation

In Domain 1, Element 5, we would give this principal feedback at the *Innovating* level. The principal and his team planned, implemented, and monitored to determine if the intervention was achieving the desired results. After determining the intervention was achieving the desired effect with the majority, the leader implemented the successful instructional techniques with all students, and ongoing data monitoring revealed that the intervention was working with all.

Achieving Desired Results

Much of our discussion in this chapter has focused on the actions and processes of the school leader, but it is important to reiterate that in the Marzano evaluation model, the leader's performance is measured by the *desired outcomes* of her actions.

What is the process for deciding if the school leader is actually achieving results? Since this is a pivotal point for each element, we would suggest that supervisors of principals offer definitive examples or evidences of the expected results. For example, when reviewing Domain 1, Element 1, if the desired result is that everyone know the school's overall goals, then the supervisor of the school leader must establish, early in the evaluative process, the evidences the school leader must present to show that she achieved the desired result.

In Element 1, the school leader may have sample artifacts such as exit slips from teams at a faculty meeting where teachers prioritize the school's goals as they relate to the goals of the students in their classes. Establishing evidence to demonstrate the leader is achieving the desired effect with the majority is necessary before the leader can make adjustments and necessary changes to achieve the *Innovating* level.

Conclusion

As we have seen, multiple formative, accurate measures tied to standards are crucial to school success. Domain 1 of the Marzano School Leader Model focuses closely on goal setting and appropriate levels of data analysis, both on the "big-picture" or macro school-wide level and on the micro level of individual students.

So far, we've been focusing on principal behaviors that impact the achievement of whole-school and individual student goals. In the next chapter, we'll turn to Domain 2—"Continuous Improvement of Instruction" to examine the practices and actions a principal takes to support improved teacher practice and empower teachers to improve their own pedagogy. These actions, in turn, impact Domain 1 for whole-school improvement.

CHAPTER 2

Continuous Improvement of Instruction (Domain 2)

Using feedback isn't confined to a classroom. Consider its role in self-regulation and lifelong learning. We all stand to benefit from knowing when to seek feedback, how to seek it, and what to do with it when we get it.
—John Hattie (2012)

The idea of instructional leadership has a long legacy, and our definition of an instructional leader continues to evolve. As early as 1930, for example, the superintendent of St. Louis public schools was emphasizing both managerial and instructional leadership for principals, noting that the school principal was responsible for "all phases of management and instruction. It is the business of the principal to secure the best possible educational results and to do this with the utmost efficiency" (Pierce, 1935, p. 56). By the early 1980s, as the school accountability movement was beginning to take shape, the tide had turned toward a focus on principals who were taking responsibility for the instructional climate of their schools. The decade of the 1980s saw renewed interest on the part of researchers and policy makers, as many educators struggled with the thorny issues of what made principals effective.

In 1983, Cheryl Chase and Michael Kane found, for instance, that a review of the literature devoted to principal practices demonstrated a good deal of confusion about what, exactly, the job description entailed. Chase and Kane determined that the literature focused on three dilemmas related to the school leader's role: (1) how the principal determined his relationship to teachers and students; (2) how principals managed their time compared to managers in industry; and (3) what characteristics effective principals shared. Instructional leadership, they found, was largely left to the principal's discretion—or as Elmore (2000) put it later, to the principal's individual interest (or lack of it) in pedagogy. The authors concluded that instructional leadership could be improved by a more structured definition of the role, a defined evaluation system, and a district plan for professional development.

Other researchers of the period wrestled with similar questions. Was it possible, for instance, for a school leader to make the difference between a "successful" and an "unsuccessful" school (as measured in increased student achievement scores)—and to what extent did the administrator influence instruction? In a report published in July 1978, Jean Wellisch and colleagues note that in successful schools, the administrator was highly concerned with instruction, communicated instructional views openly; took responsibility for instructional decisions, coordinated instructional programs, and emphasized academic standards (Wellisch, MacQueen, Carriere, & Duck, 1978).

A 1987 study by Richard Andrews and Roger Soder made a clear connection between principal leadership and student achievement. Their findings suggested that "teacher perceptions of the principal as an instructional leader are critical to the reading and mathematics achievement of students, particularly low achieving students" (p. 11).

For our purposes in this chapter, an instructional leader is defined as a person who develops and supports a school culture focused on *continuously improved learning* and *continuous growth* for all—teachers, students, and the leader herself. An instructional leader influences instructional standards and actively participates in instructional actions by articulating a vision for what instruction should look like in the school.

We know more about best practices in classroom instruction for improving student achievement than ever before. The heyday of "the sage on the stage" is waning; teachers are doing less and less lecturing, and student engagement is a high priority. New research in the fields of neuro-anatomy, psychology, and sociology have offered us refined lenses with which to view optimum learning environments—and technology (whiteboards, clickers, online platforms, student interest inventories) has transformed the way we gather student data and receive and analyze feedback. With the introduction of college and career readiness standards, the focus has sharpened on cognitively complex thinking skills that will stand students in good stead as the 21st century unfolds.

Moreover, as teachers learn to use refined classroom strategies aligned with higher-order thinking skills, they are more likely to see clearer, more objectively defined results of their hard work. But changing old habits and practices is never easy—all the more reason that a school leader's dedication to continuous improvement of instruction truly matters.

The Marzano School Leader Evaluation Model is designed to work effectively with any teacher evaluation model; we consider the coherence between teacher and leader models a priority when it comes to continuous improvement of instruction. The model does require that the school have a coherent vision of effective instruction and common language of instruction, or, in a best-case scenario, formalized model of instruction. In this sense, the school leader evaluation model also helps focus and refine *teacher* evaluation.

Of course, many districts across the United States have chosen to use the Marzano leader and Marzano teacher evaluation models together for a fully comprehensive evaluation system with numerous benefits. Over time, we believe that most successful school districts will adopt some form of such highly aligned evaluation systems.

The Marzano school leader model, as we have said, positions the school leader as an instructional leader whose primary purpose is, above all others, to help teachers improve their classroom practice and thereby drive growth in student achievement. As Hallinger and Heck (1998) note, the behaviors of the school leader "have a measurable, though *indirect* effect on school effectiveness and student achievement" (p. 186). School leader behaviors support and facilitate teacher effectiveness.

The school leader must, first of all, have a vision for what effective classroom instruction looks like and what the desired outcomes of effective instruction should be—such is the focus of Domain 2. The elements in Domain 2 are the leading indicators, or the actions a school leader must take to obtain the desired results of improving instruction. This domain helps create a comprehensive approach to planning, implementing, reflecting, sharing, and mentoring around a common vision of instruction.

Continuous Improvement of Instruction

Continuous improvement of instruction is a relatively new area of focus in teacher and leader evaluation, in part because of new research in this area but also because advances in technology have made analysis of data and formative feedback both faster and more accurate. In essence, continuous improvement of instruction posits that teachers are expected to continually enhance their pedagogical skills, with particular attention to the strategies that have the highest probability of producing learning when implemented at the appropriate level and appropriate part of the lesson. Continuous improvement asks that teachers reflect on their practice, develop growth plans, and adapt their teaching strategies and behaviors based on student learning data and feedback from supervisors, colleagues, coaches, mentors, and students.

As we have seen, an effective school leader is primarily focused on helping teachers steadily improve their classroom practice from year to year, with a powerful cumulative effect on student learning. The school leader's role is as lead learner and teacher, a person with a clear implementation plan for an instructional model or a common language of instruction.

An effective principal from Lake County, Florida, shared with us that she focused on continuous improvement of instruction in her school by creating academies of professional learning within professional learning communities (PLCs). During these academies, teachers and school leaders focused on level two and level three data analysis to identify root causes for achievement gaps. Teachers started this process by reviewing data from their teacher-created common formative assessments. Data analysis allowed students who needed additional support to be identified before the summative assessments. The principal then asked her curriculum support personnel—instructional coaches, paraprofessionals, permanent substitutes, retired teacher volunteers, and lead teachers—to provide specific standards-based tutoring for the identified students.

Building Pedagogical Skills Throughout the School

The actions and behaviors in this domain help ensure that the school as a whole as well as individual teachers perceive teacher pedagogical skill as one of the most powerful instruments in enhancing student learning. The school is committed to enhancing pedagogical skills on a continuous basis. The five interrelated elements that comprise Domain 2 of the Marzano School Leader Evaluation Model have been identified by research as crucial practices and behaviors for successful school leadership and student achievement. The Wallace Foundation report, *Learning from Leadership* (2010), for example, details the school leader practices that best supported improved classroom instruction (Seashore-Louis, Leithwood, Wahlstrom, & Anderson, 2010). Those practices included focusing the school on goals and expectations for student achievement (behaviors that correspond to Domain 1, Element 1). Blase and Blase (2004) identify three primary elements of successful instructional leadership: conducting instructional conferences, providing staff development, and developing teacher reflection. These three behaviors are addressed in Domain 2, Elements 2, 4, and 5.

Further, Marzano, Waters, and McNulty's Meta-Analysis of School Leadership, published in *School Leadership That Works* (Marzano et al., 2005), categorizes twenty-one "Responsibilities of the School Leader." For example, the school leader

- Ensures faculty and staff are aware of the most current theories and practices and makes the discussion of these a regular aspect of the school's culture
- Is directly involved in the design and implementation of curriculum, instruction, and assessment practices
- Is knowledgeable about current curriculum, instruction, and assessment practices

These behaviors correspond to Elements 1, 2, and 3 of Domain 2. Figure 2.1 illustrates the five elements of Domain 2.

Figure 2.1. The five elements of Domain 2

Domain 2

**Continuous Improvement
of Instruction**

Element 1:
The school leader
provides a clear vision
as to how instruction
should be addressed in
the school.

Element 2:
The school leader
effectively supports and
retains teachers who
continually enhance
their pedagogical skills
through reflection and
professional growth
plans.

Element 3:
The school leader is
aware of predominant
instructional practices
throughout the school.

Element 4:
The school leader
ensures that teachers
are provided with clear,
ongoing evaluations of
their pedagogical
strengths and
weaknesses that are
based on multiple
sources of data and are
consistent with student
achievement data.

Element 5:
The school leader
ensures that teachers
are provided with job-
embedded professional
development that is
directly related to their
instructional growth
goals.

These interrelated elements together form a cohesive plan to support, monitor, measure, and ensure that all teachers in the school share a commitment to improving their practice. Element 1 sets and communicates the vision of instruction. Element 2 ensures that professional growth plans are in place and that teachers who continuously grow and reflect are retained in the school. Element 3 ensures that the school leader has a deep understanding of instruction in order to be able to observe, coach, and provide effective feedback. Element 4 ensures that the school leader uses multiple sources of data, including classroom observations, to determine teachers' strengths and weaknesses and see that teachers focus on classroom strategies with the greatest impact on student achievement. Finally, Element 5 focuses on professional learning directly related to, and supportive of, teacher growth goals.

Challenges

In our work with school leaders, we have identified a number of the most common and significant challenges a school leader faces in helping teachers develop their expertise in order to impact student achievement. Leaders should be aware of these points of tension in advance, so they can devise creative strategies to mitigate their effect.

1. Creative tension between roles

As we have said, the school leader's role is lead learner and teacher, a person with a clear implementation plan for the common language or model of instruction.

There are naturally some challenges for a school leader who expects to fully support continuous improvement of instruction. First and foremost, the leader must walk the delicate line between the role instructional leader, on the one hand, and evaluator/supervisor, on the other.

To support teacher growth that ultimately leads to student growth, school leaders as lead learners and teachers juggle many subroles. They want to maintain strong interpersonal relationships and continually improve their own craft knowledge and the craft knowledge of teachers. Craft knowledge is the "wisdom of teaching"; as in any profession, it is developed over time with practice, reflection, and feedback (Van Driel & De Jong, 2001). Leaders must support teachers in their professional growth, but they must also evaluate teachers. The divide between these roles may create tension.

Tension, however, is not always necessarily a bad thing. It's possible to resolve tension so that *meaning* is created within the space of conflict—so that the tension results in growth. In *The Fifth Discipline*, Peter Senge (1990) identifies this tension between reality and what could be—calling it "creative tension."

Creative tension is the difference between shared vision and current reality. The gap between where we are and where we want to be results in a desire for change. Creative tension will drive committed group members toward organizational goals, closing the gap.

In other words, the tension between the school leader's roles as lead learner/teacher and evaluator can open the door for positive, system-wide growth. Steps toward resolving this tension might include formal and informal conversations, dialogue, active listening, questioning, and other collaborative strategies common to mentoring relationships.

Developing positive mentoring relationships requires the leader to have productive, collegial conversations. Effective leaders become coaches to their teachers and know how to effectively communicate goals and objectives that support professional growth and student achievement. An administrator in Pasco County, Florida, calls these "courageous conversations." It is a delicate balance to faithfully implement an evaluation system that produces professional growth.

2. Hiring, retention, and termination

The instructional leader must also hire teachers most likely to demonstrate an eagerness to develop professionally, and retain teachers who are committed to growth. A 2011 study from MetLife finds that only 44 percent of teachers are "very satisfied" with their jobs (an 18 percent decline since 2008) and that, depending on demographics, as many as 66 percent planned to leave the profession in the next five years (MetLife, 2012). Confirming these trends, a new report on America's top K–12 teachers from The New Teacher Project (TNTP) notes that, in a survey of the most distinguished teachers in the United States, a full 60 percent said they were planning to leave the profession within five years (TNTP, 2013). In almost any other industry or profession, such a planned exodus would constitute a crisis (imagine 60 percent of surgeons leaving the profession, or 60 percent of engineers!). Hiring and retaining teachers who are willing to self-assess, reflect, and implement personal growth plans may be a significant challenge.

3. Becoming a reliable observer

Most school leaders need training, practice, and feedback to become reliable observers. In this way, the learning curve for a school leader implementing a model of instruction is as steep as it is for teachers. A school leader conducting an observation has to be able to locate evidence that the teacher is using strategies effectively; but more than that, the observer must also note when strategies were called for but not used in that particular lesson or unit.

Further, to be truly helpful, an observer has to diagnose which teacher behaviors contribute to weaknesses (and strengths) of instruction and formulate prognoses for improvement. Which practices should the teacher continue to use? Which should be retired? Which need more reflection to produce desired results? And which new strategies or behaviors should the teacher incorporate?

4. Providing formative feedback

School leaders who hope to foster an environment where instruction is continually improving also make sure that assessments or evaluations are formative as well as summative. When teachers can assess their skills early on in the unit or year, they have the opportunity to practice and refine. Good teachers are aware of the value of practice: In response to the TNTP survey, 100 percent of America's best teachers strongly agreed that "practice in the form of trying different lessons and teaching methods over time" had the highest impact on helping them improve (2013, p. 12). Ninety-three percent found observation of other teachers very helpful. Advice and feedback from colleagues and students were close behind.

Although 83 percent of teachers surveyed agreed that their evaluator's honest feedback had helped them improve, "a significant subset of respondents indicated that they are not receiving useful feedback on a regular basis. Almost one in four teachers (27 percent) at least somewhat disagreed that they "get regular, constructive feedback on their teaching" (TNTP, 2013, p. 12).

In regard to feedback, Blase and Blase (2004) find that teachers respond most positively when the suggested action is *purposeful*, the teacher has the *ability to perform* it, and the suggestion does not *offend* the teacher (pp. 30–31).

In an informal survey we conducted with leaders from more than thirty districts, leaders reported that the number one reason they failed to give teachers accurate feedback regarding their teaching practices was "relationships"—in other words, school leaders worried that honest feedback might damage or strain an otherwise good working relationship. Finding the right balance between targeted, honest feedback and collegial support will continue to be an ongoing challenge for school leaders.

5. Analysis of data

A final challenge is the school leader's ability and willingness to analyze data to inform and direct instructional practice throughout the school. In the previous chapter, we discussed a number of ways to do this. Technology tools are available to make data on teacher performance instantly accessible and guide growth planning and goals. One such technology platform, iObservation, is covered at the end of this chapter.

Providing a Clear Vision of Instruction (Domain 2, Element 1)

The school leader provides a clear vision as to how instruction should be addressed in the school.

Domain 2, Element 1 contains two interrelated pieces. First, the school leader must establish a *clear vision of instruction*—what good teaching looks like and how to get there. To this purpose, the school leader will likely implement a model of instruction (such as the one embedded in the Marzano Teacher Evaluation Model) or at the very least a common language of instruction. The second, unstated, construct of Element 1 is that the establishment of a vision rests on *clearly communicating the goals and expectations* around that vision to staff, parents, students, teachers, and the community. The leader must have a vision and an eye on the desired result of Domain 2—continuous improvement of instruction. The desired result of Element 1 is that everyone knows the instructional model.

The more the leader can minimize wide discrepancies of instructional practice from classroom to classroom, the better. Therefore, it is extremely important to implement and support a school-wide common language of instruction and encourage understanding of, and agreement about, best classroom practices—specifically those practices most closely correlated to gains in student achievement.

A model of instruction like the one embedded in Domain 1 of the Marzano Teacher Evaluation Model, for example, can go a long way to iron out the misunderstandings and pedagogical misalignments between teachers and students, teachers and teachers, and teachers and supervisors on the one hand, and the larger community on the other. Our position is that a robust model of instruction provides a frame, a vocabulary, a research base, and a measurement system to ensure that every member involved in the school knows what is expected of classroom behaviors and practices—and what the intended results, or desired effects, are of those behaviors. In such a system, each teacher is provided feedback using a common language of instruction.

Creativity and Autonomy Within an Instructional Model

A model of instruction in no way attempts to standardize or straightjacket teacher practice. Within the frame, teachers may devise creative lesson plans and exercises and experience a great deal of autonomy. Middle school language arts teacher Kerin Steigerwalt, who uses the Marzano instructional model with her students in Pennsylvania, explains, for example, her process for creating experimental inquiry lessons for the language arts students in her class (Element 22 of Design Question 4 in the Marzano Teacher Evaluation Model). Steigerwalt developed a lesson asking students to hypothesize about the qualities of an ancient Greek hero, investigate different myths, and then generate a personality quiz of the sort you might find in a fashion magazine. The students begin with the question "Are you a hero?"

> And then [they] ask a series of questions: Did you die a tragic death? Has someone been trying to kill you since birth? Did you fulfill some terrible prophecy?

They start out, of course, thinking a hero is going to be tall, blond, good looking, strong, and rich. And then they realize that none of the Greek heroes and heroines were at all what they were expecting. (Personal communication, June 2012)

Master teachers like Steigerwalt report that they don't see their creativity suffering in the classroom, even as they implement a model of instruction and use data to improve their classroom strategies.

Characteristics of a Model of Instruction

In our research and field experience, we have identified five major characteristics of the most effective model of instruction. The model should set clear definitions and measurements, help inform decisions, facilitate collaboration, and allow for efficient use of data, as outlined here:

1. A model of instruction defines and describes effective teaching based on the most current research on classroom strategies in order to improve student learning. This foundation allows for successful unit and lesson planning along with the strategies to meet instructional objectives.

2. The model provides a means for assessment, reflection, and deliberate practice.

3. The model functions as a transparent framework for making decisions about how to adjust instruction based on student data, formative and summative assessments, and other feedback.

4. The model provides a framework and common language for professional conversations, collaboration between teachers, and coaching.

5. And finally, the most useful models will incorporate a system to collect, analyze, and distribute data.

The most helpful models, as we have noted, will provide a coherent means to provide formative and summative feedback about instruction. As Showers, Murphy, and Joyce (1996) famously note in their groundbreaking work on the effects of formative assessment and coaching, only 5 percent of learners transfer a new skill into practice as a result of learning theory alone; 20 percent will make the transfer if they practice the skill during trainings; but a full 90 percent transfer the skill once feedback during training and job-embedded coaching are added to the mix.

Successful models of instruction provide for such job-embedded coaching— in many forms, from teacher mentors to supervisors to collaboration partners. As we indicated earlier, the principal as lead learner has a responsibility to balance instructional coaching with evaluative feedback.

One major advantage of a school-wide (or district-wide) instructional model is that formative and summative feedback may be more focused, specific, and actionable. Because teachers in classrooms across the school intentionally implement agreed-upon classroom strategies to improve student learning, feedback from formal or informal observations, walk-throughs, and teacher visits have a common ground. This shared understanding and focus makes it possible for supervisors to provide the type of feedback most likely to help teachers move up the performance scale; and as the leading indicator of teacher effectiveness improves, so will the lagging indicators of student test scores.

Building and Communicating a Vision for Instruction Without a Model of Instruction

A model for instruction provides the necessary communication to the teaching staff about what the building will consider effective instruction. Recently, when a group of teachers on a school leadership team were asked, "How would your building staff describe effective instruction?" the group struggled for a few minutes to determine what everyone in the building would consider effective instruction and if this description could be identified in every classroom. We can expect that instruction is likely to vary from classroom to classroom unless the school leader takes steps to ensure that everyone knows how the building staff describes effective instructional practice.

In the absence of a detailed model of instruction, the school leader can still build and communicate a vision for instruction through a series of well-thought-out steps:

1. The school leader develops a timeline and plan, communicating what the expectations are for students based on the analysis of data. The leader determines benchmarks for subsequent performance.

2. The school leader provides time and resources to allow teachers to interact and develops the format and structure for those interactions.

3. The school leader shares best practice instructional strategies with staff, parents, and students and provides time for teachers to model and observe.

Whether or not a detailed model of instruction exists, the questions are the same.

Key Questions

1. Is there a common language regarding instructional strategies?

2. Do all teachers understand the model of instruction?

3. What evidence is used to monitor teachers' understanding of and effective use of the model of instruction?

4. Does everyone in the school know the school leader's vision for what effective instruction should look like in the school?

5. When teachers discuss and plan instruction, do they use the common language of instruction?

6. What evidence is there that teachers see a relationship between their use of instructional strategies and student achievement?

7. What kinds of job-embedded professional development are provided to teachers to improve their instructional strategies?

Scale and Evidences for Domain 2, Element 1

The school leader provides a clear vision as to how instruction should be addressed in the school.

Figures 2.2 and 2.3 illustrate the scale and evidences for Domain 2, Element 1. Note that as with all the scales in the model, the school leader is expected to set level 3 (*Applying*) as the target goal and grow to at least that level over time. The *Applying* level always includes the "monitoring" component, which requires, in Element 1, that the school leader has a very good grasp of how well the teachers in the school recognize and know the school's model of instruction or common instructional language.

Figure 2.2. Scale for Domain 2, Element 1

Scale Value	Description
Innovating (4)	The school leader continually examines and makes adjustments so that all faculty and staff understand the nuances of the instructional model and integrates new instructional initiatives into the school instructional model.
Applying (3)	The school leader ensures that a school-wide language or model of instruction is in place AND monitors the extent to which the faculty and staff understand the instructional model.
Developing (2)	The school leader ensures that a school-wide language or model of instruction is in place.
Beginning (1)	The school leader attempts to ensure that a school-wide language or model of instruction is in place but does not complete the task or does so partially.
Not Using (0)	The school leader does not attempt to ensure that a school-wide language or model of instruction is in place.

Figure 2.3 details sample evidences for Domain 2, Element 1.

Figure 2.3. Sample evidences for Domain 2, Element 1

Sample Evidences for Domain 2, Element 1
• A written document articulating the school-wide model of instruction is in place.
• The school-wide language of instruction is used regularly by faculty in their professional learning communities and faculty and/or department meetings.
• Professional development opportunities are provided for new teachers regarding the school-wide model of instruction.

(Continued)

Go to www.learningsciences.com/bookresources to download figures and tables.

| • Professional development opportunities are provided for all teachers regarding the school-wide model of instruction. |
| • New initiatives are prioritized and limited in number to support the instructional model. |
| • The school-wide language of instruction is used regularly by faculty in their informal conversations. |
| • When asked, teachers can describe the major components of the school-wide model of instruction. |
| • When asked, teachers can explain how strategies in the instructional framework promote learning for the school's diverse population. |

Scenario

Mr. Hayes has been the principal at Tides Middle School for three years. During this time, he has become familiar with the teaching practices of the staff. This year, he has the responsibility to help teachers understand the new instructional model adopted at the district level as they enter the second year of implementation.

Using a staff survey, Mr. Hayes identifies the staff's level of comfort with the new model after their first year of using it and their feeling about related upcoming professional development. From this information, Mr. Hayes elects to meet with a team of staff representatives to discuss needs assessment and identify a plan for professional development around the model.

The team reports that teachers understood the system for implementation, but lacked clarity on the common language of the model. Teachers, they feel, need more practice to deepen their understanding. Specifically, most teachers can identify the structure but are still unclear on the desired-effect component of the model. The team decides that revisiting the elements and emphasizing the desired effect for each would be a good starting point for Year 2.

Throughout the second year, Mr. Hayes ensures that the team makes connections to the instructional model and that they have multiple opportunities to focus solely on the model's elements and desired effects.

As a follow-up, Mr. Hayes provided opportunities for collaborative planning, requiring all teachers to participate regardless of subject area. Exit tickets helped to monitor progress, as did midyear and end-of-year surveys. These measures indicated that the teachers had an improved understanding of the model, particularly in the area of desired effects.

Explanation

Mr. Hayes operated at the *Applying* level, or possibly at *Innovating*, depending on whether he could provide evidence that he had ensured that all teachers, not just the collective group, had a better understanding of the instructional model. To rate this principal at the *Innovating* level, we would want to hear more about how he regularly helps staff make connections between new initiatives and the instructional model. A conversation on how he monitored the understanding of all of the teachers could help ensure that he was operating at the *Innovating* level.

Since professional development connected to the use of effective instructional practices in the instructional model was an integral part of this scenario, an evaluator might want to discuss professional development plans further to also provide a rating in Domain 2, Element 5 (*the school leader ensures that teachers are provided with job-embedded professional development that is directly related to their instructional growth goals*). To challenge Mr. Hayes' thinking, an evaluator might ask him how he helped teachers understand the predominant practices in the building and worked to help them identify effective versus ineffective practice. The answers to these questions may provide evidence connected to Domain 2, Element 3 (*the school leader is aware of predominant instructional practices throughout the school*).

The school leader with a vision for how teachers should use a common language to improve instruction will clearly communicate his vision for the instructional model and will in turn use teacher evaluation as a tool for providing targeted, specific feedback. The school leader will monitor how well the teachers understand the instructional framework and make corrections if some teachers fail to understand the model. Once again, in this way the elements of the school leader model are tightly interconnected and also aligned to the model for teacher evaluation.

We often ask principals to describe their vision for instruction. We ask them to tell us what they expect to see on any given day in any classroom in their building. Next, we ask, "How do your teachers know this is what you expect?"

As we discussed in the previous chapter, it is important to communicate goals for student achievement with teachers and for teachers to communicate and develop goals for individual students with the students. When goals are clarified in this way, it is more likely that schools will see positive outcomes.

Supporting and Retaining the Right Teachers (Domain 2, Element 2)

The school leader effectively supports and retains teachers who continually enhance their pedagogical skills through reflection and a professional growth plan.

> *Coaching done well may be the most effective intervention*
> *designed for human performance.*
> —Dr. Atul Gawande (2011)

The authors of this book maintain an expectation that all teachers can increase their expertise from year to year, which can produce gains in student achievement with a powerful cumulative effect. We believe that an expectation for growth should guide decisions about hiring and retention. The best

opportunities for teacher growth happen within the areas of intentional planning, classroom instruction, and deliberate practice.

Deliberate Practice for Deliberate Growth

> [*School leaders*] *realize that most teachers expand their teaching range only with
> carefully designed support and assistance. This is a startling revelation for principals
> who had always assumed intuitively that when given minimal information
> and assistance most teachers would analyze their own teaching and formulate
> and act on growth plans in a self-directed and constructive manner.*
> —Blase and Blase (2004)

One of the most effective ways for teachers to enhance their pedagogical skills
is through a method of deliberate practice, first identified by Anders Ericsson
as a proven route to expertise for athletes, musicians, and other high perform-
ers. More recently, deliberate practice—a system where the practitioner identifies
specific skills for improvement and hones those skills based on feedback from
a coach—has been applied as a way to improve teacher pedagogy. In the past,
feedback to improve teacher performance has been intermittent or, at worst, non-
existent in many schools and districts. Deliberate practice offers a solution.

As Marzano (2011) notes,

Research suggests that the supervisory and feedback systems in place in many districts do little to systematically enhance teacher expertise (Toch & Rothman, 2008;
Weisberg, Sexton, Mulhern, & Keeling, 2009). Fortunately we can develop expertise
through deliberate practice (Ericsson, Krampe, & Tesch-Romer, 1993). Deliberate
practice involves more than just repetition; it requires activities that are designed to
improve performance, challenge the learner, and provide feedback. (p. 82)

Figure 2.4 illustrates a continuous improvement cycle based on deliberate
practice and intentional planning.

Figure 2.4. Continuous improvement with deliberate practice and intentional planning

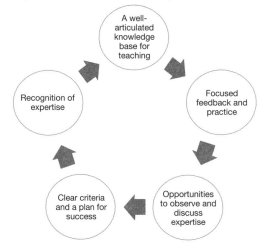

Go to www.learningsciences.com/bookresources to download figures and tables.

Deliberate practice, when applied to teaching, is a mindful, systematic, highly structured effort to relentlessly seek solutions to clearly defined problems. Rather than getting stuck in a loop of trial and error, teachers and school leaders use deliberate practice to grow expertise through a series of planned activities, reflection, and collaboration.

In other words, it is a focused plan to improve, no matter how high the level of current expertise. Deliberate practice empowers both teachers and their supervisors. To work effectively, deliberate practice requires

- *Effort.* Individuals are motivated to practice because practice improves performance.
- *Perseverance.* Expert performance doesn't happen overnight.
- *Brainpower.* Experts' practice causes brains to develop better systems for storing, organizing, and accessing information.
- *Metacognition.* The learner must possess a keen awareness of her own thinking processes.
- *Feedback.* A coach provides suggestions, questions, and prompts to improve thinking about performance.

It should be noted that all the activities illustrated in Figure 2.3 involve coaching to a greater or lesser degree; the school leader functions as "head coach" in the same way that she operates as "lead learner." The school leader, in providing feedback from observations, is certainly acting in the role of coach, although additional coaching responsibilities and opportunities may be delegated to an assistant principal or master teachers. In any event, coaching requires certain conditions to be effective—trust, focused feedback, and opportunities to observe and discuss teaching, among them.

Marzano (2011) identifies four major components of deliberate practice in schools: a common language of instruction; a focus on specific strategies; tracking teacher progress; and opportunities to observe and discuss expertise. We discuss two of these components related to Domain 2, Element 2, below.

A Focus on Specific Strategies

We generally recommend that teachers, with support from their coaches and administrators, select a small number of strategies for specific improvement each year. If the school is using the Marzano framework, this might mean one routine strategy, one content strategy, and one strategy enacted on the spot, for example. Teachers should have some autonomy in choosing the strategies to work on (although they should consider feedback from previous observations and evaluations). The strategies they select should relate to some aspect of the instructional model. The vision for instruction serves as the umbrella for this domain; each element fits beneath that umbrella in its relationship to the vision for instruction.

Teachers respond positively when feedback is constructive and focused. Kathleen (Katie) Breakey, a first-grade teacher at Allapattah Flatts K–8 in St. Lucie County, Florida, puts it this way:

> The feedback that I've been getting this year from my principals and administration versus years past with other evaluation tools is more specific. The feedback is targeted at a certain element, and therefore it's easier for me, as a teacher, to go back and hone in on that skill that I need to practice, that I need to develop further, that I need to work with the students to decide what we can do to make this better in our classrooms.
>
> I'm focused on [those skills], and it just helps me be a better teacher. I'm more focused deliberately on what we're doing right in that math lesson or right in that phonics lesson. I'm more specific and intentional about my teaching. (Personal interview, 2014)

David Worrell, who taught with the Leon County School District for more than 40 years, served as president of the teacher's union, and helped coach teachers using the new Marzano evaluation system, also found that using deliberate practice as part of the new teacher evaluation system helped him improve:

> A veteran teacher might think that there is no room for improvement and that because they've been teaching for a number of years they have arrived, they've got it, that's all there is—that's simply not so. And the "ah-ha" moment came when I realized that this is a continuous process, and our practice will become more deliberate. (Personal interview, 2012)

Tracking Teacher Progress to Improve Pedagogical Skills

Once a teacher has chosen which strategies to practice deliberately, coaches, observers, and supervisors can track improvement using a generic scale, for example, from *Not Using* to *Innovating*, as in the Marzano model; from "needs improvement" to "proficient"; or other rubrics. The goal of the coach will be to help the teacher move up the scale in improved performance. *Not Using*, for example, would mean that the strategy is called for, but the teacher is not using it. A *Beginning* teacher is using the strategy incorrectly or with parts missing. *Developing* indicates that the teacher is using the strategy with no major errors or omissions but in a mechanistic way.

Level 3 of the Marzano scale—*Applying*—is the minimum target for developing expertise. At this level, the teacher not only uses the strategy without error but also monitors to see whether the strategy has the desired effect on students. At the highest level of the scale—*Innovating*—the teacher knows the strategy so well that he has developed adaptations specific to the needs of every student in the class.

A teacher's scores may initially be quite low—either *Not Using* (unsatisfactory, needs improvement, etc.) or *Beginning*—because the teacher is focusing on areas where he would like to improve. Throughout the year, teachers can monitor their progress through self-ratings, walk-throughs conducted by administrators and instructional coaches, and comprehensive observations conducted by supervisors.

Figure 2.5 illustrates a system that supports teacher growth through professional growth planning, and formative and summative feedback.

Figure 2.5. A comprehensive system of feedback

A System of Feedback

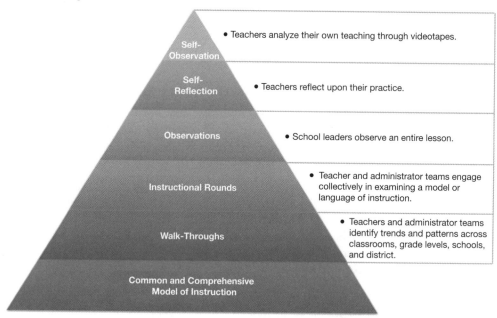

Additionally, school leaders will make announced and unannounced, *formal and informal observations* to provide formative and summative feedback. Using all of this data, teachers are able to *self-reflect* upon their own pedagogy and make plans to target specific skills or strategies that they need to practice. At the top of the pyramid teachers may be able to *self-observe* by watching videos of themselves teaching and analyze their classroom behaviors even more thoroughly.

For Evaluators of School Leaders

The preceding descriptions provide guidance for evaluators to gather evidence for Element 2. Evaluators can expect to see evidence of a comprehensive system of feedback in the schools of effective leaders. Figure 2.6 illustrates the scale for Domain 2, Element 2, and Figure 2.7 the evidences for Domain 2, Element 2.

Key Questions

1. Do all teachers have written professional growth plans?
2. What process is in place for teachers to track their own growth?
3. What process do you have in place to provide feedback to teachers on their professional growth plans?
4. What support do you make available for teachers who are not progressing adequately in their professional growth?
5. Do you have specific criteria related to instruction that you use when hiring teachers?

Figure 2.6. Scale for Domain 2, Element 2

Scale Value	Description
Innovating (4)	The school leader regularly intervenes with and supports teachers who are not meeting their growth goals or adequately enhancing the achievement of their students.
Applying (3)	The school leader ensures that teachers establish growth goals regarding their pedagogical skills and track their individual progress AND monitors the extent to which teachers achieve their growth goals.
Developing (2)	The school leader ensures that teachers establish growth goals regarding their pedagogical skills and track their individual progress.
Beginning (1)	The school leader attempts to ensure that teachers establish growth goals regarding their pedagogical skills and track their individual progress but does not complete the task or does so partially.
Not Using (0)	The school leader does not attempt to ensure that teachers establish growth goals regarding their pedagogical skills and track their individual progress.

Figure 2.7 details sample evidences for Domain 2, Element 2.

Figure 2.7. Sample evidences for Domain 2, Element 2

Sample Evidences for Domain 2, Element 2
• Individual teachers have written pedagogical growth goals.
• Individual teachers keep track of their progress on their pedagogical growth goals.
• Evaluation results, growth plans, and interventions for struggling teachers are available.
• Meetings are regularly scheduled with teachers regarding their growth goals and tracking of their progress.
• A system is in place to effectively evaluate and revise the school's new teacher induction program.
• The school leader has demonstrated a track record of hiring effective teachers.

(Continued)

Go to www.learningsciences.com/bookresources to download figures and tables.

• The school leader has a track record of retaining effective teachers.
• When asked, teachers can describe their progress on their pedagogical growth goals.
• When asked, teachers can share documented examples of how reflection has improved their instructional practice.

Awareness of Instructional Practices (Domain 2, Element 3)

The school leader is aware of predominant instructional practices throughout the school.

The majority of classroom teachers enter their classrooms at the beginning of each day and start the daily process of teaching and learning. Some call it an isolated process, but we suggest that if we want teachers to embrace a vision for a school-wide model of instruction, and perhaps embrace the practice of adding new instructional strategies to their pedagogical tool kit, the first step is for school leaders to identify the predominant instructional practices in the school and make teachers aware of these practices. In our discussion of Domain 4 (Cooperation and Collaboration), we will talk about ways to ensure that teachers have opportunities to observe other teachers. But in Domain 2, we explore *why* teachers should be aware of and understand the school's predominant instructional practices, what can happen with that information, and how it can be one of the first steps in changing instructional practice. To foster this awareness, the school leader will have to help break down a longstanding tendency toward teacher isolation.

As Jacob Mishook notes in a 2011 commentary for the Annenberg Institute:

> The traditional "egg-crate" model of teaching and learning has been dominant in the United States for decades, where individual teachers are isolated behind the closed doors of their classrooms (Johnson 2010). This traditional model has been discarded by most of the world's successful school systems, which recognize that having highly qualified but isolated teachers is not enough (Fullan 2010). Developing schools with a high level of human capital (i.e., a staff of individual teachers who have advanced skills and knowledge) *and* a high level of social capital (i.e., where teachers interact regularly with each other) is necessary for all teachers and students to succeed. But new human capital reforms, which evaluate teachers individually, and district decentralization, which isolates schools from one another and pits them against one another as competitors, actively work against the notion of teachers utilizing each other to become better practitioners.

Element 3 says that the school leader must know the predominant practices; however, before this can happen, a set of identified instructional practices must be in place. Although this leadership framework supports the common language of the Marzano Teacher Evaluation Model, by design it adapts to any instructional model. The key to Element 3 is that the leader must be able to identify instructional strategies during walk-throughs and informal and formal observations.

What is the desired outcome of a leader knowing the predominant instructional strategies? If one of the first steps to improvement is awareness of a behavior, the desired result is that *all teachers in the school* are aware of the predominant teaching practices, setting the foundation for professional dialogue for feedback on these strategies. We discussed tension between roles for a school leader in an earlier section. Tensions are eased when all are aware of common expectations and effective practices.

For example, after completing several weeks of walk-throughs, a principal notes that during the majority of time teachers are in front of their classes, they are reviewing past content and then introducing new content. Teachers are spending scant time *processing* or *practicing* before rushing on to yet more new content. In such a case, the principal would probably identify teacher-directed lecturing as a predominant strategy in the school. The leader would share this trend data with teachers to make them aware of it and then focus continuous improvement on instructional strategies related to classroom processing and practice.

Element 3 is closely related to Element 5, in which the school leader provides teachers with job-embedded professional development. Part of the process of providing meaningful professional development begins with teachers and leaders knowing the school's instructional patterns and trends and using this data to design and implement individual professional development. Figures 2.8 and 2.9 illustrate the scale and evidences for Domain 2, Element 3.

Figure 2.8. Scale for Domain 2, Element 3

Scale Value	Description
Innovating (4)	The school leader regularly intervenes to ensure that ineffective instructional practices are corrected and effective instructional practices are proliferating.
Applying (3)	The school leader ensures that information about predominant instructional strategies in the school is collected, regularly interacts with teachers about the effectiveness of these strategies, AND monitors the extent to which the information is used to identify effective and ineffective practices.
Developing (2)	The school leader ensures that information about predominant instructional strategies in the school is collected and regularly interacts with teachers about the effectiveness of these strategies.
Beginning (1)	The school leader attempts to ensure that information about predominant instructional strategies in the school is collected and regularly interacts with teachers about the effectiveness of these strategies but does not complete the task or does so partially.
Not Using (0)	The school leader does not attempt to ensure that information about predominant instructional strategies in the school is collected.

Go to www.learningsciences.com/bookresources to download figures and tables.

Figure 2.9 details sample evidences for Domain 2, Element 3.

Figure 2.9. Sample evidences for Domain 2, Element 3

Sample Evidences for Domain 2, Element 3
• Walk-through or other informal observation data are aggregated in such a way as to disclose predominant instructional practices in the school.
• Forthright feedback is provided to teachers regarding their instructional practices.
• Systems are in place to monitor the effect of the predominant instructional practices for all subgroups in the school.
• Data are available to document the predominant instructional practices in the school.
• The school leader can describe effective practices and problems of practice.
• When asked, teachers can describe the predominant instructional practices used in the school.

Key Questions

1. What data source do you use to track instructional strategies used in your building?

2. How do you make teachers aware of the predominant instructional strategies used throughout the building?

3. How do you address problems with instructional strategies that are not being used appropriately?

Scenario

During the first grading period, Mr. White, school principal, walks through every classroom each week collecting observational evidence regarding the instructional strategies the teachers are implementing. Through his performance management system, he is able to disaggregate the observational evidence to determine which instructional strategies teachers are using; he also analyzes the data to determine if teacher use of a strategy is having the desired results.

At a monthly staff meeting, Mr. White shares the trends in the instructional strategies he has observed and leads a discussion to explain the relationship between the use of the strategies and whether they are achieving the desired effect. Mr. White specifically addresses the alignment of the strategy to the achievement standards for each content area. As part of the process, he guides teachers in the review, and the group notes that the majority of teachers are using teacher-centered strategies. There is little or no evidence of teachers using teaching strategies that require students to generate or test hypotheses. He asks teachers to think about how they can work as a team to begin changing their instructional practices.

Go to www.learningsciences.com/bookresources to download figures and tables.

Explanation and Feedback

A supervisor or observer reviewing the constructs of Element 3 would see that Mr. White is demonstrating that he can identify the predominant instructional practices of the school. Based on this evidence, Mr. White would be rated at the *Developing* level. Think about what feedback we would give him to help him move up the scale to *Applying*. The focus of Domain 2 is to improve instruction, and a necessary first step in the process to improve instruction is for everyone to know the school's predominant instructional practices. In this case, the predominant practices are teacher centered, and teachers have not begun to shift to student-centered strategies that deepen understanding or challenge students to utilize knowledge. (Note that we continue this scenario in our discussion of Domain 2, Element 5.)

Conducting Ongoing Evaluations (Domain 2, Element 4)

The school leader ensures that teachers are provided with clear, ongoing evaluations of their pedagogical strengths and weaknesses that are based on multiple sources of data and are consistent with student achievement data.

Knowing trends in instructional practices is a starting point, but school leaders are charged with giving each teacher accurate feedback about their pedagogical strengths and weaknesses. Note that the scale and evidences for Element 4 (Figures 2.10 and 2.11) contain multiple embedded constructs:

- Teachers are provided with clear, ongoing evaluations of their teaching strengths and weakness.
- Evaluations are based on multiple sources of data.
- Evaluation data are consistent with student achievement data.

Figure 2.10. Scale for Domain 2, Element 4

Scale Value	Description
Innovating (4)	The school leader ensures that teacher evaluation processes are updated regularly to ensure the results are consistent with student achievement data.
Applying (3)	The school leader ensures that specific evaluation data are collected on each teacher regarding his/her pedagogical strengths and weaknesses and that these data are gathered from multiple sources AND monitors the extent to which teacher evaluations are consistent with student achievement data.
Developing (2)	The school leader ensures that specific evaluation data are collected on each teacher regarding his/her pedagogical strengths and weaknesses and that these data are gathered from multiple sources.

(Continued)

Go to www.learningsciences.com/bookresources to download figures and tables.

Beginning (1)	The school leader attempts to ensure that specific evaluation data are collected on each teacher regarding his/her pedagogical strengths and weaknesses and that these data are gathered from multiple sources, but does not complete the task or does so partially.
Not Using (0)	The school leader does not attempt to ensure that specific evaluation data are collected on each teacher regarding his/her pedagogical strengths and weaknesses and that these data are gathered from multiple sources.

Figure 2.11 details sample evidences for Domain 2, Element 4.

Figure 2.11. Sample evidences for Domain 2, Element 4

Sample Evidences for Domain 2, Element 4
• Highly specific scales are in place to provide teachers accurate feedback on their pedagogical strengths and weaknesses.
• Teacher feedback and evaluation data are based on multiple sources of information including but not limited to: direct observation, teacher self-report, analysis of teacher performance as captured on video, student reports on teacher effectiveness, and peer feedback to teachers.
• Teacher evaluation data are regularly used as the subject of conversation between school leaders and teachers.
• Data show that the school leader provides frequent observations and meaningful feedback to teachers.
• Ongoing data are available to support that teacher evaluations are consistent with student achievement data.
• When asked, teachers can describe their instructional strategies that have the strongest and weakest relationships to student achievement.

Can one yearly observation serve as a mechanism for changing a teacher's instructional practice? Most states require only one annual evaluation observation for teachers with more than three years of teaching experience. For teachers with one to three years teaching experience, most states recommend up to four observations annually. We propose that the purpose of evaluation is to refine and improve teachers' instructional practices through targeted feedback. In this case, clearly, one evaluation per year will not identify areas for improvement in a teacher's practice. The challenge we must confront is, do we ensure that teachers are provided ongoing evaluations of their performance?

No single data point can paint a complete picture of a teacher's performance. Obtaining a true score representing a teacher's instructional practice would require a commitment to have an observer in the classroom daily. *Therefore, to achieve the fairest picture of a teacher's performance, evaluation systems should use multiple measures to determine whether teachers have met performance expectations.*

Go to www.learningsciences.com/bookresources to download figures and tables.

In The New Teacher Project's 2010 paper, *Teacher Evaluation 2.0*, the authors argue that, whenever possible,

> multiple measures should include objective measures of student academic growth, such as value-added models that connect students' progress on standardized assessments to individual teachers while controlling for important factors such as students' academic history. Other possible measures include performance on districtwide or teacher-generated assessments, and classroom observations centered on evidence of student learning.

In addition to observation data, we advise that evaluators draw on multiple data sources, which might include student survey data, teacher self-evaluated video, peer feedback, and student artifacts. If the true measure of teacher effect is student outcomes, Element 4 says that there should be a relationship between a teacher's instructional practice evaluations and the achievement of the students in that teacher's classroom.

The process does not have to be complex. If a teacher consistently earns the highest rating for instructional practice, it follows, logically that the students in that classroom benefit from the instruction, and their achievement should show steady improvement. Thomas Kane and Stephen Cantrell in the Measures of Effective Teaching Project, a three-year project published in 2013, suggest that strong teacher performance positively impacts student learning and may in fact be the best predictor of student achievement.

Test Case: Pilot Project Using Multiple Measures in a Large Urban School District

In 2012–2013, Learning Sciences International conducted a pilot project with a large urban school district to test the use of multiple measures for accurate teacher performance assessment. Regardless of the process utilized for considering multiple data sources to assess teacher proficiency, it's not possible to achieve an improvement in teacher pedagogy without multiple layers of coaching and support. Participants in the pilot can attest to the level of commitment necessary to positively impact student achievement.

This pilot relied on formal observation data to determine its effectiveness. But in reality, the designers of the pilot were aware that it would be extremely difficult to formally observe all teachers in the district four times per year (a challenge many school districts must confront). Therefore, multiple measures of teacher proficiency and growth were deliberately built into the pilot: student surveys, informal walk-throughs by instructional coaches, instructional data chats, and student artifacts.

A novel measure for teachers in the pilot was the use of student surveys. Students were asked to rate the effectiveness of their teacher's learning goals and accompanying scales. Additionally, students were asked to describe the current unit scale and address their perception of their most recent achievement along the scale. Many teachers were concerned that students wouldn't give accurate accounts of their understanding of the scales. To address these concerns, the leader's formal observation data was compared to student perceptions as a check for possible student bias or inaccuracy. In addition to student survey data, instructional coaches routinely conducted informal, nonevaluative walk-throughs to determine teacher proficiency. The focus of the walk-throughs was centered on the use of learning goals and scales and tracking student progress, Elements 1 and 2 of the Marzano Teacher Evaluation Model. Student artifacts and results from instructional data chats were also used to measure teacher proficiency.

Stephen Cantrell and Thomas Kane (2013) for the Bill and Melinda Gates Foundation describe the causal relationship between student test data and the effectiveness of teacher instruction. Data chats can be defined this way: conversations centered around student achievement based on formative and summative assessment data. These routinely scheduled data chats were useful in determining how well teachers taught critical information from their shared lesson plans.

Data chats were conducted during scheduled weekly PLC meetings made up of grade- and subject-level teams—for example, sixth-grade math teams. During the PLC meetings, in addition to time devoted to common planning, conversations were scheduled to discuss data from common student formative and summative assessments. Information from data chats was used to assist observers in determining the effectiveness of the agreed-upon instructional strategies that teachers were using and to impact planned instruction. Teachers were able to determine if adaptations to future lesson plans and remediation would be needed before progressing to the next planned unit. Information from the chats was also used to identify students who could benefit from planned interventions, such as "pull-out" groups and after-school tutoring.

Focused collegial conversations during PLCs and supportive job-embedded coaching from instructional coaches, along with student survey data, assist in molding future instructional practices, all with the expressed intent of improving student achievement and teacher pedagogy.

It requires a high level of professionalism and passion to be reflective and intentional in the use of instructional strategies. Teachers, whether they are in a pilot or not, deserve recognition for the courageous effort needed to move beyond a cookie-cutter model to a researched-based, adaptive, shared collective approach to teaching.

If teacher behavior is the leading indicator for the lagging indicator of student achievement, we might ask why most reform initiatives have goals to improve student achievement without an accompanying focus on improving teacher pedagogy. No Child Left Behind, for example, focused on improving achievement of subgroups and meeting proficiency targets but lacked an emphasis on how to improve student achievement.

The federal Race to the Top initiative did include a focus on building great teachers and leaders as a major element of its reform project. The Marzano School Leader Evaluation Model builds on and reinforces those efforts.

Key Questions

1. How do you manage your schedule to allow maximum opportunities to observe teaching?

2. What are at least three different sources of data that you consider when evaluating teachers?

3. What data sources do you use to compare teacher evaluation data with student achievement data?

4. What are different ways that you provide teachers ongoing feedback as a part of their evaluation?

Providing Job-Embedded Professional Development, (Domain 2, Element 5)

The school leader ensures that teachers are provided with job-embedded professional development that is directly related to their instructional growth goals.

Element 5 should be the culmination of continuous improvement. The emphasis on teacher development implies the associated need for professional development directly related to teachers' areas of weakness. Element 5 asks the school leader to ensure that teachers are provided with differentiated professional development that will demonstrably help them achieve their instructional growth goals (Figures 2.12 and 2.13).

Figure 2.12. Scale for Domain 2, Element 5

Scale Value	Description
Innovating (4)	The school leader continually reevaluates the professional development program to ensure that it remains job-embedded and focused on instructional growth goals and intervenes with teachers who are not making sufficient progress toward achieving growth goals.
Applying (3)	The school leader ensures that job-embedded professional development that is directly related to their instructional growth goals is provided to teachers AND monitors the extent to which teachers improve their instructional practices.
Developing (2)	The school leader ensures that job-embedded professional development that is directly related to their instructional growth goals is provided to teachers.

(Continued)

Go to www.learningsciences.com/bookresources to download figures and tables.

Beginning (1)	The school leader attempts to ensure that job-embedded professional development that is directly related to their instructional growth goals is provided to teachers but does not complete the task or does so partially.
Not Using (0)	The school leader does not attempt to ensure that job-embedded professional development that is directly related to their instructional growth goals is provided to teachers.

Figure 2.13 details sample evidences for Domain 2, Element 5.

Figure 2.13. Sample evidences for Domain 2, Element 5

Sample Evidences for Domain 2, Element 5
• Online professional development courses and resources are available to teachers regarding their instructional growth goals.
• The school leader tracks teacher participation in professional development activities.
• Teacher-led professional development is available to teachers regarding their instructional growth goals.
• Instructional coaching is available to teachers regarding their instructional growth goals.
• Data are collected linking the effectiveness of professional development to the improvement of teacher practices.
• Data are available supporting deliberate practice in improving teacher performance.
• When asked, teachers can describe how the professional development supports their attainment of instructional growth goals.

Key Questions

1. How do you determine what professional growth to provide to the entire faculty?

2. How do you differentiate professional growth opportunities to meet individual needs?

3. What are different sources of professional development that you provide?

4. What evidence do you have that teachers are participating in professional development opportunities and that teacher practices are improving as a result?

5. What structures are in place to allow for peer coaching?

Scenario

In this scenario we revisit Principal White from Element 3. Mr. White identified the predominant instructional practices in the school and asked teachers to think about how they could change them. In Element 5, we find that Mr. White has continued to monitor the predominant instructional practices and further

Go to www.learningsciences.com/bookresources to download figures and tables.

identified individual teachers who need professional development in specific instructional strategies. Using data from the school's performance management system, he is able to identify targeted professional development for individual teachers and groups of teachers that will address their instructional weakness. Once he compiles the data, Mr. White works with the leadership team to develop a schedule for the instructional coach to model the use of targeted strategies for identified teachers.

Mr. White also schedules mini professional development sessions for other teachers utilizing resources and services provided by the district's professional development department. As part of this process, he works with teachers to develop instructional growth plans that focus on their specific pedagogical growth needs. He schedules time for teachers to observe other teachers in the building who are proficient in the identified instructional strategies.

By the end of the year, Principal White has collected evidence that teachers are forming small study groups to learn more about the strategies in which they need to grow. On a report that documents each teacher's in-service hours, he also notes that teachers are selecting classes that relate to their growth plans. The observation data in the performance management system reveals that teachers are making shifts in their instructional strategies. (For an example of a performance management system, see the final section of this chapter, devoted to the iObservation platform.)

Explanation and Feedback

At the end of the year, Mr. White's supervisor will give him feedback at the Innovating level, as he has offered multiple sources of evidence that teachers have been provided job-embedded professional development. Mr. White has achieved the desired results: observable shifts in every teacher's instructional practices. Note how closely Elements 3 and 5 are interrelated and how evidence collected in one element is often relevant to others.

Technology-Based Platforms for Data Collection, Feedback, and Collaborative Learning

Technology platforms are now available to simplify data collection for evaluation, growth, and collaborative learning. Although there are a number of such platforms available, we focus in this section on the platform developed by Learning Sciences International, iObservation, to illustrate the role such platforms play in providing feedback for formative assessment and tracking growth as part of the evaluation process for school leaders.

Platforms such as iObservation allow unprecedented access to resource libraries, communication and conferencing, video examples of classroom strategies, and other documents to help both teachers and school leaders monitor for desired effects. iObservation reports real-time data from classroom walk-throughs, teacher observations, school leader observations, confidential self-assessments, instructional rounds, and evaluations conducted by school leaders or the supervisors of school leaders. Such electronic tools and professional development resources enable users to focus on instructional leadership while maintaining compliance with state and district requirements. Technology platforms allow observers to send feedback to teachers or school leaders immediately following a classroom or school visit for a transparent and effective process.

A supervisor may, for example, use the platform to inform school leaders of upcoming observations and preconference meetings and share relevant resources for preconference review. Scales, evidences, and desired effects for each domain are loaded into the platform for easy reference; an observer/evaluator is able to indicate observed strategies or elements and add notes and recommendations to provide instant feedback.

Such platforms further encourage discussion between teachers and school leaders and between school leaders and their supervisors, with resources embedded in the conversational thread. Figure 2.14 illustrates how the iObservation platform, for example, fosters and enhances professional development.

Professional development is often seen as fragmented and irrelevant to instruction (Lieberman & Mace, 2010). Platforms such as iObservation can pull all the threads together in one place so that resources are shared by leaders, teachers, and other district personnel responsible for evaluation.

Figure 2.14. Examples of iObservation's online conferencing capabilities and forms for tracking school leader growth in Domain 1

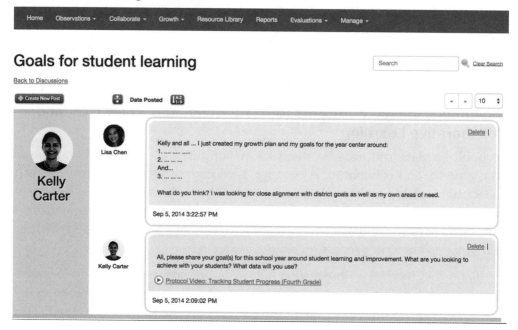

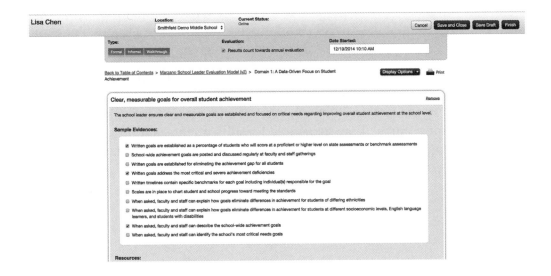

Conclusion

Teaching is not a static occupation: The demands of the 21st century require that we continually strive to improve our practice for the benefit of our students. The Programme for International Student Assessment (PISA) report of 2012 has set a recent challenge for American students, who currently rank 26th in math, 21st in science, and 17th in reading, findings US Education Secretary Arne Duncan called "a portrait of educational stagnation." Rapid technological advances put further pressure on teachers, and whole schools, to continuously improve. From the newest first-year teacher to the seasoned veteran, becoming better educators must be a nonnegotiable goal.

The good news is that educational research and innovations in systems and technology are giving us better knowledge and tools to meet those challenges. We know more than ever about how collaborative cultures can work to meet school goals; how performance evaluations can function as an integrated aspect of a model of instruction; and how the cycle of deliberate practice can be a major component of building pedagogical expertise.

The primary purpose of the school leader evaluation model outlined here, and certainly the focus of Domain 2, is to foster a culture of continuous improvement, one "that shatters the norms of isolation and autonomy . . . thus leading to the establishment of an 'educational practice' that trumps the notion of teaching as an art, a craft, or a style" (City, Elmore, Fiarman, & Teitel, 2009, p. xi). We are seeing a definitive trend away from "islands of excellence" toward a comprehensive landscape where all educators are connected in a common project to improve public education and raise the achievement of our students.

In our work with districts, we usually recommend that districts weigh Domain 2 at 40 percent of the final evaluation score for the school leader. For a full description and analysis of our recommended weighing system, see Chapter 6.

So far, we've been focusing on principal behaviors that foster continuous growth for teachers and, therefore, whole-school improvement. In the next chapter, we turn to Domain 3—A Guaranteed and Viable Curriculum—to look at how a uniform curriculum, accessible for all students, supports the goal of further focusing and refining the practices that drive student achievement.

CHAPTER 3

A Guaranteed and Viable Curriculum (Domain 3)

Preparing All Students to Be College and Career Ready

The past decade has seen a strong shift toward the recognition that student achievement should be the central focus of public education, and that rigorous, uniform standards hold great hope for significantly improving student achievement (Scherer, 2001). Since 2007, the National Governor's Association and the Council of Chief State School Officers have been investing heavily in plans to implement Common Core State Standards—standards designed to resolve a number of troubling issues in public education. Some states have addressed this challenge by opting to put in place their own college and career readiness standards. In either case, rigorous standards go some way to resolving the problem of variation in uneven expectations and measurements of student achievement between states; they meet international benchmarks; and they resolve what some critics have labeled the "scattershot and cumbersome" standards in many states that are nearly impossible for teachers to implement faithfully (Resmovits, 2014). Fully preparing students for college and career has become a national goal.

Policy makers are also deeply involved in sorting through the issues around implementation of new standards and updates to existing ones. A report in *Education Week* (Ujifusa, 2014) identifies 270 unique bills moving through state legislatures related to academic content standards, more than double 2013's number (107 of these are related to assessments), with a prediction that the number of standards bills will rise significantly in 2015.

As of this writing, most states have put subject-specific standards in place, along with state assessments and other accountability measures to measure student achievement on these state-adopted standards.

However, to implement standards effectively, Marzano and others have long suggested that the number of state standards should be cut dramatically. As early as 2001, Marzano pointed out that a sampling of state standards documented by McREL (Mid-continent Research for Education and Learning) found 130 standards across 14 subject areas—representing 3,500 benchmarks—an accumulation of knowledge and skills that would be impossible to acquire in a mere twelve years of schooling. To make the standards manageable, Marzano argues, they would have to be cut by nearly one-third (Scherer, 2001).

A second and related problem was the lack of uniformity in standards from state to state; there could be a wide divergence in what constituted proficiency (see, for example, *Mapping State Proficiency Standards onto NAEP Scales: 2005– 2007*, released by the U.S. Department of Education, 2009a). Until the adoption of Common Core or other college and career readiness standards, it was virtually impossible to reliably compare the achievement of students across state borders. Further, the United States was one of the few developed countries to lack national standards.

Both of these issues have been addressed with the adoption of national standards. When the final Common Core State Standards (CCSS) were released in June 2010, they were expected to go a long way to address issues of unequal standards and uneven proficiency expectations between states.

The designers of the CCSS emphasized that the Common Core was created to align grade-level expectations and internationally benchmarked standards to college and work expectations. The standards include both rigorous content *and* application of knowledge through high-order skills.

The creators of CCSS and other state-adopted college and career readiness standards recognized that preparing students for the 21st century would raise new challenges. Our definition of *readiness* must be more precise than ever. As K. J. Pittman notes in a 2010 issue of *School Administrator*, the idea of "readiness" is highly relevant to the future of both students and society at large. Pittman cites evidence that currently only three in ten seniors are college ready and four in ten high school seniors are work ready.

Given such sobering news, the need for rigorous standards across states could not be clearer.

As with any reform movement, the process of rolling out college and career readiness standards has not been without challenges, including helping the public and parents understand that the 21st century requires a large shift in our approach to teaching and learning. Nevertheless, despite some anxiety around the new methods, and questions that continue to surface about implementation, cost, and testing of the more rigorous standards, many parents and educators agree that "teaching students to think" rather than memorize by rote and giving them the opportunity to dive deeply into a text or problem—to take it apart, turn it every which way, and put it back together again—are precisely the challenges the students of today will face in the workplace of tomorrow.

Further weighing in on the standards movement is the consideration that we are a more mobile society than ever before. Implementing standards that are uniform between states is crucial, as has been putting in place standards within states that align between districts and between individual schools.

No one who loves public education favors a cookie-cutter approach to teaching and learning—and if uniformity can sometimes feel like "teaching to the test," there is an important caveat here. New standards are designed to help *all* students become college and career ready.

Defining a Guaranteed and Viable Curriculum

Domain 3 of the Marzano School Leader Evaluation Model addresses these recent, rapid changes as schools and districts are required to meet multiple demands, including adopting new rigorous college and career readiness standards and other state and federal curriculum reform efforts.

In order to fully understand this domain, we should establish and clarify our definitions. Marzano coined the phrase "a guaranteed and viable curriculum" in *What Works in Schools* (2003), based on his analysis of the literature on effective schools. The term has strong implications for what should be expected of effective leaders. Marzano defines *curriculum* as the essential content to be addressed in specific courses at specific grade levels. Further, a *guaranteed* curriculum is designed to *optimize learning for all students* by ensuring that classroom teachers follow the curriculum and address specific content in specific courses at specific grade levels.

In other words, a guaranteed curriculum imposes the expectation that this content is available to *all* students, not just specific populations. And finally, we want to add the concept of *viability*: the *time* to address the essential content with all students.

We might summarize our definition with the following formula: *Curriculum + Opportunity to Learn (OTL) + Time = A Guaranteed and Viable Curriculum.*

Unpacking the Concept of Guaranteed

In the absence of a guaranteed and viable curriculum, it is possible to imagine, for example, triplets attending the same school but with different teachers and learning a widely divergent curriculum. Until recently, teachers tended to teach lessons that were more or less idiosyncratic—lessons derived from individual textbooks and favorite sources or units that reflected their own choices. While individual schools may well have approved these lessons and inspired and motivated students, there was no focus on ensuring that a standards-based curriculum was being taught across all classes, frequently even at the same grade level. We could not guarantee that the triplets would learn the same curriculum.

A guaranteed curriculum may mean that occasionally teachers must give up cherished lessons they've relied on for many years—of course, if those lessons cannot be uniformly applied across a grade or subject or they do not teach the concepts needed to meet state standards. Lessons that do not incorporate the complexity of today's standards will no longer do. Teachers must develop new, standards-aligned instructional units and lessons and identify new resources that they may not have used in the past. The school leader's pivotal role is to ensure alignment of planning and teaching to adopted standards. To apply a guaranteed curriculum, school leaders must ensure that *all* students in the same grade are exposed to the same *essential content* and that the agreed-upon essential content is aligned to required standards.

Ensuring Equal Opportunity to Learn to Standards

A related question for Domain 3 is this: *How can the school leader guarantee that every student has an equal opportunity to learn to the required standards?*

A principal relates a painful story about an honors advanced algebra class in her school that brought this question home for her. Visiting district personnel sat in on the advanced class. At the end of it, they asked the principal if only kids of one racial background at her school were smart.

The principal was taken aback. She asked what they meant.

"None of the kids in this class are African American or Latino," the visitors pointed out.

The principal realized to her chagrin that the criteria for entrance into the advanced math class set the bar so high that it was effectively preventing some student subpopulations from learning the higher math skills they would need to succeed in college and career readiness courses. Rather than *all* the students in the school learning the critical content, only *some* were. The realization shook her, and she was able to make appropriate corrections to ensure that the students in her school would have the opportunity to learn critical content.

This principal is hardly alone. For many years it was not uncommon for students to be required to score above the 80th percentile on a norm-referenced test in order to take Algebra 1. In states that maintain these stringent requirements, Algebra 1 is still a gateway to advanced mathematics classes. In such cases, it may be necessary for the school leader to reevaluate the structure of that gateway and adjust the necessary requirements to allow all students equal opportunity to pass through it.

Unpacking the Concept of Viability

A viable curriculum is one that can be taught in the instructional time available to teachers.

New standards can appear daunting at the outset. Many principals may wonder how teachers will still manage to cover so much material at the appropriate level of rigor within given time constraints. For most instructional leaders, it is not simply a question of exposing students to content—it's also about maximizing the instructional time available to teachers.

Indeed, one of the most common long-term complaints we hear from teachers is that they don't have time to teach all the required content for their standards. As a result, teachers often feel that, by necessity, their approach is to apply a broad brush when it comes to content: cover many things, but with less depth than is really optimal for learning that results in students using and applying authentic learning experiences. In many cases, teachers continue to have more standards in a given year than it is ultimately possible to teach (Senechal, 2011). The challenge will be to shift the focus from an emphasis on simply covering content to an emphasis on *depth* of content, which requires more time for students to process and utilize knowledge at the highest level of complex cognitive processing.

We see the potential for technology to play a role in this shift from low-level thinking to higher levels of knowledge utilization. This shift will require changes in instructional practices. As students have vast quantities of information at their fingertips via the Internet, it has become less necessary to learn by rote the kinds of information students learned at the turn of the 20th century.

This is just the beginning, but it is good news for students and teachers, as the demands of applied learning become realistic in a standards-focused curriculum. As we have noted, we are gradually moving away from having too many standards. But teachers still need assistance from school leaders in identifying essential standards in order to effectively manage classroom time.

Managing Time for Essential Standards

One of the school leader's duties in this regard is to ensure that the stated curriculum is continuously analyzed, and if too many standards are in place, to determine the *essential standards* and make sure that all teachers in the school also understand which standards are essential. While most states have pared down the number of essential standards, often schools have not entirely realigned their master or bell schedules to ensure that lesson time is available to teach at the necessary depth of cognitive complexity.

There are many actions a school leader might take to protect and maximize instructional time. It can begin as simply as reducing the number of disruptive announcements during the day, for instance, or carefully scheduling core subjects so that all students will have opportunities to enroll in classes appropriately challenging. The school leader must assess, monitor, and develop ways to prevent students from leaving the classroom for other activities; offer additional interventions that don't interfere with students' core subject classes; and monitor attendance data to identify potential scheduling conflicts. The savvy school leader will design a master schedule focused on meeting the needs of students who have multiple interests (e.g., a student who wants to be in the jazz band but also needs AP biology, which is scheduled during the same period).

Challenges for School Leaders

One of the school leader's challenges in Domain 3 is to ensure that time is available for all teachers to teach *all* students the necessary skills, concepts, and strategies to make the curriculum viable.

A related challenge, and one that is even more daunting, is the school leader's role in helping teachers understand that all students must have equal opportunities to learn. In this sense, Domain 3 is highly interconnected with Domain 1 (A Data-Driven Focus on Student Achievement). Recall that in our discussion of Domain 1 in Chapter 1, with Elements 4 and 5, for example, the school leader's responsibility is to monitor data to ensure individual student growth and also that programs and practices are in place to help students meet their achievement goals. A guaranteed and viable curriculum for all students plays a dynamic role in helping students meet their individual achievement goals. Analysis of data allows school leaders to look at the student populations represented in individual classes and ensure that subpopulations are not prevented from accessing any essential learning experiences.

Three Elements

1. The school leader ensures that the school curriculum and accompanying assessments adhere to state and district standards.
2. The school leader ensures that the school curriculum is focused enough that it can be adequately addressed in the time available to teachers.
3. The school leader ensures that all students have the opportunity to learn the critical content of the curriculum.

Ensuring That Curriculum Adheres to Standards (Domain 3, Element 1)

The school leader ensures that the school curriculum and accompanying assessments adhere to state and district standards.

One of the principal jobs of the school leader is to ensure that curriculum is aligned to essential state standards. It is imperative for all teachers to have a solid understanding, first, of what content is essential to teach for each grade level or course and, second, the level of rigor required to meet state standards. If the district has not already done so, the school leader can put processes in place to examine state standards with groups of teachers and curriculum directors to determine which standards are essential. Resources like test specification, released test items, or previously released tests can be invaluable to leaders in determining essential standards.

Using Formative Assessments to Keep Curriculum on Track

In this era of high-stakes accountability, where teachers and school leaders are typically held responsible for student achievement outcomes on state assessment tests, school leaders must guarantee testing measures they can administer periodically and that will be so closely aligned with the tested standards that these tests will show student progress toward achieving the standards. School leaders can ensure that school curriculum and accompanying assessments are aligned to state and district standards by using a *formative approach* to testing, as we touched on in Chapter 1.

In *District Leadership That Works* (2009), Marzano and Waters cite Black and Wiliam's (1998a) definition of formative assessment: "All those activities undertaken by teachers and/or by students which provide information to be used as feedback to modify the teaching and learning activities in which they are engaged" (pp. 7–8). Wiliam and Leahy (2007) emphasize that the purpose of formative assessment is determined by "the extent that information from the assessment is fed back within the system and actually used to improve the performance of the system in some way (i.e., that the assessment *forms* the direction of improvement)" (p. 31).

Therefore, the formative assessments teachers develop and use must be tightly aligned to college and career readiness standards. Teachers must ensure that their assessments incorporate all levels of the taxonomy. In other words, teacher assessments should measure higher-order thinking skills and knowledge utilization. In the past, too many assessments have fallen short of rigor and therefore failed in the formative sense defined earlier—as a tool to provide feedback and guide modifications in pedagogy. As Black and Wiliam (1998b) note, "The tests used by teachers encourage rote and superficial learning even when teachers say they want to develop understanding; many teachers seem unaware of the inconsistency" (p. 5).

Brookhart (2010) suggests the following:

> Observing and discussing student reasoning directly can be a powerful way to assess higher-order thinking. Give students an assessment, and use it formatively. Have conversations with students about their reasoning, or give substantive written feedback. The conversations and feedback should be based on your learning target and criteria. Exactly what sort of thinking were you trying to assess? How should students interpret the quality of their thinking? What are some ways they might extend or deepen that thinking? (p. 31)

Formative assessments can be an extremely valuable tool to give teachers early feedback on whether the time allotted to a lesson or unit has been sufficient. School leaders will have to be sure teachers are provided with formative assessments that are rigorous and specific enough to give teachers the targeted feedback they need to hone their lessons and identify struggling students.

Managing Time With Shared Leadership

Schools can no longer rely on programs, textbooks, or supplemental materials to guide curriculum decisions. School leaders are now called upon to make focused, systematic plans for implementation of targeted programs to guarantee that teachers teach the intended curriculum. While this may sound like a very tall order for school leaders who are already stretched thin, there are practical ways to accomplish the goal of an aligned curriculum with shared leadership responsibilities.

For example, school leaders can use grade-level team meetings, PLC (professional learning community) teams, and professional development days to work on common assessments. Depending on available resources, a school leader who does not already have content teams developing common assessments may plan to put those teams in place. Successful common assessments will align with both content (the curriculum) and level of rigor (the standards). To illustrate: if the standard for a unit demands analysis, the assessment would test students in their ability—for example, to compare and contrast.

If developing such teams is not an option, the leader may follow up with individual teachers to check for curriculum alignment to state standards. During postobservation conferences, for example, the school leader might ask a teacher how her lesson plan and assessments are aligned with the curriculum and standards. A large part of Element 1 in Domain 3, as in other domains, is fostering a *cultural shift* where every teacher understands the requirement and is self-monitoring to ensure, first, compliance, and second, demonstrated results.

Written Versus Taught Curriculum

Although we've touched on this topic earlier, it's important to stress that there is often a conflict in school buildings between the *written* curriculum and *taught* curriculum (Gehrke, Knapp, & Sirotnik, 1992) or more recently in the Second International Mathematics Study (SIMS) model, the *intended* curriculum, *implemented* curriculum, and *attained* curriculum. As Marzano (2003) notes in *What Works in Schools*,

> The intended curriculum is content specified by the state, district, or school to be addressed in a particular course or at a particular grade level. The implemented curriculum is content actually delivered by the teacher, and the attained curriculum is content actually learned by students. The discrepancy between the intended curriculum and the implemented curriculum makes OTL [opportunity to learn] a prominent factor in student achievement—a factor that since SIMS has continued to show a very strong relationship with student achievement (Brewer & Stacz, 1996; Herman, Klein, & Abedi, 2000; Robitaille, 1993). (p. 22)

There may still be a gap between what teachers are actually teaching in the classroom (e.g., their favorite dinosaur unit) and the agreed-upon curriculum for that grade or unit (e.g., the organization and development of living organisms, including growth and reproduction). In this case, the school leader will help the teacher adjust instruction to ensure that dinosaur lessons will happen in the context of, perhaps, comparing the reproductive behaviors of mammals and reptiles. Students taught this unit will have the same essential knowledge about living organisms as students in other third-grade classes when it comes time to take a formative assessment or end-of-year achievement test.

These conflicts and confusions often arise when teachers or administrators conflate textbooks with curriculum rather than perceive textbooks as one *resource* toward implementing the intended curriculum. There may be many resources dedicated to implementing an agreed-upon curriculum—but resources do not a curriculum make.

To unpack this a bit further, the point is to ensure that there is consistency in the material teachers cover in the same subjects between classrooms and that it is covered at the level of rigor the state standards require. Common formative assessments will supply the proof in the measured outcomes.

Key Questions

1. How do you ensure that all staff members have copies of the most current curriculum standards?
2. How do you ensure that the intended curriculum is the taught curriculum?
3. Who is responsible for providing formative assessments correlated to the rigorous, standards-based curriculum?
4. What evidence do you have that current formative assessments adequately prepare students to meet state standards?
5. What structures do you have in place to monitor, on an ongoing basis, that the intended curriculum is the taught curriculum?

Scenario

As the mandated transition to college and career readiness standards approached, Ms. Casper decided to work with grade-level representatives to help lead teams in using the new curriculum maps developed centrally with teams of teachers the previous summer. As a result of the new maps, she developed a schedule of meetings for the teams to review the maps and discuss them in terms of their lesson planning. The teams met throughout the year, led by teacher leaders identified by Ms. Casper from the initial team.

Ms. Casper met with the teams after the first quarter to hear more about their progress. She determined that the teams seemed to be working well together and appeared, from the reports of the leaders, on task in using maps for planning. She did not meet with the leaders or any of the teachers after this follow-up meeting in November. She did, however, attend a few meetings after the new year began in January. In February, she reviewed lesson plans to determine if the teams had begun to incorporate the new standards into their lesson plans. Teachers were using the maps in their planning and were on target with their pacing. Ms. Casper did not always check for the connection to the new standards or curriculum maps during the observation process.

At the end of the year, Ms. Casper asked teachers for feedback about their work. Most reported that they understood the new standards and mapping. Some reported that they had not met recently; others reported concerns about the way their teams had worked in the meetings.

Explanation and Feedback

Ms. Casper did not monitor frequently enough to ensure that teachers were deepening their understanding of the transition to college and career readiness standards. She assumed that teachers were able to continue the work she had initiated. Ms. Casper could not determine if teachers were teaching the newer version of the curriculum. An evaluator might further engage Ms. Casper in considering how she might have connected this work to the professional development plan considered in Domain 2, Element 5 (*ensuring that teachers are provided with job-embedded professional development directly related to their instructional growth goals*). Based on the information provided in the scenario, the leader would be rated at the *Developing* level.

Scale and Evidences for Domain 3, Element 1

Let's take a look at the scale and evidences for Domain 3, Element 1. Figure 3.1 illustrates that as a baseline, the school leader is ensuring that written curriculum and accompanying assessments adhere to state standards. As leaders move up the scale of expertise, they are monitoring for adherence and intervening with individual teachers.

In Figure 3.2, evidences for these behaviors include being able to provide information correlating the taught curriculum with the written curriculum; the success of assessments in accurately evaluating this alignment; and that teachers understand curricular goals.

We might say the desired result of Element 1 is that there is universal alignment between taught curriculum in the school, state standards, and the accompanying assessments that measure the progress toward the standards.

Moving Up the Scale From Not Using to Innovating

Let's apply the scale in a hypothetical situation. Principal Smith knows the state has adopted curriculum standards that school leaders must implement in every school building before the beginning of the year. Principal Smith's evaluator schedules a conference six weeks into the year and asks Principal Smith for the school's published curriculum. The principal offers an apology, saying it was a busy summer with hiring and readying resources for the new year, but the curriculum team will get started on the process.

Figure 3.1. Scale for Domain 3, Element 1

Scale Value	Description
Innovating (4)	The school leader ensures that the assessment and reporting system focuses on state and district standards and intervenes with teachers who do not follow state and district standards.
Applying (3)	The school leader ensures that both the written curriculum and accompanying assessments adhere to state and district standards AND monitors the extent to which the curriculum is delivered and the assessments measure the curriculum.
Developing (2)	The school leader ensures that both the written curriculum and accompanying assessments adhere to state and district standards.
Beginning (1)	The school leader attempts to ensure that both the written curriculum and accompanying assessments adhere to state and district standards but does not complete the task or does so partially.
Not Using (0)	The school leader does not attempt to ensure that both the written curriculum and accompanying assessments adhere to state and district standards.

Figure 3.2. Sample evidences for Domain 3, Element 1

Sample Evidences for Domain 3, Element 1
• Curriculum documents are in place that correlate the written curriculum to state and district standards.
• Rubrics or proficiency scales are in place that clearly delineate student levels of performance on essential elements of the state and district standards.
• Information is available correlating what is taught in the classroom (i.e., the taught curriculum) and the written curriculum.
• Information is available examining the extent to which assessments accurately measure the written and taught curriculums.
• School teams regularly analyze the relationship between the written curriculum, taught curriculum, and assessments.
• Evidence is available demonstrating the assessments are accurately measuring the state and district standards.
• When asked, teachers can describe the essential content and standards for their subject area(s) or grade level(s).
• When asked, teachers demonstrate understanding of how the curriculum and assessments are aligned.

Go to www.learningsciences.com/bookresources to download figures and tables.

At this point, the school leader would be scored at *Not Using*, level 0, on the performance scale. The evaluator would ask the principal to begin the process of developing and publishing the school's curriculum and accompanying assessments.

In a subsequent visit, the principal has started working with the district curriculum department to align the school's curriculum, but progress is minimal. The evaluator gives Principal Smith a rating of *Beginning* (level 1) and offers specific feedback to facilitate moving the principal toward *Developing* (level 2).

To move toward the *Developing* level, Principal Smith will establish weekly curriculum meetings with teacher teams to analyze the relationship between what they are teaching (the taught curriculum) and the district standards (the written curriculum). Teachers will participate in the process of developing common assessments aligned to measure the adopted standards.

In this district, the standards are published and assessments are in place, but Principal Smith does not have a systematic process for ensuring that the school's curriculum is aligned to the district/state curriculum standards. After the evaluator's observation and a conference session, the principal works with teachers to establish that the school's curriculum is aligned with state and district standards.

However, as we have discussed, the desired proficiency level is *Applying* (level 4). At the *Applying* level, Principal Smith is monitoring for results, which in this case would mean that the majority of teachers use the published curriculum, and there is evidence that the accompanying assessments measure the curriculum. During the course of the year, Principal Smith monitors formative and benchmark assessment results and notes that all teachers are using the adopted curriculum standards, but the assessments in some cases do not reflect the rigor required to gauge students' application of the content. The principal provides these teachers resources to help them develop common assessments that incorporate cognitively complex items.

By the end of the year, assessment data shows that curriculum and assessments are aligned and that they appropriately assess the taught standards. Now, Principal Smith is rated at the highest level (level 5), *Innovating*.

Note that in scoring elements, the scores are not cumulative. Principal Smith's scores are not averaged over the course of the year. Instead, they reflect Principal Smith's final score. For more information on scoring, see Chapter 6.

The School Leader Determines What Is Nonnegotiable

The taught curriculum must be aligned with district and state standards, as we have discussed, but the school leader must also determine which elements of district and state standards are nonnegotiable.

In order to determine what curriculum content is nonnegotiable, a school leader might use the following questions for consideration:

1. Who currently does the work of developing standards-based content in your district or school? Who determines which content is essential and responsible for alignment? Who ensures the opportunity to learn the content in the classroom? Who instructs in the essential content? What type of professional development is offered, and is it aligned to the school's nonnegotiable goals?

2. How do teachers, building leaders, and district leaders share in these aspects of education? What evidence might be considered to measure the effectiveness of that involvement?

3. How is your school leadership regarding curriculum positively affecting student outcomes?

4. What sources of evidence could demonstrate that these practices are effective in creating a viable and guaranteed curriculum?

It's important to emphasize that one role of the school leader in Domain 3 is communication channel and buffer. Teachers are not, for the most part, equipped to create curriculum guides or common summative assessment items on their own or deal with thorny issues of developing and aligning curriculum to standards. This is not to say that teachers should not participate in decision-making processes about curriculum. But a school leader who has her ear to the ground, in terms of the kind of help teachers want and need, can be a voice in the district to ensure that the necessary curriculum mapping and accompanying assessments are developed.

The school leader then becomes a guide or coach who can support teachers to determine how to group standards into effective units, and so on.

The work related to Domain 3 can serve as an undergirding for the work we have done in establishing goals for student achievement in Domain 1 and for reinforcing that instructional vision captured in Domain 2. We may consider, in this first element, how the principal connects the work around assuring a standards-aligned curriculum to the feedback he gives to teachers around their lesson planning and their responsive planning after the review of their data.

For the Evaluation
A school leader being evaluated in Domain 3 will most likely be asked to provide evidences for application of the elements and their results. In many cases the school leader will provide a summary document to the evaluator demonstrating some of the possible evidences we saw in Figure 3.2 or outlining scenarios that have taken place around these elements. Team meeting notes, PLC notes, staff meeting agendas, the data in technology platforms such as iObservation, pre- and post-conference notes with individual teachers—all are examples of possible evidences. The most compelling evidence, of course, will provide

documentation that the school leader is obtaining the desired results for each of the three elements discussed here.

Ensuring Viability of the Curriculum (Domain 3, Element 2)

The school leader ensures that the school curriculum is focused enough that it can be adequately addressed in the time available to teachers.

Element 2 addresses the viability of the curriculum, which we discussed in some detail early in this chapter. The question for school leaders here is whether they have created a focused curriculum with the essential standards that can be accomplished in the scope of a school year. The essential standards and content must be determined collaboratively, not by individual teachers.

Savvy school leaders examine data and talk to teachers about how to design a plan so that they have enough instructional time in class to meet the standards. In our conversations with teachers, we frequently hear the same refrain. Research compiled by Learning Sciences Marzano Center, based on classroom observations logged in the iObservation database, suggests that teachers are currently spending the majority of their instructional time introducing new content and far too little time on deepening knowledge and higher-order thinking skills. As little as 5 percent of class time is devoted to the kinds of higher-order thinking skills—analysis, comparison and contrast, generating hypotheses, and problem solving—that are the foundation of what we mean when we use the term *rigor*. Teachers like to call this allocation of classroom time the "mile-wide, inch-deep" syndrome.

The intention of college and career readiness standards is to narrow the standards so that mile-wide and inch-deep lessons become less prevalent. Standards alone, however, are not enough to overcome a long history of pedagogical focus on new content.

Figures 3.3 and 3.4 illustrate the scale and possible evidences for ensuring that critical content and higher-order thinking skills can be addressed in the time allotted. Possible evidences might include that the school leader has conducted a curriculum audit; teams meet regularly to assess pacing guides, curricular maps, and the like; and student surveys indicate that students feel they have enough time to learn the expected material.

This element reminds us also of the work we do in Domain 2 around assuring effective instruction in our classrooms. Recently, a survey of teachers in one district indicated the teachers felt they did not have enough time to teach the standards identified in district curriculum guides. A visit to the classrooms by school leaders revealed opportunities where instructional time could have been used more efficiently. Teachers were spending inordinate amounts of time on activities that were developed with loose connections to the standards. For example, one grade-level team was implementing lessons that required students to *identify* whether a statement was a fact or opinion. But the standard required students to *analyze* the impact of the statement with regard to whether it was a fact or opinion with the goal of comprehending the text. Teachers were spending time on lower-level activities that did not impact the students' mastery of the standards. The principal had the opportunity to help teachers better understand standards-aligned instruction through feedback connected to lesson planning.

Figure 3.3. Scale for Domain 3, Element 2

Scale Value	Description
Innovating (4)	The school leader ensures that essential elements of the curriculum are regularly examined and revised with an eye toward making instruction more focused and efficient.
Applying (3)	The school leader ensures that the written curriculum has been unpacked in such a manner that essential elements have been identified AND monitors the extent to which the essential elements are few enough to allow adequate time for students to learn them.
Developing (2)	The school leader ensures that the written curriculum has been unpacked in such a manner that essential elements have been identified.
Beginning (1)	The school leader attempts to ensure that the written curriculum has been unpacked in such a manner that essential elements have been identified but does not complete the task or does so partially.
Not Using (0)	The school leader does not attempt to ensure that the written curriculum has been unpacked in such a manner that essential elements have been identified.

Figure 3.4. Sample evidences for Domain 3, Element 2

Sample Evidences for Domain 3, Element 2
• A written list of essential elements is in place.
• A curriculum audit has been conducted that delineates how much time it would take to adequately address the essential elements.
• Teams regularly meet to discuss the progression and viability of documents that articulate essential content and timing of delivery (e.g., pacing guides, curriculum maps).
• Time available for specific classes and courses meets the state or district specifications for those classes and courses.
• Data are available to show that students are ready to be contributing members of society and participate in a global community.
• Data are available to show that students are college and career ready.
• A plan is in place to monitor that the curriculum is taught in the time available to teachers.

(Continued)

• When asked, teachers can describe which elements are essential and can be taught in the scheduled time.
• When asked, students report they have time to learn the essential curriculum.

Key Questions

1. As a school leader, what is your role in assessing whether the essential standards are in place?

2. How do you monitor that teachers are using standards as the basis for unit and lesson planning?

3. What indicators do you monitor to determine if teachers have enough time to teach the required standard?

4. What evidence will you use to document that essential standards are being met in all the classrooms in your school?

5. What evidence will show that your teachers are teaching the essential standards within the prescribed time and that all students have an opportunity to learn the critical content?

Ensuring Opportunity to Learn Critical Content (Domain 3, Element 3)

The school leader ensures that all students have the opportunity to learn the critical content of the curriculum.

We touched on the focus of Element 3 earlier in this chapter with the story of the principal who realized her school had set the bar too high for entrance into an essential math class. If the focus of the new state standards is college and career readiness, it can't be emphasized often enough that this means readiness for *all* students (see Figures 3.5 and 3.6).

Figure 3.5. Scale and sample evidences for Domain 3, Element 3

Scale Value	Description
Innovating (4)	The school leader intervenes with teachers whose students do not have adequate access to essential elements and instructional strategies that most strongly increase their chances of learning the essential elements.
Applying (3)	The school leader ensures that all students have access to the courses and classes that directly address the essential elements of the curriculum AND monitors the extent to which those courses and classes utilize instructional strategies that most strongly increase their chances of learning the essential elements.
Developing (2)	The school leader ensures that all students have access to the courses and classes that directly address the essential elements of the curriculum.

(Continued)

Go to www.learningsciences.com/bookresources to download figures and tables.

Beginning (1)	The school leader attempts to ensure that all students have access to the courses and classes that directly address the essential elements of the curriculum but does not complete the task or does so partially.
Not Using (0)	The school leader does not attempt to ensure that all students have access to the courses and classes that directly address the essential elements of the curriculum.

Figure 3.6. Sample evidences for Domain 3, Element 3

Sample Evidences for Domain 3, Element 3
• Tracking systems are in place that examine each student's access to the essential elements of the curriculum.
• Parents are aware of their child's current access to the essential elements of the curriculum.
• All students have access to advanced placement or other rigorous courses.
• All students have a prescribed program of study that documents access to courses.
• Data are available to show teachers have completed appropriate content area training in their subject area courses.
• Data are available to verify student achievement in critical content and standards.
• When asked, teachers can describe the content strategies that result in the highest student learning for specific courses and topics.
• When asked, students report they have the opportunity to learn the critical content of the curriculum.

In his survey of college and career readiness, K. J. Pittman (2010) outlines the sobering results of the "readiness gap" between student subpopulations and what the inevitable consequences of that gap might be:

Up to a fourth of all first-year students at four-year colleges do not return for their second year. The dropout rates are particularly high for African American, Hispanic, and first-generation college students, according to a report by the Urban Institute and the Harvard Civil Rights Project.

Employers, while acknowledging the need for 21st-century skills, are not equipped to train in these deficiency areas. According to a 2009 Corporate Voices for Working Families study, 40 percent of the business respondents that offer some workforce-readiness training have no on-the-job trainings to offer in these high-need areas.

Youth, especially low-income minorities, are having a hard time finding quality jobs during and after high school. Teen employment is now the lowest it has been in more than half a century. Low-income, minority youth are least likely to find work, even with high school diplomas.

Go to www.learningsciences.com/bookresources to download figures and tables.

The school leader's responsibility is to foster a school culture where teachers have high expectations for all students. Students should be placed in appropriately rigorous classes, and the school leader should ensure that honors and AP classes are not available to one subset of students at the expense of others.

Such a mission sounds very clear in theory, but it can become murky in practice. The building leader's role is as an arbiter, the person who makes sure, in the final count, that no student is denied the opportunity to succeed in college and career. If Jake needs a reading intervention and the reading specialist is available only during Jake's math class, then Jake is going to either miss math or the reading intervention. Such conflicts are not insoluble if everyone, from teachers to parents to instructional support staff, is aware that missing either vital math or equally vital reading instruction is simply not an option.

Key Questions

1. What structures are in place to track whether all students have the opportunity to learn the critical content of the curriculum?

2. How do you determine which students will have access to higher-level courses?

3. What structures are in place to ensure that all students have access to and will be successful in higher-level courses?

4. When you identified gaps between students' opportunities to learn, did you take appropriate action to fill these gaps?

5. What structures are in place to ensure that parents are aware of their child's current access to the essential elements of the curriculum?

Scenario

Applegate High School, a large comprehensive school in a midsize southern town, houses multiple learning communities, each with an academic focus. The school's demographics reflect the diversity of the town's growing minority population. One learning community, the Achievement Academy, is designed to challenge students with the most rigorous college preparatory classes. It is known throughout the state for the number of graduates who receive Ivy League college scholarships.

A new principal, Mr. Sterling, was recently assigned to the school, and when reviewing the master schedule of the school and the students enrolled in the courses for the Achievement Academy, he discovered a major void in the course offerings. He noted that a course code for advanced or honors did not identify the majority of courses. Except for those courses offered to students enrolled in the Achievement Academy, the opportunity for students to take challenging academic courses was quite limited. Mr. Sterling met with other administrators at the school to discuss a plan that would create the opportunity for *all* students to enroll in challenging courses.

Mr. Sterling noted a problem: recent achievement data clearly showed the school had many students whose current scores did not qualify them for entrance to the Achievement Academy. But those same students had had high achievement scores when they entered Applegate High. Because there were too few advanced or honors classes to accommodate all students with high scores, these students had been placed in basic-level classes. The data showed that after two years in basic-level classes, their achievement scores were rapidly declining.

Mr. Sterling shared concerns that these students did not have an opportunity to learn critical content, which was affecting their academic performance. After presenting the evidence and meeting with the team, the team decided that it was too late in the summer to change the master schedule and find teachers who could teach advanced courses, so the team postponed the change until the following year.

Explanation and Feedback

Where would you rate the principal on this element? What feedback would you provide?

This principal could be rated at the *Beginning* level for Element 3, as the process was started but not completed. To move to the *Developing* level, *all* the constructs of the element would need to be in place. At *Developing*, the principal would *ensure all students have the opportunity to learn critical content*.

A supervisor might, in fact, decide to give this principal feedback at the *Not Using* level since there was no *attempt to ensure* all students had access to challenging courses. Such a decision would call for a discussion between principal and supervisor about why no attempt was made.

Let's say, for example, that during that discussion, Mr. Sterling informs his supervisor that very few teachers at Applegate High have the credentials to teach advanced courses. Even if the schedules had been adjusted to accommodate higher-level courses, not enough teachers were qualified to teach them. If Mr. Sterling outlines a plan for getting more teachers qualified, the supervisor would then revise the rating from *Not Using* to *Beginning*.

Conclusion

When it comes to curriculum decisions, the role of the school leader is to help teachers identify and work with the designated curriculum—one designed by the district or collaboratively by school-based teams. The school leader clears the brush from the path, or, as one principal put it, knows enough to "get off the dance floor and get up on the balcony." The school leader needs to remain cognizant of the big picture.

The Marzano School Leader Evaluation Model is designed to be collaborative; it should facilitate real dialogue and communication about professional development and foster ongoing conversations. The building leader's role, now more than ever, is to create a culture where teachers and administrators can support each other. The principal's primary role here is as a conduit for the free flow of information and communication.

In our next chapter, we turn to a discussion of how cooperation and collaboration (Domain 4) work to enhance this supportive culture and support the goals of the previous three domains.

CHAPTER 4

Cooperation and Collaboration (Domain 4)

Great discoveries and improvements invariably involve the cooperation of many minds.
—Alexander Graham Bell

A great deal has been written about the need for cooperation and collaboration as a means to improve schools and student learning outcomes. But what do we mean by *cooperation* that is specific to educational systems, as opposed to, for example, business systems? How is *collaboration* within the K–12 environment both like and different from the kinds of collaboration called for in other professions and industries? And what might we learn from them?

Most school systems have programs and structures in place to foster cooperation and collaboration throughout the entire network of participants. Professional learning communities (PLCs) encourage collaboration between teachers (DuFour, 2004; DuFour & Marzano, 2011). School board meetings ideally foster collaboration between parents, the community, and school administrators (Office of Superintendent of Public Instruction, 2004). Conferences between teachers and parents build connections (Graham-Clay, 2005). Celebrations, games, and sports set a foundation for cooperation and goodwill between students, teachers, parents, administrators, and the community at large (Bolman & Deal, 2003). The purpose of all these activities and interactions is to build a vibrant, cohesive, and productive school culture—a culture that sets in motion widening spheres of influence that impact the larger community, like a stone tossed into a pond.

Clearly, cooperation and collaboration in the school environment go far beyond just "getting along." The ultimate goal is to develop what Philip C. Schlechty and others have called "civic capacity." Civic capacity, Schlechty notes in *Leading for Learning* (2009), "refers to the ability of business leaders, union leaders, civic leaders, educational leaders, and leaders of other significant organizations to work together on behalf of common goals" (p. 187). Developing such civic capacity builds trust, a common identity, and the willingness to work with shared purpose for the success of the school or schools within the system.

Writing on the connection between teacher and administrator relationships and student learning in the *Stanford Social Innovation Review*, Carrie Leana notes, "When the relationships among teachers in a school are characterized by high trust and frequent interaction—that is, when social capital is strong—student achievement scores improve" (2011).

Another way of looking at such a flourishing school community is what Marzano has called a "purposeful community." In *School Leadership That Works* (2005), Marzano, Waters, and McNulty define the purposeful community as "one with the collective efficacy and capability to develop and use assets to accomplish goals that matter to all community members through an agreed-upon process" (p. 99). Marzano et al. go on to elaborate on the four concepts embedded in this definition:

1. *Collective efficacy.* Collective efficacy occurs when group members share the perception or belief that they can dramatically enhance the effectiveness of an organization; in other words, that they can make a difference. This sense of collective efficacy has been correlated to student achievement.

2. *Development and use of all available assets.* Available assets include both tangible assets, such as financial and physical resources, the talent of the school's personnel, and technology, but also intangible assets such as the shared ideals and beliefs about the school's core mission.

3. *Accomplishment of goals that matter to the community members.* The school functions as a community created for a specific purpose with specific goals to meet that purpose. Sergiovanni (2004) has called such groups "communities of hope."

4. *Agreed-upon process.* An agreed-upon process enhances communication among community members, provides efficient reconciliation of disagreements, and keeps members attuned to the status of the community.

Domain 4 of the Marzano School Leader Evaluation Model supports the school leader's capacity to develop such a community of purpose. Marzano et al. (2005) identify nine primary responsibilities of the school leader that help him move toward that goal. Those responsibilities include the capacity for the leader to be an *optimizer* (an inspiration and driving force) who practices *affirmation* (recognizing and celebrating school accomplishments) and clearly articulates *ideals* and *beliefs*. The leader is a person of high *visibility*, with a similarly high degree of *situational awareness* (the ability to honestly appraise the state of the organization), who cultivates *relationships*; hones effective *communication*; creates a strong, cohesive culture; and cultivates and invites teacher, student, and community *input*.

Marzano et al. (2005) also found the following behaviors were associated with "the responsibility of Culture":

- Promoting cohesion among staff
- Promoting a sense of well-being among staff
- Developing an understanding of purpose among staff
- Developing a shared vision of what the school could be like

In previous chapters we have focused primarily on the impact that individual leaders, and by extension individual teachers, can have on student achievement. But as DuFour and Marzano note in *Leaders of Learning*:

> The research has concluded that focusing on individual development does not develop the interdependence, collaboration, and collective effort essential to improving results (Carroll, 2009; Kruse et al., 1995; Little, 2006; McCauley and Van Velsor, 2003). (2011, p. 66)

DuFour and Marzano (2011) go on to note that Newmann and Wehlage (1995):

> found many schools that had competent individual teachers lacked the organizational capacity to raise student achievement because meeting that challenge "is beyond the skills of individual staff" and requires instead the organization of "human, technical, and social resources into an effective collective effort" (pp. 29–30). More recently, Fullan (2010) has argued emphatically that strategies that focus solely on improving individuals will fail to improve schools because meeting that challenge requires building collective capacity. (p. 66)

In other words, as we have discussed, an effective school leader must have a strong vision of her purpose and goals for the school. But the individual visionary is not enough. The effective school leader relies on the support of an extended team of teachers and community members to accomplish those goals—as Alexander Graham Bell put it, *the cooperation of many minds*.

Domain 4 of the Marzano School Leader Evaluation Model offers research-based strategies to meet the challenge to build collective capacity. *The actions and behaviors in this domain help ensure that teachers and staff have, and engage in, opportunities to address issues critical to the optimal functioning of the school and operate as a cohesive team.*

Creating a Social Space for Collaboration to Flourish

In *The Answer to How Is Yes: Acting on What Matters* (2003), the philosopher Peter Block suggests that asking how questions too early in the change process undermines the power of dialogue and potentially encourages early closure that could derail solutions. As Marzano et al. note in *School Leadership That Works* (2005),

> Block suggests that effective leaders are social architects who create a "social space" that enhances the effectiveness of an organization. The ideal social space is one conducive to solving even the most perplexing of organizational problems. For Block, critical leadership skills include convening critical discussions, naming the question, focusing the discussion on learning as opposed to premature closure on solutions, and using strategies for participative design of solutions. (pp. 19–20)

In our consultations with schools across the United States, we have identified a number of factors working within the social space that help ensure effective collaboration in schools:

- Effective school collaboration means teachers are interacting with other teachers around the subject of effective instruction. Teachers may be participating in instructional rounds or PLCs, conducting lesson studies where they are modeling planned instructional strategies, discussing planned interventions, and generally modeling *learning in action.*

- Effective school instruction means that teachers have a say in decisions important to the school. They are aware of new initiatives and participate in planning for those initiatives. Formal processes are in place to ensure that teachers have a way to voice concerns and provide other input.

- The school also has in place formal structures for becoming an effective learning organization. These structures might include systems for collective decision making, the implementation of a research-based instructional model, establishment of key roles for leadership and action, thoughtful allocation of resources, attention to the social needs of the group, and so on.

- There is evidence of shared leadership. *Shared leadership* is a term often used in school effectiveness literature. In a nutshell, shared leadership means that the school leader has been able to identify teachers and non-classroom personnel who have the ability to build capacity within the school and larger community and that the school leader is secure enough in his role to encourage this to happen.

Learning Organization or Learning Community?

In *Leading for Learning* (2009), Phillip C. Schlechty makes a distinction between a "learning community" and "learning organization" that sharpens the focus on this sense of *purposefulness* Marzano identified. Schlechty defines learning organizations as the larger organizational structure inside of which learning communities flourish. Learning organizations are

> formal social organizations that purposefully create, support, and use learning communities and communities of learners as the primary means of inducting new members; creating, developing, importing, and exporting knowledge; assigning tasks and evaluating performances; and establishing goals and maintaining direction. Learning organizations create and maintain networks of learning communities and use these networks as the primary means by which the work of the organization is accomplished. (p. 115)

Schlechty (2009) emphasizes that the learning organization lends legitimacy to the learning community or communities, such as professional learning communities (PLCs) and teacher learning communities (TLCs) under its larger umbrella. Bureaucracies are the enemies of learning communities (and learning organizations) because bureaucracies do not assume either participatory decision making or open dialogue between leaders and followers. "In bureaucracies, the key questions are 'What is the rule?' and 'Who is in charge?' In a learning organization the key questions are 'What is the problem?' and 'Who is likely to know what to do about it?'" (p. 117).

Schlechty concurs with Marzano in naming the necessary conditions to support a successful learning organization, to create the social space Marzano has identified. There must be "sufficient cohesion within the school and district so that cooperation with others does not needlessly threaten the internal integrity of the system" (Schlechty, 2009, pp. 237–238). Shared authority is crucial, he says, but that does not mean the abandonment of authority.

Second, school leaders must shed their identities as managers and become leaders who encourage and support varied interactions between members so that the social space becomes "permeable." And lastly, all members must have a clear sense of the school's mission and vision.

With these characteristics in place, the school leader can create a culture that "drives out fear, encourages responsible risk taking, separates unsuccessful tries from punishment" (Schlechty, 2009, p. 235). He adds, "Only organizations that have clear beliefs to which most members are committed can collaborate without fear of compromising their mission and their integrity" (p. 238). Schlechty emphasizes that collaboration is necessary for the "disruptive innovations needed to ensure a healthy future for public education in America" (p. 237).

Effective Communication Breaks Down Isolation

The assumption is that in order to foster such a social space or build civic capacity, the school leader must be an excellent communicator. In the absence of communication, the school leader will not be able to establish a collaborative environment that builds shared leadership, and will be unable to de-velop a coherent succession plan for new school leaders and instructional leaders. Because teaching has, in the past, been such an isolated profession (Lortie, 1975; Scholastic & the Gates Foundation, 2012), it will be up to the school leader to help teachers build the bridges they need to become effective collaborators.

Successful leaders will see that teachers get out of their own classrooms to observe other teachers, participate in study and planning groups, and otherwise become aware and engaged in what is happening throughout the entire building. Communication in this sense involves the entire community, not just top-down communication from the school leader.

A school leader we know shared a story that sheds some light on the impor-tance of school-wide communication. She was working to get the teachers in her high school to leave their classrooms and explore and learn from their peers. Many of the teachers in this high school were seasoned veterans with fifteen to thirty years' experience. But a large number of veteran teachers were using inef-fective instructional strategies. The school leader encouraged peer observations or instructional rounds, with the focus of pairing some seasoned veterans with more novice teachers who were using student-centered strategies and getting good results.

The veteran teachers were initially hesitant. It was the first time a school leader had suggested peer observations, and many were afraid that their peer data would be used against them in some way. To curtail these fears, the school leader met with the more vocal of these hesitant teachers and took their sugges-tions. She didn't shy away from having the conversations.

Based on their feedback, the first change she made was the term *instruc-tional rounds*. She renamed the observation practice "Watch and Grow." She also changed the form for discourse to a simple yellow smiley-face Post-it note and the reflection form to a green smiley-face Post-it. Instead of *requiring* that teach-ers share their suggestions with administrators, it was just strongly suggested. Finally, the school leader created a contest as an incentive. The teacher with the most smiley-face Post-its and the teacher with the most reflective evidence won a prize: an assistant leader would cover their assigned duty for a week. Because she had welcomed open dialogue and made crucial changes to the original plan, the collegial process of learning from peers and sharing effective instructional practices was a success. The peer observation process has now been successfully integrated into the school's culture for half a decade.

We always recommend that teachers have structured opportunities to ob-serve other teachers to assess their practice against the teaching strategies of their peers. The school leader's job is to facilitate and encourage those interactions. The school leader who fails to do this will, in the long run, be inhibiting the growth of teachers, who will remain isolated.

Building Evidence of Collaboration

The actions and behaviors within this domain help ensure that teachers and staff have and engage in opportunities to address issues critical to the optimal functioning of the school and operate as a cohesive team.

The central question the school leader will ask in Domain 4 is this: Do I honestly have *evidence* that I have built a cooperative and collaborative environment?

Let's take a look at the five elements of Domain 4. These elements focus on collaboration around effective teaching, participation in decision making, team building for issues around curriculum and assessment, and formal ways for staff to provide input about school-wide policies and procedures. They also address the need for students, parents, and the wider community to be positively engaged.

1. The school leader ensures that teachers have opportunities to observe and discuss effective teaching.
2. The school leader ensures that teachers have formal roles in the decision-making process regarding school initiatives.
3. The school leader ensures that teacher teams and collaborative groups regularly interact to address common issues regarding curriculum, assessment, instruction, and the achievement of all students.
4. The school leader ensures that teachers and staff have formal ways to provide input regarding the optimal functioning of the school and delegates responsibilities appropriately.
5. The school leader ensures that students, parents, and community have formal ways to provide input regarding optimal functioning of the school.

The unstated but important premise that underlies Domain 4 is that it is crucial for the school leader to get teacher buy-in before putting sequential action steps in place. As we noted earlier, it's important not to foreclose discussion too early in the process, before the community has had the chance to digest, assess, contribute, and refine. The social architect is one part engineer, one part businessperson, and one part artist. As Block (2003) puts it, the answer to *how* is *yes*.

Observation and Discussion of Effective Teaching (Domain 4, Element 1)

The school leader ensures that teachers have opportunities to observe and discuss effective teaching.

Figures 4.1 and 4.2 illustrate the scales and evidences for Domain 4, Element 1.

Figure 4.1. Scale for Domain 4, Element 1

Scale Value	Description
Innovating (4)	The school leader intervenes and supports teachers who do not actively participate in opportunities to interact regarding effective instructional practices.
Applying (3)	The school leader ensures that teachers have regular opportunities to interact regarding effective instructional practices and observe specific examples of effective teaching virtually or in person AND monitors the extent to which teachers who actively participate in these opportunities improve their pedagogy.
Developing (2)	The school leader ensures that teachers have regular opportunities to interact regarding effective instructional practices and observe specific examples of effective teaching virtually or in person.
Beginning (1)	The school leader attempts to ensure that teachers have regular opportunities to interact regarding effective instructional practices and observe specific examples of effective teaching virtually or in person but does not complete the task or does so partially.
Not Using (0)	The school leader does not attempt to ensure that teachers have regular opportunities to interact regarding effective instructional practices and observe specific examples of effective teaching virtually or in person.

Figure 4.2. Sample evidences for Domain 4, Element 1

Sample Evidences for Domain 4, Element 1
• Teachers have opportunities to engage in instructional rounds.
• Teachers have opportunities to view and discuss video-based examples of exemplary teaching.
• Teachers have regular times to meet and discuss effective instructional practices (e.g., lesson study, professional learning communities).
• Teachers have opportunities to interact about effective teaching via technology.
• Instructional practices are regularly discussed at faculty and department meetings.
• Video segments of instructional practices are regularly viewed and discussed at faculty and department meetings.
• Procedures are in place for scheduling teachers to observe and discuss effective instructional practices.

(Continued)

Go to www.learningsciences.com/bookresources to download figures and tables.

> • Data are available to document that teachers who participate in observational rounds improve their pedagogy.
>
> • When asked, teachers report their participation in observing other teachers results in individual self-reflection and pedagogical growth.

Moving From Isolation to Collaboration

Teachers do collaborate. They just don't get to collaborate as much as they would like to. The *MetLife Survey of the American Teacher* published in 2009 reports that on average, teachers spend just 2.7 hours per week in structured collaboration with other teachers and school leaders. And less than one-third spent time observing other classroom teachers and providing feedback:

> By far, the least common collaborative activity is teachers observing each other in the classroom and providing feedback to each other. Much fewer teachers (22%) and leaders (32%) report it occurring always or often, with 44% of teachers and 26% of leaders saying it happens rarely or never. However, new teachers are more likely than other teachers to report teacher observation and feedback at their school (32% vs. 20%). (p. 10)

Furthermore, 67 percent of teachers and 78 percent of leaders responded that greater collaboration among teachers and school leaders would have a major impact in improving student achievement. In schools with high levels of collaboration, teachers and leaders held markedly different attitudes about the role of collaboration and collective responsibility.

> Teachers and leaders in schools with higher levels of collaboration are more likely than others to strongly agree that teachers in a school share responsibility for the achievement of all students and that greater collaboration among teachers and school leaders would have a major impact on improving student achievement. . . . Most striking is the higher level of trust in more collaborative schools. (Schools with) higher levels of collaboration are more likely to strongly agree that this level of trust exists (teachers: 69% vs. 42%; leaders: 78% vs. 60%). Furthermore, teachers in schools with higher levels of collaboration are more likely to be very satisfied with teaching as a career (68% vs. 54%). (p. 11)

The Gates Foundation supports this view, reporting that nearly 90 percent of US teachers believe that collaboration with colleagues is crucial to retaining good teachers (Scholastic & the Gates Foundation, 2012).

Marzano (2013) identifies a number of "leading indicators" for effective classroom instruction. One of these is that teachers have opportunities to observe and discuss effective teaching—for example, by engaging in instructional rounds, virtual discussions, and other forms of collaboration (p. 28).

Element 1 of Domain 4 helps ensure that teachers are fully engaged in the conversation about effective teaching: what it looks like in the classroom, how

Go to www.learningsciences.com/bookresources to download figures and tables.

to plan for it, and the effect of specific strategies in specific lessons for specific results.

The school leader developing capacity in this element might ask the following questions:

1. How do I, as a leader, help teachers see the benefit of observing other teachers?

2. Is there a schedule in place to facilitate opportunities for teachers to observe other teachers?

3. Do teacher know why they are observing other teachers? Are there boundaries or guidelines?

4. What would the desired effect be for this element?

Another way of looking at this element, as we have noted, is that the school leader is working against the tendency of teachers to isolate themselves. Dan Lortie, in his classic 1975 book *Schoolteacher*, proposes that without a solution to this tendency for teachers to work behind closed doors, it would be virtually impossible for schools to improve. Historically, the teacher

> spent his teaching day isolated from other adults; the initial pattern of school distribution represented a series of "cells" which were construed as self-sufficient. (p. 14)

In her recent book *The Smartest Kids in the World: And How They Got That Way* (2013), Amanda Ripley describes the extent to which teachers in countries like Finland, which outperformed nearly all other countries on the 2013 PISA (Programme for International Student Assessment) tests, collaborate with their colleagues. Finland's success, she argues, is due primarily to the extraordinary talent of teachers, who are selected from the top tiers and given lengthy and rigorous training and interact with each other around instructional improvement to an extent unheard of in the United States. Similarly, Thomas Del Prete, in *Teacher Rounds: A Guide to Collaborative Learning in and from Practice* (2013) reminds us that teaching hospitals have engaged in instructional rounds for decades—and that a similar model would very likely improve teacher performance.

It should be emphasized that the purpose of classroom visits, or regular instructional rounds, is not to evaluate the teacher being observed, but rather to provide an opportunity for teachers to share their knowledge and self-assess their practice. The school leader here is creating a culture that embraces the sharing of ideas.

One leader we know shares her experience with creating such a culture. In her middle school, she made sure to create opportunities for visits to other classrooms. Teachers reported they were often surprised that even the best teachers in the school were not consistently using what were agreed to be highly effective practices, such as inquiry-based learning. The purpose was certainly not to reprimand the teachers observed; instead, the sixth-grade teachers internally devised a system, which they titled Teachers Teaching Teachers, where they scheduled hours devoted to sharing their practice with other teachers, in facilitated discussions of effective teaching. Although the sixth-grade teachers had begun this practice independently with support from the leader, it was so successful that it eventually spread from grade to grade.

Building Evidence of Collaboration

School leaders must create structured periodic opportunities for teachers to meet, either as a whole or in small groups, to discuss effective instructional strategies based on current research. As teachers propose classroom strategies they would like to try, the leader's role is to provide examples of such effective strategies, either through classroom observation or other coaching. The school leader will further monitor these activities to ensure that all teachers are actively participating. The key is that the school leader must be deliberate and intentional in planning and allocation of resources to allow teachers to actively engage in these professional collaborative conversations and define and set expectations. It's important that the pedagogical examples provided are consistent with the critical needs of students.

What would the desired effect be for this element? The desired effect would be evidence of ongoing collaborative meetings and classroom visits. Over time, there should also be evidence that pedagogy throughout the school continues to improve. To measure the desired effect, the school leader would set up a system to facilitate participation, provide data about the outcome, and ensure full accountability.

Real-World Example

Recently, we worked with Principal Wendy Ivory at John Young Elementary School in Orange County, Florida. Her district was implementing the Marzano instructional model. Ms. Ivory worked relentlessly with the staff to better understand the model and was very transparent about her efforts as a learner in conjunction with her efforts as a leader. Ms. Ivory first engaged her leadership team in becoming more familiar with the framework and each of its components. Next, she and the team practiced reviewing videos of teacher classroom performance that they could score with teachers to help them better understand the model. The team then moved on to observing live classroom instruction and discussing the feedback they would give teachers, in addition to a rating that would serve as a coaching opportunity.

Ms. Ivory followed this practice by having teachers volunteer to be observed or to be an observer as part of a teacher team. She noted that she was surprised not only by the number of teachers interested in observing but the number of teachers who were willing to have their peers observe them. The conversations the staff had about the teaching and learning relationship using the model served to grow the principal's understanding, and it served as professional development for the teaching staff. The enthusiasm and depth of the conversation "brought tears to my eyes," Ms. Ivory reported after three months of the process.

In this scenario, we see the principal retaining the authority of her position but functioning in an open, nonthreatening way as the "chief learner" in the building. Her openness to this process yielded excellent results: teachers were enthusiastic about engaging in conversation around collegial instruction, and as a result, showed significant improvement.

Key Questions

1. What specific structures are in place to allow teachers to discuss effective teaching practices?

2. How do you monitor that these collaborative discussions are taking place?

3. What specific evidence do you look for to support that having opportunities to observe effective teacher practices is resulting in changes to teachers' pedagogy?

4. What specific evidence do you look for that the collaboration is resulting in teachers discussing effective teacher practices?

5. Do you intervene with staff members who are not utilizing opportunities to observe effective teachers and changing their practice based on that collaboration?

Scenario

Dr. Darby believes strongly in providing teachers with the opportunity to observe other teachers.

At the beginning of the year, Dr. Darby explained to teachers that as part of improving their instructional practices, they were expected to participate in peer observations with the goal of observing and sharing effective teaching practices. She met with grade-level representatives to establish a set of "look for" questions that would guide a teacher's visit to a colleague's classroom. The representatives also set up guidelines for visits.

Dr. Darby took a careful approach to this new initiative by asking for volunteers who would allow other teachers to observe in their classrooms. She also asked teachers to identify teachers they would like to observe. This left Dr. Darby with the job of crafting a schedule to accommodate all the special requests, along with scheduling teachers who did not make any requests. As part of the established procedures, participating teachers completed short reflection questions following their observations. To preserve teachers' privacy and autonomy, Dr. Darby was not able to view these reflection questions, which were recorded in the school's performance management system. But she *was* able to track which teachers chose to participate. At the end of the year, she surveyed participants with an anonymous survey tool to ask them for feedback explaining how visiting another teacher's class impacted their practice. When she reviewed the report, she learned that less than 60 percent of the volunteers had participated.

Explanation and Feedback

Dr. Darby should be rated at the *Developing* level as she carefully implemented all the constructs of the element, but it appears she was so focused on implementation that she did not provide ongoing monitoring to determine if the teachers were achieving the desired results. To move to the *Applying* level, she would need to have evidence of monitoring for the desired results.

Involving Teachers in Decision Making (Domain 4, Element 2)

The school leader ensures that teachers have formal roles in the decision-making process regarding school initiatives.

Domain 4, Elements both 2 and 4, address the various formal roles that teachers play in making decisions at the school. Many schools struggle with the number of initiatives that the district meted out, but the key is to involve teachers in the decision making about how those initiatives will be implemented at their school.

In his 8-Step Process for Leading Change, John Kotter (2012) emphasizes the importance of clearly communicating a vision for any new initiative that facilitates stakeholder buy-in. Kotter maintains that most organizations undercommunicate their vision of large scale change efforts by at least a factor of ten. An effective leader will work tirelessly to communicate an essential vision and strategy in a way that is simple, vivid, repeatable (the message can be spread by anyone to anyone), and invitational (opening avenues for two-way communication).

Element 2 helps ensure that the school faculty is involved in constructive conversations about important school issues, including academic initiatives like scheduling, placement of students, or college and career readiness standards. The key here is to define initiatives clearly and continue to articulate the message often. Figures 4.3 and 4.4 illustrate the scale and evidences for Domain 4, Element 2.

Collective Decision Making

One of the goals of Domain 4 is to initiate the growth of a culture where decisions are made collectively more often than they are from the top down. Teacher leaders can play important roles in implementing, planning, and monitoring new projects.

Key Questions

1. What is the process for involving staff members in key decisions regarding new initiatives in the building?

2. What is the process for ensuring that all staff members feel represented in routine decisions throughout the year?

3. How do you ensure that staff members feel that the administration has heard their opinions?

4. What evidence is critical to indicate you are getting the desired results?

Figure 4.3. Scale for Domain 4, Element 2

Scale Value	Description
Innovating (4)	The school leader continually seeks new venues for teacher input regarding important decisions.
Applying (3)	For specific types of decisions, the school leader ensures that formal processes are in place to collect data from all teachers regarding their preferences AND monitors the extent to which those data are used to make decisions and the transparency of those decisions.
Developing (2)	For specific types of decisions, the school leader ensures that formal processes are in place to collect data from all teachers regarding their preferences.
Beginning (1)	The school leader attempts to ensure that formal processes are in place to collect data from all teachers regarding their preferences on specific decisions but does not complete the task or does so partially.
Not Using (0)	The school leader does not attempt to ensure that formal processes are in place to collect data from all teachers regarding their preferences on specific decisions.

Figure 4.4. Sample evidences for Domain 4, Element 2

Sample Evidences for Domain 4, Element 2
• Teachers are advised of the specific types of decisions in which they will have direct input.
• Data-gathering techniques are in place to collect information from teachers.
• Notes and reports are in place that describe how teacher input was used when making specific decisions.
• Electronic tools are utilized to collect and report teacher opinions regarding specific decisions (e.g., online surveys).
• Groups of teachers are selected and utilized to provide input regarding specific decisions.
• Teacher leaders are enabled to proactively initiate, plan, implement, and monitor projects.

(Continued)

Go to www.learningsciences.com/bookresources to download figures and tables.

• The school leadership team has critical roles in facilitating school initiatives.
• Data are available to show input is used by the school leader.
• When asked, teachers report they feel their input is valued and used by the school leader.

Scenario

Purvis Middle School wants to implement a new behavior management program. The faculty is aware that there are problems with discipline in the school, and they have seen other schools using a specific structured behavior management program with highly effective results. While some school leaders might simply announce the new program and begin planning implementation, perhaps requiring teachers to attend a professional development day on the new program, Element 2 specifically calls for faculty input for decisions. Therefore, a school leader at the *Developing* level would provide information about the new system and survey the staff, disseminate and discuss the current research, and perhaps send a representative to observe the strategies in classrooms in other schools and report back. The staff, or key members of the team, might then meet to discuss how to personalize the strategies to meet the specific needs of the school.

At the *Applying* level, the school leader would do everything required for the *Developing* level, but she would also monitor whether the faculty feels that they have been closely involved. The leader might survey the staff, asking for feedback on the initiative, along with feedback on the process and their reported satisfaction with their level of input. Does the faculty feel included in the planning and processing of this critical initiative? At the *Innovating* level, the leader would continue to meet with faculty and seek input as the program is implemented.

Good sense will tell you that leaders do have to make decisions that may at times contradict the wishes of the staff. Especially in the case of emergency procedures and other critical health and safety issues, what's best for students is always nonnegotiable. Not every decision will be made democratically. But it is critical for leaders to maintain transparency, show the steps along the way and the reasoning behind why they have made decisions, and demonstrate that opposing views have been not only heard, but deeply considered. Once the school leader has gathered input from teachers, he may follow up with teachers to discuss how that input was used in making the final decision (Glanz, 2009; Nye & Capelluti, 2003).

The desired effect for Element 2 is that teachers know they have formal roles in decision making, that their input plays a critical role, and that the process is very transparent. In a collaborative environment, teachers also feel that they are professional, contributing members of the school community. Specific persons are appointed to represent departments or groups within the school, online tools or open forum meetings are made available to facilitate input, and so on.

Go to www.learningsciences.com/bookresources to download figures and tables.

Leadership teams are tasked with representing their groups' input and taking information from the administration back to the group.

Giving teachers opportunities for input about the implementation process not only taps into the collective wisdom, but it allows leaders to build enthusiasm and momentum for the initial implementation. Teachers who spend time developing the new behavior program are much more likely to be enthusiastic during its rollout and less likely to criticize it as problems arise. Additionally, the collaborative team developing the plan for the initial implementation becomes the same collaborative team that identifies solutions to problems arising after the program is launched. There is more protective ownership of the program's success (Conzemius & O'Neill, 2001).

Ensuring Teacher Collaboration (Domain 4, Element 3)

The school leader ensures that teacher teams and collaborative groups regularly interact to address issues regarding curriculum, assessment, instruction, and achievement of all students.

Sometimes Element 3 is referred to as the PLC element because of its focus on collaboration and cooperation among teachers. Element 3 helps create an environment where teachers routinely come together, in communities of practice, to discuss curriculum, build units, and examine and share practices that build student achievement. Because teachers don't have the autonomy to change their schedules, the school leader must build time into the schedule for teachers to have these supportive, collaborative opportunities, and prioritize these sessions so they are guarded from intrusions.

Role of PLCs in School Culture

Early in this chapter, we touched on some ways in which professional learning communities play a crucial role in facilitating collaboration and communication. It may be useful at this juncture to take a look at what educators and researchers consider the defining characteristics and goals of an effective PLC.

In 1997, Shirley Hord published *Professional Learning Communities: Communities of Continuous Inquiry and Improvement*, a literature survey of the concept of the PLC. In her introduction, Hord discusses what she identifies as "change-ready" schools:

> It seemed to me that if we could better understand the phenomenon of producing change-ready schools (those that value change and seek changes that will improve their schools), we could develop a more effective strategy for pursuing continuous school improvement. Jeannie Oakes, from her studies in school context, maintains: "there is evidence that a 'professional' staff will work to-

ward implementing strategies and programs to improve results" (1989, p. 194). (Preface, para. 7)

Hord's literature review sought to:

1. Define and describe what the literature referred to as "professional learning communities"
2. Describe what happens "when a school staff studies, works, plans, and takes action collectively on behalf of increased learning for students"
3. Reveal what is known "about how to create such communities of professionals in schools" (1997, p. 5)

Hord (1997, Intro, para. 2) focuses on what Astuto, Clark, Read, McGree, and Fernandez (1993) label a *professional community of learners*, one "in which the teachers in a school and its administrators continuously seek and share learning, and act on their learning. The goal of their actions is to enhance their effectiveness as professionals for the students' benefit." Hord notes that the arrangement could also be termed *communities of continuous inquiry and improvement*.

Many of the principles that Hord identified in her review have persisted in our current understanding of the characteristics and value of professional learning communities, including the work of many researchers studying the positive effect of PLCs on student achievement (Berry, Johnson, & Montgomery, 2005; DuFour & Marzano, 2011; Hollins, McIntyre, DeBose, Hollins, & Towner, 2004; Phillips, 2003; Strahan, 2003; Supovitz, 2002; Supovitz & Christman, 2003). British researcher Dylan Wiliam (2012) notes that an effective PLC can raise the PISA test scores of students in a school by 16 percent in two to three years.

Hord lists the following attributes of the PLC: supportive and shared leadership; collective creativity; shared values and vision developed from an unswerving commitment to student learning; supportive conditions for collective learning, including peer feedback, classroom observations, and other forms of shared personal practice; and physical conditions and human capacities to support the operation (1997, p. 24).

Hord also notes that building effective PLCs requires a large paradigm shift "both in the public and in teachers themselves about what the role of teacher entails." She points to studies comparing how teachers around the world spent their time, noting that in Japan, for instance, "teachers spend a greater portion of their time in planning, conferring with colleagues, working with students individually, visiting other classrooms, and engaging in other professional development activities (Darling-Hammond, 1994, 1996)" (p. 25).

With these characteristics and goals in mind, let us now turn to a closer examination of Domain 4, Element 3. Figures 4.5 and 4.6 illustrate the scale and evidences for Element 3.

Figure 4.5. Scale for Domain 4, Element 3

Scale Value	Description
Innovating (4)	The school leader ensures that group goals relative to curriculum, assessment, and instruction are regularly revised to reflect the changes in student achievement data and intervenes and supports teacher teams whose goals do not adequately address the achievement of all students.
Applying (3)	The school leader ensures that formal teams or collaborative groups of teachers and other relevant staff meet regularly and have specific goals relative to curriculum, assessment, and instruction AND monitors the extent to which these goals are designed to enhance the achievement of all students.
Developing (2)	The school leader ensures that formal teams or collaborative groups of teachers and other relevant staff meet regularly and have specific goals relative to curriculum, assessment, and instruction.
Beginning (1)	The school leader attempts to ensure that formal teams or collaborative groups of teachers and other relevant staff meet regularly and have specific goals relative to curriculum, assessment, and instruction but does not complete the task or does so partially.
Not Using (0)	The school leader does not attempt to ensure that formal teams or collaborative groups of teachers and other relevant staff meet regularly and have specific goals relative to curriculum, assessment, and instruction.

Figure 4.6. Sample evidences for Domain 4, Element 3

Sample Evidences for Domain 4, Element 3
• Professional learning communities (PLCs) are in place and meet regularly.
• PLCs have written goals.
• The school leader regularly examines the PLCs' progress toward goals.
• Common assessments are created by PLCs.
• Student achievement and growth are analyzed by PLCs.
• Data teams are in place and have written goals.
• The progress of each data team toward reaching its goals is regularly examined.
• To maintain a focus on student achievement, the school leader collects and reviews minutes, notes, and goals from meetings.
• When asked, teachers can explain how being a member of a PLC has helped them grow their pedagogy.
• When asked, teachers can explain how PLCs analyze data to identify appropriate instructional practices.

Go to www.learningsciences.com/bookresources to download figures and tables.

The school leader should not only make time for PLCs but provide direction, set expectations, and monitor the results of what happens during these community meetings. Here is the time and place where teachers and leaders can together address assessments and draw on student data to gauge how well students are meeting their goals. These resources allow teachers to adjust instructional strategies and build units and lessons to directly meet the needs of individual students.

Teachers may also use this time for lesson study, a very focused protocol for teachers to observe and discuss effective instruction. In this case, teams of teachers get together to plan a detailed lesson and discuss which classroom strategies are most effective for delivering that lesson. In some lesson studies we have worked with, one teacher is designated to teach the lesson, while other members of the group observe to determine whether the lesson is getting the desired effect from students. Depending on the observers' feedback, the group may make adjustments in the strategy and, over time, develop best practices for the type of lesson. Lesson studies that operate this way are becoming more frequent as schools implement more rigorous college and career readiness standards. The school leader's responsibility is to guide and monitor these groups to ensure the activities are aligned with school-wide goals.

The Role of Collaboration in a PLC

In *Leaders of Learning* (2011), DuFour and Marzano emphasize that they believe PLCs are crucial to developing a school's collective capacity:

> The best strategy for improving schools and districts is developing the collective capacity of educators to function as members of a professional learning community (PLC)—a concept based on the premise that if students are to learn at higher levels, processes are in place to ensure the ongoing, job-embedded learning of the adults who serve them. (p. 21)

The PLC concept, as DuFour et al. have refined it, represents "an ongoing process in which educators work collaboratively in recurring cycles of collective inquiry and active research to achieve better results for the students they serve" (DuFour, DuFour, Eaker, & Many, 2010, p. 11).

As DuFour and Marzano (2011) elaborate, "It is not a program to be purchased, it is a process to be pursued but never quite perfected" (p. 22), and as Sparks (2004) says, it's "an ethos that infuses every single aspect of a school's operation" (p. 48).

DuFour and Marzano (2011) identify three big ideas that drive the PLC process:

1. The fundamental purpose of school is to ensure that all students learn at high levels.

2. If we are to help all students learn, it will require us to work collabora-
    tively in an effort to meet the needs of each student.

3. Educators must create a results orientation to know if students are learn-
    ing and use that evidence to drive continuous improvement of the PLC
    process. (p. 24)

What conditions are necessary to make a PLC effective? What are the challenges a school leader may expect to face in setting up, supporting, and monitoring
the PLC?

Let us offer an example. To help ensure that PLCs were faithfully implemented, one school district we know of gave teachers an hour of early release
time each Monday afternoon so staff could participate in focused collaborative
groups. Setting up early release time throughout the county was no simple task.
It required careful coordination: buses had to come early, some parents had to
arrange child care, an after-school program had to be put in place, and a host of
other administrative decisions. But by doing so, the county very clearly signaled
that time for collaborative PLCs was a priority for teachers. Teachers responded
by taking and using the time seriously.

Other districts have put in place half-day releases on a bimonthly basis. The
school leaders in these cases ensure that once this major shift is accomplished,
the time is regarded as sacred.

The goal of Element 3 is to help ensure that structured professional learning
communities meet for regular and consistent collaboration on the subjects of developing curriculum, assessments, and effective instruction. Ideally, the goals of
the PLC relate to furthering school-wide goals. PLCs may develop common assessments that allow tracking of learning goals. For example, they may develop
procedures for disaggregating data from assessments or decide how best to use
the data from those assessments.

The desired effect for Element 3 is that teachers work as a PLC to measurably improve. Teachers working as a team can create better outcomes than
individuals working alone, but effective teamwork doesn't just happen on its
own. Leaders must create the conditions for teams to work together, managing interactions and guiding activities, so they can operate effectively and
efficiently.

The desired effect is that teacher teams collaborate on issues related to curriculum, assessment, instruction, and achievement of all students. Teaching and
student achievement improves.

Key Questions

1. What specific structures are in place to allow teachers to collaboratively
    plan for instruction?

2. What specific structures are in place to allow teachers to work collaboratively with other teachers to monitor their instructional pedagogy?

3. How do you monitor the effectiveness of these PLCs or collaborative structures?

4. How do you know that they are improving instruction?

5. How do you determine the extent to which these collaborations are focused on improving student learning?

Ensuring Staff Input and Delegating Responsibilities (Domain 4, Element 4)

The school leader ensures that teachers and staff have formal ways to provide input regarding the optimal functioning of the school and delegates responsibilities appropriately.

Like Element 2, Element 4 focuses on ways that the school leader involves teachers in the design and implementation of important decisions and policies. Element 4 takes the idea further, because in addition to ensuring teacher input, the school leader must delegate authority, create a succession plan, and ensure that the right staff is in the right leadership seat. Figures 4.7 and 4.8 illustrate scale and evidences for Element 4.

Figure 4.7. Scale for Domain 4, Element 4

Scale Value	Description
Innovating (4)	The school leader intervenes and provides support when delegation of authority and teacher input is not working to optimize the function of the school.
Applying (3)	The school leader ensures that input is regularly collected from teachers and staff, appropriately delegates responsibilities, AND monitors the extent to which the inputs and delegations are contributing to the optimal functioning of the school.
Developing (2)	The school leader ensures that input is regularly collected from teachers and staff and appropriately delegates responsibilities.
Beginning (1)	The school leader attempts to ensure that input is regularly collected from teachers and staff and appropriately delegates responsibilities but does not complete the task or does so partially.
Not Using (0)	The school leader does not attempt to ensure that input is regularly collected from teachers and staff and does not appropriately delegate responsibilities.

Figure 4.8. Sample evidences for Domain 4, Element 4

Sample Evidences for Domain 4, Element 4
• Data collection systems are in place to collect opinion data from teachers and staff regarding the optimal functioning of the school.
• Data are archived and reports are regularly generated regarding these data.
• The manner in which data are used is made transparent.
• The school improvement team provides input to the leader regarding the school improvement plan.
• Appropriate faculty and staff are identified and mentored for succession planning and provided appropriate growth opportunities.
• Faculty and staff are assisted with career planning and continuing educational opportunities.
• Teacher leaders and other faculty are empowered to share in the leadership of the school.
• Potential leaders are identified and guided in career development.
• The school leader can cite examples of where teacher input has resulted in effective change at the school.
• The school leader demonstrates ongoing mentoring of teacher leaders.
• When asked, teachers explain formal ways they have to give input regarding optimal functioning of the school.
• When asked, teachers can identify examples of when their input has resulted in effective change at the school.

Obtaining Teacher and Staff Input

Some research, such as Silins, Mulford, and Zarins (2002), suggests that school effectiveness is proportional to the extent that teachers participate in all aspects of the school's functioning, not only in instructional and curricular decisions but also in school policy decisions and review. Such participation is necessary to foster a coherent sense of direction and understanding of the wider school community.

To create a collaborative culture, a school leader might begin refining skills within this element by asking the following questions:

1. What factors should be considered when defining the optimal functioning of the school?

2. What are the formal processes in place to solicit input from teachers and staff?

3. What is the process for deciding which responsibilities should be delegated?

4. How is it determined if leadership capacity is being developed within the school?

Go to www.learningsciences.com/bookresources to download figures and tables.

A supervisor evaluating a school leader might ask:

1. What data can be used for demonstrating the school leader's achievement in this element?

2. What data would be important to distinguish between levels of *Applying* and *Innovating*?

In Element 4, as in Element 2, the school leader actively seeks staff input. Formal processes for collecting input might include teacher surveys, formal committee recommendations, school advisory committees, and the like. Decisions require collective conversations that may, for example, result in formal resolutions. School advisory committees must become not just a matter of compliance, but important drivers of collective efficacy.

Transparency of decision making, as we noted with Element 2, is paramount. The desired effect of Element 4 is that teachers and staff have input when it comes to decision making and that the school actually does function at the optimal level. Responsibilities are distributed, and there is evidence that leadership is shared throughout the school.

We have identified at least five possible steps for achieving shared leadership in your school:

1. Develop a strong school leadership team.
2. Distribute responsibilities throughout the leadership team.
3. Select the right work.
4. Identify the order of magnitude implied.
5. Match management style to the order of magnitude of the change.

Getting the Right People in the Right Seats

As we have discussed, in Element 4 the school leader identifies future leaders and continues to build leadership capacity.

Related to the challenge of developing shared leadership is that the school leader must place the right people in the right seats; in other words, the leader must delegate responsibility appropriately. The school leader who delegates responsibility effectively is doing far more than just handing out projects to key team members. She will be providing growth opportunities for teachers who aspire to be leaders. The leader will be designing a succession plan and building capacity for leadership within the school. The overarching idea is that the school becomes self-functioning—in other words, the school will continue to operate at a high level under successive generations of leaders. If the leader provides clear guidance—articulating a vision and ensuring that teacher leaders are motivated toward promotion opportunities—the school culture built on such a solid foundation will carry on for many years (Fullan, 2007). One former school leader we know reports that many of the policies and procedures she put in place at her elementary school 20 years ago are still operating today—and that the vision she and her team established is still strong.

Key Questions

1. Who are the future leaders in your building?

2. What is your process for identifying future leaders?

3. What growth opportunities do you provide future leaders?

4. How do you monitor the effectiveness of their leadership in the building?

5. How do you determine which responsibilities to delegate and which must be made only by administrators?

6. What evidence reveals that your school is functioning at an optimal level?

Ensuring Community, Parent, and Student Input (Domain 4, Element 5)

The school leader ensures that students, parents, and community have formal ways to provide input regarding optimal functioning of the school.

Most schools have at least a rudimentary process for involving students, parents, and the community in school initiatives. The goal of Element 5 is to help school leaders refine the process so that the input they gather from the community can be effectively utilized in decision making.

As Marzano notes in *What Works in Schools* (2003), parental and community involvement has been identified in most attempts to synthesize the research on effective schooling. Research has shown that positive involvement from family and community is correlated with higher grades, better attendance, more positive attitudes toward school, higher graduation rate, and greater enrollment in college (Henderson & Berla, 1994). Parental involvement has been associated with a .26 effect size, which translates into a percentile gain of 10 percent in student achievement. Marzano has identified three features that define effective parental and community involvement: communication, participation, and governance.

Communicating With Parents and Community

Strong two-way channels of *communication* are a defining feature of effective parent and community involvement (Antunez, 2000). In other words, the medium of communication will be most effective if it allows parents and community members to participate and respond. Technology has made two-way communication much easier to achieve in recent years. Many schools rely on social media (blogs, Twitter, Facebook, etc.) in addition to traditional avenues of communication such as bulletins, newsletters, and flyers.

These two-way channels of communication naturally lead to increased *participation* and community involvement in the day-to-day running of the school. As Marzano (2003) notes, "Involved parents sense that the school values and welcomes not only their ideas but also their physical participation" (p. 48). As an added benefit parent and community involvement can significantly add to a school's resource base (Tangri & Moles, 1987, cited in Marzano, 2003), which can include access to expertise, community contacts, financial contributions, and donation of equipment.

Governance is related to participation and communication in that it allows parents and community to participate in key school decisions. Marzano notes that a 1982 survey of parents in six southwestern states (Stallworth & Williams, 1982) found that parents were very interested in decisions regarding programs and practices that bore directly on the achievement of their children.

The revised Interstate School Leaders Licensure Consortium (ISLLC) Standards for School Leadership issued in October 2014 reflect the growing understanding of the importance of community engagement, with an emphasis on the school leader's role in collaborating with communities as learning partners.

Figures 4.9 and 4.10 illustrate the scale and evidences for Domain 4, Element 5.

Some planning questions to consider for Element 5 include the following:

- In what ways can you ensure that data is collected from students, parents, and the community regarding school policies?
- How will you use that data and plan for follow-up?
- What are your specific challenges when tapping into community input, and how can you address them?
- What kinds of decisions can be made collaboratively around school policies and initiatives?

In building a positive relationship with the larger community, the school leader will, as we have suggested, not only put workable communication and feedback systems in place and make transparency a priority, but also carefully consider that the community is a diverse place. The leader will have implemented formal ways to cross any cultural or language barriers, for example, and processes to get all parents engaged in school initiatives and policies. The leader might hold physical or virtual town hall meetings, set up interactive websites, hold focus groups, and speak at community events.

Figure 4.9. Scale for Domain 4, Element 5

Scale Value	Description
Innovating (4)	The school leader intervenes and provides support when student, parent, and community input is not working to optimize the function of the school.
Applying (3)	The school leader ensures that input is regularly collected from students, parents, and community AND monitors the extent to which the inputs are contributing to the optimal functioning of the school.
Developing (2)	The school leader ensures that input is regularly collected from students, parents, and community.
Beginning (1)	The school leader attempts to ensure that input is regularly collected from students, parents, and community but does not complete the task or does so partially.
Not Using (0)	The school leader does not attempt to ensure that input is regularly collected from students, parents, and community.

Figure 4.10. Sample evidences for Domain 4, Element 5

Sample Evidences for Domain 4, Element 5
• Data collection systems are in place to collect opinion data from students, parents, and community regarding the optimal functioning of the school.
• Data are archived and reports regularly generated regarding these data.
• The manner in which these data are used is made transparent.
• Data are available to show that input from the school's diverse population is valued and used.
• An interactive website is provided for students, parents, and community to provide input.
• Appropriate social networking technologies (e.g., Twitter, Facebook) are utilized to involve students, parents, and community.
• Focus group meetings with students and parents are routinely scheduled.
• The school leader hosts or speaks at community/business luncheons.
• The school leader can explain how the use of input from the school community has resulted in improved functioning of the school.
• The school leader can demonstrate how data gathered from subpopulations at the school are incorporated in school planning.
• When asked, students, parents, and community members report their input is valued and used by the school leader to better the functioning of the school.

It's crucial that the school leader is known to the community. He must be active in making opportunities to connect with parents, students, business leaders, and the public. Strong participation in noneducation-related community meetings helps connect with business leaders for potential partnerships; the school

Go to www.learningsciences.com/bookresources to download figures and tables.

leader can also invite community members in for face-to-face chats, set up parent advisory committees, and survey local organizations for useful feedback.

A school leader who would like to make a change in the school's tardy policy, for example, would do well to enlist the input and support of all stakeholders whom the policy might affect, before making or announcing any formal decision. The leader might ask for feedback on the updated guidelines and use this data to adjust the policy, if necessary. It will be much easier in the long run to implement any new policy if the leader can show that a larger group made the decision rather than a single administrator or small committee.

The desired effect for this element is similar to some of the other elements we have discussed. Input from the community is being considered as part of the decision-making process. The community feels that they are valued, participatory members in decision making. This process helps the community feel more connected, which may have multiple positive results: increased participation in parent activities, increased student attendance, increased support for school initiatives, and a general sense that the school is performing well and people want to be part of the school community.

Role of Student Participation

So far, we have discussed ensuring teacher, parent, and community input, but it's important to understand that students, too, can play critical roles in giving feedback. Students, after all, are usually the members of the community that new policies and procedures most affect. A student advisory committee can be surveyed formally or informally—but we find that all too often this doesn't happen.

Our interviews with multiple school leaders have found scant evidence that student input is either routinely gathered or used to influence decisions. But a truly cooperative environment includes *all* stakeholders. The fact is, students can make or break initiatives. Without student buy-in, many new policies will have a tough time taking root. And when students are "the last to know," it's likely their reactions will be similar to adults who have been left out of a process—particularly when the issues affect them directly.

Teachers will often pass along informal feedback they get from students, and with a few caveats, this can be useful. Often the most vocal students are not representative of all students. The school leader will need to develop ways to get input on important policies from *all* students. When this begins to happen, it builds trust between students and administrators. Students trust a leader who shows that she will act on the problem.

Key Questions

1. What formal structures are in place to gather input from parents and community members?

2. What formal structures are in place to gather input from students?

3. How do you communicate important information to parents, community, and students?

4. What data will you use to monitor stakeholder involvement in critical decisions?

5. What evidence will you gather to document that you are achieving the desired effect for this element?

Scenario

At Atlantic High School, a survey of parents indicated that students felt rushed during their thirty-minute lunch period; they reported very little time to actually eat lunch. Parents requested that the school add an additional lunch period. Principal Collins understood their suggestion, but she also knew that reorganizing the entire school schedule wasn't a viable option.

Instead, Dr. Collins assigned members of the leadership team to observe all three lunch periods for three days. The team determined that students who purchased their lunch spent an average of twenty-two minutes in the lunch line, leaving them only eight minutes to eat. The cafeteria manager told Dr. Collins that there were no more personnel to assist in serving lunch. So Dr. Collins decided to restructure teacher's duty assignments. Since no teachers were currently assigned to the cafeteria, she reorganized their duty assignments to the cafeteria during lunch period. The nutrition manager could then move her personnel from supervising students to cashier duty, shortening the time it took for students to purchase lunch from twenty-two minutes to ten minutes. The average student now had twenty minutes to eat.

Dr. Collins and other school staff followed up with parents and students through formal and informal conversations. They continued to observe the cafeteria and posted a feedback comment section on the school's website. A large number of parents offered online feedback, expressing that they were pleased with the changes, and students reported that they had more time to eat, use the restroom, talk to friends, and go to their locker before lunch was over.

During the monitoring process, Dr. Collins learned that students who arrived last for lunch still had less time to eat. After consulting with staff, she asked that three classes dismiss students to lunch three minutes later, to create a small staggering effect. This simple move resulted in all students having ample time to eat. While monitoring school-wide data, the leadership team noted that, surprisingly, the extra time decreased the amount of tardiness to classes that followed lunch.

Explanation and Feedback

Based on the information early in this scenario, Dr. Collins clearly demonstrated behaviors at the *Developing* level when she set up the parent survey, identified the problem, and made staff changes to allow more time for students to eat.

She moved up to the *Applying* level when she monitored that the changes were contributing to the optimal functioning of the school (e.g., observing that students now had a full twenty minutes to eat lunch). When Dr. Collins noted that the change in the lunch procedure was still not obtaining the desired results (i.e., some students still didn't have enough time to eat), she made a further adjustment—staggering class schedules slightly and monitoring the data to note reduced tardiness after lunch. Therefore, the final feedback would be at the *Innovating* level.

Conclusion

> *Most school variables have at most small effects on learning. The real payoff comes when individual variables combine to reach critical mass. Creating the conditions under which that can occur is the job of the leader.*
> —The Wallace Foundation (2012)

Not every school leader is lucky enough to come into a school culture that is a fully functioning and effective community. But the good news is it is possible to turn an ailing school culture around.

A leader relates that more than ten years after she left her school, a teacher new to that school told her on first meeting: "I feel like I've always known you. I've learned that many of the things you started so many years ago are still in place. I want to make sure they are carried on." Once put in place, strong legacies can be passed on indefinitely. The effective leader could help define those legacies by hiring and developing the staff most likely to work well cooperatively. This school leader made a conscious effort to do so—and the result? In the years since her last day as leader of that school, a very small percentage of the teachers she originally worked with have left the school.

In the next chapter we discuss the final domain, Domain 5, which looks at the research on school climate and the actions a leader can take to build a school environment where both students and staff can flourish.

CHAPTER 5

Positive School Climate (Domain 5)

A great deal of research is beginning to accumulate around the connection between school climate and student achievement, as well as other factors that continue to affect well-being and success long after students have left school. A joint paper, *The School Climate Challenge*, published by the National School Climate Center, the Center for Social and Emotional Education, and the National Center for Learning and Citizenship at the Education Commission of the States sums up the effect school climate has on learning this way:

> There is a compelling body of research that underscores the importance of school climate. Positive school climate promotes learning, academic achievement, school success and healthy development, as well as effective risk prevention, positive youth development and increased teacher retention. However, these research findings are not consistently reflected in current educational policy, practice and teacher education efforts. (2007, p. 7)

Indeed, the authors find, school climate has a relationship to truancy, violence, bullying, cyber bullying, risky sexual behavior, drug abuse, rate of student suspension, attendance, rate of graduation, and physical health, all factors that indirectly affect student achievement. But there is also a *direct* correlation between positive school climate and higher levels of student achievement. In *What Works in Schools*, Robert Marzano ranked school climate as fourth of five school-level factors that impact student achievement. Positive school climate was associated with an effect size of 0.22, which translates into an 8 percent gain in student achievement (Marzano, 2003, p. 19).

The authors of *The School Climate Challenge* caution that we still have much to learn about how school climate affects student achievement, but they summarize the relationship this way:

> We are still learning why positive school climate leads to academic achievement and positive youth development. In broad strokes, it seems a positive school climate leads to greater focus and attunement to what students need to learn and teachers need to teach. (National School Climate Center, 2007, p. 7)

Furthermore, a positive climate contributes to building precisely the kind of learning environment conducive to new college and career readiness standards focused on 21st-century skills (Partnership for 21st Century Skills, 2002):

> When students, in partnership with educators and parents, work to improve school climate, they promote essential learning skills (e.g., creativity and innovation skills, critical thinking and problem solving skills, communication and collaborative skills) as well as life and career skills (e.g., flexibility and adaptability, initiative, social and cross culture skills, productivity and accountability, leadership and responsibility) that provide the foundation for 21st century learning. (p. 6)

But what exactly do we mean by *school climate*? ASCD's *A Lexicon of Learning* (n.d.) defines school climate as "the sum of the values, cultures, safety practices, and organizational structures within a school that cause it to function and react in particular ways." In a 2004 best practices brief, *School Climate and Learning*, produced by University Community Partnerships at Michigan State University, the authors define school climate as follows:

> School climate reflects the physical and psychological aspects of the school that are more susceptible to change in that they provide the preconditions necessary for teaching and learning to take place. . . . School climate . . . is evident in the feelings and attitudes about a school expressed by students, teachers, staff, and parents—the way students and staff "feel" about being at school each day. (Michigan State University, 2004, p. 2)

It should come as no surprise that students who feel safe and valued are likely to do better academically. Research has added to our understanding of the long-term impact of school climate.

We might define a *positive school climate* as the extent to which a school creates an atmosphere that students perceive as orderly and supportive. A positive school climate correlates with students attending school regularly and staying in school longer with lower dropout rates. Students who stay in school are more likely to have better lifelong health and higher incomes (Jensen, 2009; Kolata, 2007; Rumberger, 2011).

As Murphy and Torre (2014) write:

> A supportive learning community provides a "protective power" (Garmezy, 1991, p. 427) while attacking social problems that place students in peril (Christle, Jolivette, & Nelson, 2005; Crosnoe, 2011). It helps create a "social environment that neutralizes or buffers home stresses" (Alexander & Entwisle, 1996, p. 77) and community problems and individual characteristics that foster social marginalization and academic disengagement (Demaray & Malecki, 2002; Garmezy, 1991). Concomitantly, supportive learning environments create assets, social and human capital, to draw youngsters into the hard work that is re-

quired to be successful in school (Ancess, 2003; Goddard, 2003; Supovitz, 2002, 2008) (pp. 52–53).

Because of the profound influence of school climate on learning and student well-being, the school leader must ensure that the school climate fosters a rich and collective sense of a shared enterprise among all stakeholders in the system. Indeed, the updated ISLLC (Interstate School Leaders Licensure Consortium) Standards for School Leaders, released in 2014, place increased emphasis on the leader's role as a "community builder," a person who "ensures the formation of a culture defined by trust" and who ensures that students are "enmeshed in a safe, secure, emotionally protective, and healthy environment" (ISLLC, 2014). The authors of the revised standards call this environment a "Community of Care."

This focus on the cultivation of positive school and community environment(s) is threaded throughout the 2014 ISLLC standards. In his unpublished paper explaining the foundations of the revised 2014 standards, Murphy (2014) references three "distinct but related dimensions" of the school leader as community builder. The first is the *extended school environment*, where the school leader honors the voices of parents and members of the larger community. In the second sphere, the school leader acts as guardian of *communities of learning* for teachers and staff (emphasized in Marzano Domain 4). And in the third, she builds and safeguards *caring learning environments* for students (ensuring opportunity to learn, as in Domain 3, and continuous improvement of instruction, as in Domain 2).

It's important to note that school climate as generally understood by educators refers to the *subjective experience* of the school, rather than the *actual* state of the school, which is our understanding of school *culture*, our focus in the previous chapter. This is an important distinction. Boisterous classroom activity, for example, might be one aspect of a school's culture—but how people *feel* about it ("the kids are running wild" vs. "students here are full of energy and enthusiasm") reflects the school climate.

We often think of school culture as simply "the way things are done"—that is, norms and traditions, whether the environment is closed or open, collaborative (as we discussed in Domain 4) or not. Climate is the "way it feels," usually as the result of the culture at a school. Do people feel safe? Valued? Is the school inviting? Most perceptions are a result of the way things are done at a school.

With an eye on the continuous improvement of the school, in order to promote a positive school climate, the purpose and values of the school must be shared and unified to foster work that is productive and meaningful. In this way the actions reflected in Domain 4 and perceptions reflected in Domain 5 are closely related. Domain 4 is largely focused on collective efficacy and the school leader's role as an "optimizer." Domain 5 focuses on the positive perceptions of staff and community that will encourage the communication and collaboration of Domain 4 to flourish and positions the school leader as a model of behavior and actions for all the educators in the school.

Building Evidence of a Positive School Climate

The actions and behaviors in this domain help ensure that all constituents perceive the school as positive and well-functioning.

The central question the school leader will ask in Domain 5 is this: Do I honestly have evidence that I have taken specific actions to foster a positive school climate?

Six specific categories of school leader actions and behaviors constitute this domain:

1. The school leader is recognized as the leader of the school who continuously improves his professional practice.
2. The school leader has the trust of staff and is guided by what is best for all students.
3. The school leader ensures that the staff perceive the school environment as safe and orderly.
4. The school leader ensures that students and parents perceive the environment as safe and orderly.
5. The school leader manages resources to focus on student achievement.
6. The school leader acknowledges the success of the whole school and individuals within the school.

Domain 5 begins to pull together the goals of all the previous domains. The school leader must establish herself as a leader who continually improves professional practice (Domain 5, Element 1); this element, for example, will certainly include attention to factors related to Domain 2 (*Continuous Improvement of Instruction*), as both teachers and school leaders are expected to grow and improve their practice. Establishing a climate of trust in which actions are guided by what is best for all student populations (Domain 5, Element 2) relates back to Domain 1 (*a focus on student achievement*) and Domain 2 (*Continuous Improvement of Instruction*): a school leader with uncompromising regard for student achievement will hire the best teachers, provide them with the resources they need, and cultivate a climate where no one makes excuses—a climate that embraces the challenges of improving student achievement. Such a leader will constantly assess school initiatives to measure their impact on students and ensure that resources are secured. For such a leader, failure is not an option for students.

Therefore, the school leader's role is to model positive behavior through a process that Burns (1978), Bass (1985), and Bass and Avolio (1994) have identified as *idealized influence*. As Marzano, Waters, and McNulty (2005) explain in *School Leadership That Works*, "Idealized influence is characterized by modeling behavior through exemplary personal achievements, character, and behavior" (p. 14).

As we can see, each of the four previous domains includes areas of focus that impact school climate. Students, teachers, and parents perceive that there is a strong focus on student achievement (Domain 1); there is support for continuous improvement of instruction (Domain 2) so teachers perceive themselves as professionals who continuously build expertise; students are provided time and opportunity to learn the curriculum (Domain 3); and cooperation and collaboration are integral components of school climate (Domain 4). A safe and orderly environment allows these components to function optimally, as does the efficient and targeted use of resources. Regular opportunities to acknowledge the success of all these functioning parts contribute to a positive climate. Multiple facets of each domain are interwoven and interdependent.

The unstated but important premise that underlies Domain 5 is that the school leader has a profound influence on the way every member of the system—teachers, students, parents, and support staff—perceive the overall climate of the school, a perception that in turn impacts the performance of teachers and students.

Modeling Leadership (Domain 5, Element 1)

The school leader is recognized as the leader of the school who continually improves his or her professional practice.

What does it mean to be "recognized as a leader"? General Colin Powell famously defines leadership as "creating the conditions of trust":

> The longer I have been in public service and the more people have asked me about leadership over the years, leadership ultimately comes down to creating conditions of trust within an organization. Good leaders are people who are trusted by followers. They will follow you into the darkest night, down into the deepest valley, up the highest hill, if they trust you.

One aspect of building organizational trust is to become a model of the kinds of behavior you expect of others. Just as the school as a whole focuses on Continuous Improvement of Instruction in Domain 2, the school leader must continuously demonstrate improvement in his own professional practice by seeking out mentors and professional development and building leadership capacity.

Figure 5.1 illustrates the scale for Domain 5, Element 1.

Figure 5.1. Scale for Domain 5, Element 1

Scale Value	Description
Innovating (4)	The school leader actively seeks expertise/mentors for validation and feedback to confirm or improve leadership skills.
Applying (3)	The school leader demonstrates leadership skills and continually engages in activities to improve his/her professional practices AND monitors the extent to which these activities enhance personal leadership skills and the staff's confidence about his/her ability to lead.
Developing (2)	The school leader demonstrates leadership skills and continually engages in activities to improve his/her professional practices.
Beginning (1)	The school leader attempts to demonstrate leadership skills and engage in activities to improve his/her professional practices but does not complete the task or does so partially.
Not Using (0)	The school leader does not attempt to demonstrate leadership skills and does not engage in activities to improve his/her professional practices.

A look at the scale in Figure 5.1 tells us that the focus of this element is on building recognition as a leader and continuing professional development via the cultivation of relationships with one or more mentors. In *Mentoring Principals: Frameworks, Agendas, Tips, and Case Stories for Mentors and Mentees*, Young, Sheets, and Knight (2005) acknowledge that for school leaders, developing mentor relationships is crucial:

> Adults learn best when they are goal oriented and self-directed. They seek out experiences when facing life-changing events. New principals' success when facing the steep learning curve during the first critical years of service depends on their ability to meet external expectations, develop interpersonal relationships, turn obstacles or barriers into goals and positive outcomes, and maintain their self-esteem and sense of pleasure in the work they do. Mentors need to be attuned to the factors that impact their mentee's motivation to learn. They must also help their mentee visualize how to apply these basic concepts to the job-embedded situations they face. (p. 4)

The mentor-mentee relationship is to some extent built into the Marzano School Leader Evaluation Model. The evaluator functions as a potential mentor for the school leader in that she provides focused performance feedback in this and other domains. Supervisors of principals mentor principals; principals mentor assistant principals and other school leaders. But mentoring is not limited just to relationships between leaders and supervisors—the growing, developing school leader looks for other school leaders to serve as mentors, as well. As Brown, Collins, and Duguid (1989) note, mentorship is a crucial factor in professional growth:

Participation with others, especially members of the field of practice who are more expert in some areas (perhaps a more experienced leader), substantially extends the potential for individual leadership development. (As cited by Leithwood, Seashore-Louis, Anderson, & Wahlstrom, 2004, p. 69)

Developing relationships with mentors, participating in professional networking, and continuously improving practice is only one facet of this element. The second area of focus is how these practices can enhance the perception of teachers, staff, students, and parents that the school leader is a person who takes seriously his responsibility to continually develop professional practice—that he is a responsible leader in whom the community may place its confidence.

For Element 1, then, the desired outcome is that the leader is clearly recognized as a leader focused on personal development of leadership expertise. The evidences for this outcome might include that in Figure 5.2.

Figure 5.2. Sample evidences for Domain 5, Element 1

Sample Evidences for Domain 5, Element 1
• A written annual growth plan is in place to address how the school leader will address strengths and weaknesses.
• Professional development activities consistent with the leader's growth plan have been identified.
• Evidence of leadership initiatives is available.
• Adherence to district and state policies and procedures is evident.
• The school leader has demonstrated the ability to be a problem solver.
• The school leader has identified mentors and regularly interacts with them.
• When asked, faculty and staff identify the school administrator as the leader of the school.
• When asked, faculty and staff describe the school leader as uncompromising in regard to raising student achievement.
• When asked, faculty and staff describe the school leader as effectively communicating those nonnegotiable factors that have an impact on student achievement.
• When asked, faculty and staff generally agree as to the vision provided by the school leader.

The evaluator of the school leader may also draw on district-provided staff and teacher surveys or school climate surveys that include questions related to the school leader's visibility and communication skills or identify levels of trust or perceptions of leadership. In other words, evidence should demonstrate that the school leader is recognized as a leader: data should show that teachers and the school community support her initiatives and there is a shared perception that the leader is actively working to continuously improve the school.

Go to www.learningsciences.com/bookresources to download figures and tables.

Key Questions

1. How do you make your staff aware of your personal goals?
2. Do you have a written professional growth plan that identifies specific actions that will help you improve your practice?
3. How will you measure the effectiveness or impact of your professional growth?
4. What elements will come into play in a growth plan (i.e., deliberate practice, self-assessment, etc.)?
5. From whom will you receive coaching and feedback?
6. How do you communicate your leadership initiatives to your staff?

Evaluators should ask themselves

- What evidence would be collected to demonstrate the leader continues to grow and develop leadership expertise?
- What evidence would support the school leader is recognized as a leader?

Scenario

Principal Clark has been aware that due to the adoption of college and career readiness standards he will need to learn to assist teachers with understanding how the standards align with the school's instructional model. Mr. Clark has also been concerned about the change to student assessments scheduled this year. The new assessments were designed to be end-of-course assessments. Mr. Clark realized that he, too, must embark on learning not only the new state standards but also the new graduation end-of-course assessments for students. To this end, he elected to take advantage of the courses and professional development the State Department offered, to train both administrators and teachers.

Mr. Clark identified a professional development series the State Department designed to help teams of administrators and teachers learn more about the new assessment and deepen their understanding of the newly adopted state standards. He scheduled his team to participate.

Throughout the year, Mr. Clark regularly meets with groups of teachers and eventually carves out two meeting dates each month to develop benchmarks to help them identify content areas where students are weak. These groups work together using the materials and content information from the State Department series. At times, the groups develop training sessions for the rest of the math department, examine data, and plan small-group instructional opportunities for students. They work together to monitor the progress of both students and teachers.

When they examine the student end-of-course data, they do not see the same level of predictive power they had hoped for; however, Mr. Clark surveys teachers about the professional development they have received, and the results indicate teachers recognize his leadership in this important initiative.

Explanation

In this scenario, we would recommend feedback at the *Applying* level, as the principal has evidence that when monitoring his leadership and professional development, the survey data show he is recognized as a leader who keeps developing expertise. The actions in this scenario also support the school leader in Domain 3, Element 1 (ensuring that the school curriculum and assessments adhere to state standards) and Domain 2, Element 5 (ensuring that teachers are provided with job-embedded professional development).

Building Trust (Domain 5, Element 2)

The school leader has the trust of the faculty and staff that his or her actions are guided by what is best for all student populations.

Perception of Integrity

Element 2 is related to Element 1 in that the school leader continues to model behavior, but in this case, the behavior is related to cultivating trust and acting as an example of ethical decision making, specifically decision making related to serving the best interests of students. Element 2, in a nutshell, is about the perception of the school leader's integrity. Element 2 gauges the school leader's ability to make tough decisions that never fail to put students first. Those decisions may not always be popular with teachers and/or parents. But every decision must be measured by its impact on students. The school leader's ability to continuously make such difficult decisions with a focus on student outcomes will contribute to the perception that students are valued at the school, and the leader's integrity is uncompromised. Further, the school leader's advocacy of student interests will ideally extend even into the arena of public policy. ISSLC Standard 7, for example, emphasizes that the school leader must build and sustain productive relationships with community partners in the government and become a voice to influence policies and resources for the school community.

In their (2009) paper *Why Does Leader Integrity Matter to Followers? An Uncertainty Management-Based Explanation*, Robert H. Moorman and Stephen Grover examine how leadership integrity can affect followers' perception of risk. The authors suggest that the perception of integrity, or the link between a leader's words and actions, is one of the primary ways that followers make decisions about whether to commit to cooperation with the leader. And although the perception of "integrity" and "trustworthiness" may at first glance appear to be highly subjective, recent research sheds some light on the perception of trustworthiness between teachers and school leaders.

A 2011 study conducted by Monica Kathleen Makiewicz for a dissertation at the University of California, for example, examines this question in relation to three factors that strongly influence teacher perception of principal trustworthiness: *ability*, *benevolence*, and *integrity* (p. 11). Makiewicz notes that although teachers, like all humans, exhibit individual propensities to trust or not trust other adults, there was a strong correlation between teacher trust in a school leader and frequency of specific principal-teacher interactions. Put most simply, a highly visible and engaged school leader will be able to mitigate or modify a personal propensity on the part of individual teachers toward mistrust.

Why is trust between faculty and administrators important? Makiewicz cites several studies that have found correlations between trust among administrators and teachers, and student achievement (Bryk, Easton, Rollow, & Sebring, 1994).

Element 2, as we have said, also addresses a very specific area of trust: The faculty trusts that the school leader makes decisions that are in the best interests of all students. The desired effect of Element 2 is that the school leader does whatever it takes to improve student achievement, and the school improves as a result of the processes the leader has put in place.

Figure 5.3 illustrates the scale for Element 2.

Figure 5.3. Scale for Domain 5, Element 2

Scale Value	Description
Innovating (4)	The school leader actively seeks expertise/mentors for validation and feedback to confirm or improve how he performs or is perceived.
Applying (3)	The school leader performs with integrity and in the best interest of all students AND monitors the extent to which faculty and staff perceive him or her as an individual who will follow through with initiatives and whose actions are guided by the desire to help all students learn.
Developing (2)	The school leader performs with integrity and in the best interest of all students.
Beginning (1)	The school leader attempts to perform with integrity and in the best interest of all students but does so sporadically or inconsistently.
Not Using (0)	The school leader does not attempt to perform with integrity and in the best interest of all students.

Note that at the *Innovating* level, the school leader continues to pursue mentorship opportunities, but in this case the leader is seeking mentorship and development specifically around the concept of how the faculty and staff perceive him. With Element 2 the leader is striving to improve the perception of trustworthiness, follow-through, integrity, and the best interests of all students—a perception that will in turn improve the unity and cohesiveness of the school and positively impact student achievement.

Go to www.learningsciences.com/bookresources to download figures and tables.

Potential evidence of such disciplined leadership is shown in Figure 5.4.

Figure 5.4. Sample evidences for Domain 5, Element 2

Sample Evidences for Domain 5, Element 2
• The school leader is recognized by the school community as one who is willing to "take on tough issues."
• The school leader acknowledges when school goals have not been met or initiatives have failed and revises the plan for success.
• When asked, faculty and staff describe the school leader as an individual whose actions are guided by a desire to help all students learn.
• When asked, faculty and staff describe the school leader as an individual who will follow through with his or her initiatives.
• When asked, faculty and staff describe the school leader as one whose actions support his or her talk and expectations.
• When asked, faculty and staff describe the school leader as one who speaks with candor and "takes on tough issues."

An Example

Let us look at an example of how one school leader demonstrated evidence as a leader "willing to take on tough issues," whose actions are "guided by what is best for all students," and who "follows through on initiatives," to build trust among staff and colleagues.

A secondary school principal in a large urban middle school noted that, in studying the school's discipline incidences, certain patterns emerged. Some of the discipline incidents were occurring during class changes, before school, and after school on the bus ramp. During these times, the students were moving around campus with minimal supervision. The principal asked teachers to station themselves at their doors during class changes, to greet students and supervise what was happening in the area around their classes. Other personnel were assigned to monitor areas where some of the prior discipline incidents had occurred.

Then the principal took an even more drastic step. He asked teachers to walk their students to the cafeteria and share responsibility to walk students to the bus ramp. Because it was a large school, with more than thirty school buses, a great many students were heading to the bus at the same time. Although teachers at first were unhappy about the added responsibilities, they realized that discipline incidences were extremely high in their school. They trusted their principal and supported his initiatives. Within the first quarter, there was a more than 30 percent reduction in incident referrals and actual disciplinary incidents.

Go to www.learningsciences.com/bookresources to download figures and tables.

In time, faculty and staff feedback revealed that although at first they were reluctant to change their routines and perform extra supervision, reduction in major infractions quickly convinced teachers that the principal's initiatives were sound. The principal followed through in the face of some resistance and made the tough decision to require everyone to take responsibility for maintaining a safe and orderly environment, demonstrating that the decision was in the best interest of students. In time, as problem incidents declined, the school was gradually able to relax the policy, as students developed a greater level of self-discipline.

This element captures the decisions that principals make that may not be popular, and may be even somewhat painful to make in the short term, but help the leader develop a reputation for consistency of student-centered action and planning. Any principal has to make difficult decisions around termination of staff, reassignment of teachers, discipline, student placement, and similar decisions that are not likely to please everyone involved and impact perceptions of leadership. However, the school leader who makes decisions with student outcomes foremost in mind will eventually be seen as a consistent and fair leader.

Key Questions

1. Identify a time this year you made a tough decision that benefited the students in your school, and explain your rationale for making this decision.

2. Explain how you communicate to the staff when you make a challenging decision.

3. What actions do you take to build the trust of your faculty?

4. What evidences would support that you have the trust of your faculty?

Perceptions of Safety From Faculty and Staff (Domain 5, Element 3)

The school leader ensures that faculty and staff perceive the school environment as safe and orderly.

> *A school that has a safe and orderly environment is one in which students*
> *and teachers alike are safe and perceive that they are safe from both*
> *physical and psychological harm.*
> —Robert Marzano, "Leadership and School Reform Factors" (2007, p. 602)

There are good reasons for maintaining a safe and orderly environment for student learning. A safe and orderly environment has a measurable effect on student achievement and whole school effectiveness. Effective schools research (Levine & Lezotte, 1995) identifies a safe and orderly school as one of six correlates of effective schools. Lezotte notes that the first-generation correlate describes a school where students are free from psychological and physical harm. A second generation, or next step, might regard this standard as placing increased emphasis on not just the elimination of undesirable behaviors, such as bullying, but the cultivation of desirable behaviors, such as cooperative team learning.

In *What Works in Schools*, Marzano (2003) notes that safety and order are addressed in many studies on school effectiveness. A safe and orderly environment is critical to academic achievement (Chubb & Moe, 1990; Mayer, Mullins, Moore, & Ralph, 2000). At the federal level, Goals 2000: Educate America Act (2002) articulated a goal that by the year 2000, every school "will offer a disciplined environment conducive to learning" (p. 13).

However, our definition of what constitutes *safe and orderly* has changed a great deal since the events at Columbine and as a result of recent tragedies on school grounds in the United States and elsewhere. Previously, the concept of a safe and orderly environment focused primarily on classroom management, mutual respect between teachers and students, and maintaining order throughout the school. Post-Columbine, public schools are required to maintain and test crisis management systems and ensure that both students and faculty are practiced in crisis management procedures. Schools may have installed metal detectors, utilized drug- or weapon-sniffing dogs, or even discussed allowing security guards to carry firearms. In this context, securing a safe and orderly environment becomes much more complex. It requires a focused effort on the part of all members of the school community.

A school principal shared a decision she made as a new principal that was initially unpopular with parents and students, but student safety was an issue. Before her tenure, parents and members of the public freely walked on campus and delivered "outside" or restaurant food to the high school students during the four lunch periods. For a three-hour period, anyone could be on campus. At its worst, students would routinely walk out the school's front door to meet their parents bringing lunch. During lunch hours, to thwart these visits, the new principal immediately posted school personnel by the front doors and in the parking lot. All school doors were also locked from the inside, and parents were escorted into the building to sign into the office before walking into the school cafeteria. It wasn't a popular decision. At times, school personnel had to manage very vocal and irate parents and students, but over time, the decision to increase security and school-wide safety measures was understood as a necessary change, both locally and nationally. As a measure of goodwill for the students, the principal did survey students about their concerns with school lunch and was able to provide more healthy and tasty school lunch options.

In order to achieve the desired effect for Element 3, members of the school must perceive the school as safe and orderly so that students can stay focused on learning.

Figure 5.5 illustrates the scale for Domain 5, Element 3.

Figure 5.5. Scale for Domain 5, Element 3

Scale Value	Description
Innovating (4)	The school leader ensures that rules and procedures are reviewed and updated as necessary to ensure a safe and orderly school environment and the perception of such by school faculty and staff.
Applying (3)	The school leader ensures that well-defined routines and procedures that lead to safe and orderly conduct are in place AND monitors the extent to which faculty and staff share the perception that the school environment is safe and orderly.
Developing (2)	The school leader ensures that well-defined routines and procedures that lead to orderly conduct are in place.
Beginning (1)	The school leader attempts to ensure that well-defined routines and procedures that lead to orderly conduct are in place but does not complete the task or does so partially.
Not Using (0)	The school leader does not attempt to ensure that well-defined routines and procedures that lead to safe and orderly conduct are in place.

As indicated in the scale in Figure 5.5, rules, procedures, and routines are integral to this element. Potential actions the school leader might take, as outlined by Marzano in *What Works in Schools* (2003), include (1) establishing rules and procedures for behavioral problems resulting from the school's physical characteristics or the school's routines; (2) establishing clear school-wide rules and procedures for general behavior; (3) establishing and enforcing appropriate consequences for violations of rules and procedures; (4) establishing a program that teaches self-discipline and responsibility to students; (5) establishing a system that allows for the early detection of students who have high potential for violence and extreme behaviors.

School leaders will want to consider how they establish school-wide rules and procedures, determine and apply appropriate consequences for violation of rules, teach students self-discipline, and identify students at risk for violence or extreme behavior.

Evidences that school members perceive the school as safe and orderly might include those in Figure 5.6.

Key Questions

1. How have you determined whether everyone in the building thinks the school is safe and orderly?

2. What opportunities have you provided for staff to give input about the environment and their concerns?

3. How have you determined whether current discipline policies are or are not effective?

Go to www.learningsciences.com/bookresources to download figures and tables.

4. What training has been provided on what to do in an emergency?

5. What sources and resources have you provided for expert advice on school safety and managing emergencies?

6. What procedures have you established for emergencies during non-classroom times such as lunch, class changes, and the beginning and ending of the school day?

7. What process do you have in place to analyze the effectiveness of your emergency procedures?

8. What is your process for updating your emergency plans?

Figure 5.6. Sample evidences for Domain 5, Element 3

Sample Evidences for Domain 5, Element 3
• Clear and specific rules and procedures are in place for the running of the school.
• Faculty and staff are provided the means to communicate about the safety of the school.
• Faculty and staff know emergency management procedures and how to implement them for specific incidents.
• Evidence of practicing emergency management procedures for specific incidents is available.
• Evidence of updates to the emergency management plans, and communication of those plans to the faculty and staff is available.
• When asked, faculty and staff describe the school as a safe and orderly place.
• When asked, the faculty and staff describe the school leader as highly visible and accessible.
• When asked, faculty and staff describe the school as a place focused on learning.

Perceptions of Safety From Students, Parents, and Community (Domain 5, Element 4)

The school leader ensures that students, parents, and community perceive the school environment as safe and orderly.

As with Element 3, communication will be a key factor in the school leader's success in Element 4. Element 4 helps align the perceptions of parents and community with the perception of the school leader and faculty around the issue of school safety. The revised ISLLC standards of 2014 emphasize this aspect of school leadership practice in Standard 5: Community Care for Students. As Joseph Murphy writes in his explanation of the revised standards, *2014 ISLLC Standards* for school leaders,

> A supportive learning community provides a protective cove while attacking social problems that place students in peril. It helps buffer home stress, community problems, and individual characteristics that foster social marginalization

Go to www.learningsciences.com/bookresources to download figures and tables.

and academic disengagement. Concomitantly, supportive learning environments create assets, social and human capital, to draw youngsters into the hard work that is required to be successful in school. (Murphy, 2014, p. 6)

The 2011 documentary *Bully* makes plain that a perceptual divide can imperil the safety of students—in this film, parents who complain that their child is being bullied on the bus are told by the school leader that the situation is under control (Hirsch & Lowen, 2011). And although the principal does take some action steps to follow up on the complaint, the bullying doesn't stop, and the child's parents still continue to feel strongly that their child is not safe riding the bus. In other words, the school administrators perceive that they have dealt effectively with the problem. The child's parents have a very different perception. And in fact, the child's safety is severely compromised in the end.

It's important to note that such a cycle can begin to degrade the overall safety of the school. When children do not feel safe, the school can *actually become* less safe. Human beings who feel threatened are less likely to behave in ways that are rational and orderly. (Conversely, stress reduction programs have been found to have a positive impact on behavior; see Barnes, Bauza, & Treiber, 2003.) Children (or even teachers and administrators) who feel threatened or bullied may overreact, for example, and contribute to a downward spiral in school climate. Children who feel unsafe may resist coming to school (and, in fact, there is documented evidence that bullied children are more often absent), which can further erode positive school climate (Gastic, 2007). And even short-term stress has a documented negative effect on learning (University of California–Irvine, 2008). Therefore, the school leader must have an accurate perception of how the community perceives the school.

There are many reasons public perception of safety is crucial. Schools often function as the heart of a community (Office of Innovation and Improvement [OII], 2007). Their effect spreads far beyond the walls of the school itself. A school perceived as safe and orderly can have a profound impact—through school programs, after-school activities, volunteer opportunities, civic organizations, and local business involvement. But parents will avoid sending their children to schools perceived as unsafe (OII, 2007). The business community will not support unsafe schools. Attendance at school and at school activities will suffer. Property values may decline. In this way, school climate can have a positive or negative impact on entire communities.

An aggressive school safety plan might include interactive ways to survey students, parents, and community members on their perceptions of school safety. The leader will endeavor to address issues, correct misconceptions, and build a positive image regarding the school's safety record, including consistent communications about safety and emergency procedures, discipline policies, bullying awareness campaigns, and other measures. As with Domain 4,

Element 5, the school leader will develop accessible media so that stakeholders may have an input when it comes to policies and procedures having to do with school safety. And finally, the school leader will develop an ongoing schedule to revisit the policies and procedures related to school safety.

It is important to note that this element is about perception of safety. Some schools face challenges that occur in their communities. A principal may be assigned to a building where there are incidents of gang violence in the neighborhood, high levels of crime, and other adverse conditions. The principal must take proactive and reactive steps to manage perception about the safety and orderliness of the environment.

The effective school leader clearly communicates the positive actions she is taking. Safe schools often have an open-door policy for parents, for example, so that parents feel welcome to visit classrooms to monitor the processes put in place. Social media is an extremely effective tool for communicating initiatives related to safety. Therefore, the desired outcomes for Elements 3 and 4 are very similar.

There are many informal ways a school leader can monitor the perception of safety. Data will indicate how many students have requested to move out of the school, for example. The number of businesses willing to partner with the school can be another source of feedback. Such informal measures may go far beyond surveys to ensure that the school leader has a finger on the pulse of community perceptions. A great deal of flight from the school would indicate perceptual problems, and as we have said, school climate is all about perception. The perception of safety allows students to focus on learning.

Figure 5.7 illustrates the scale for Domain 5, Element 4.

Figure 5.7. Scale for Domain 5, Element 4

Scale Value	Description
Innovating (4)	The school leader ensures that rules and procedures are reviewed and updated as necessary to ensure a safe and orderly school environment and the perception of such by students, parents, and community.
Applying (3)	The school leader ensures that well-defined routines and procedures that lead to orderly conduct are in place AND monitors the extent to which students, parents, and community share the perception that the school environment is safe and orderly.
Developing (2)	The school leader ensures that well-defined routines and procedures that lead to orderly conduct are in place.
Beginning (1)	The school leader attempts to ensure that well-defined routines and procedures that lead to orderly conduct are in place but does not complete the task or does so partially.
Not Using (0)	The school leader does not attempt to ensure that well-defined routines and procedures that lead to orderly conduct are in place.

Figure 5.8 illustrates sample evidences for Domain 5, Element 4.

Figure 5.8. Sample evidences for Domain 5, Element 4

Sample Evidences for Domain 5, Element 4
• Clear and specific rules and procedures are in place for the running of the school.
• Social media is utilized so that students may anonymously report potential incidents.
• A system is in place for mass communicating to parents about issues regarding school safety (e.g., a callout system).
• Coordination with local law enforcement agencies regarding school safety issues is a routine event.
• Parents and community are engaged to give input regarding issues of school safety.
• When asked, parents and students describe the school as a safe place.
• When asked, parents and students describe the school as an orderly place.
• When asked, community members perceive the school as safe and orderly.
• When asked, parents, students, and community members describe the school leader as highly visible and accessible.

The authors of *School Climate and Learning* offer a number of approaches for promoting a safe and orderly environment. These include (1) maintaining buildings in good physical condition; (2) rewarding students for appropriate behavior; (3) enforcing consequences for inappropriate behavior; (4) using contracts for students to reinforce behavioral expectations; (5) posting behavioral policies on bulletin boards and periodically announcing them over the public address system; (6) initiating antibullying, conflict resolution, and peer mediation programs; and (7) engaging students, staff, and parents, in planning school safety activities (Michigan State University, 2004, p. 6).

Key Questions

1. How do you communicate with parents and community regarding safety issues at your school?

2. What procedures do you have in place for ongoing informal measures to gauge community perception of school safety?

3. How do you use social media to receive feedback?

4. What is your process for analyzing behavioral data and communicating that information to the school community?

5. What processes are in place to ensure that parents and community feel welcome at your school?

Go to www.learningsciences.com/bookresources to download figures and tables.

6. How are school-wide procedures for safety communicated to students, parents, and the community?

Managing Resources (Domain 5, Element 5)

The school leader manages the fiscal, operational, and technological resources of the school in a way that focuses on effective instruction and the achievement of all students.

> *Resources are to a complex organization what food is to the body.*
> *Resources important to a school extend well beyond books and materials.*
> —Marzano, Waters, and McNulty, *School Leadership That Works* (2005)

As with the other elements we have examined in Domain 5, a steady hand on the fiscal stewardship of the school helps create a positive climate in which student achievement can flourish. The school leader

- Manages materials, resources, and time to meet state and district specifications
- Develops, submits, and implements detailed budgets with the capacity to use a variety of resources focused on building student achievement
- Protects the time of teachers, to allow them to focus on instruction and professional development
- Provides adequate technology and training around that technology to supplement the needs of classrooms

In other words, within Element 5, the school leader is *managing resources to create the optimal climate for learning*.

These resources may include fiscal resources, curriculum materials, and human resources such as the use of staff and schedules created to maximize the human capital in the building as well as community resources.

The desired effect of Element 5 is that teachers and students have access to the resources they need to teach and learn.

In *School Leadership That Works* (2005), Marzano et al. cite the work of Deering, Dilts, and Russell (2003) for a broad definition of the concept of "resources." The authors note that successful organizations will be fluid enough to respond quickly to new circumstances. "This involves the alignment of several levels of resources," Marzano et al. note, "necessary to analyze, plan, and take action in response to opportunities and threats that the future brings" (2005, p. 34). Resources, as we have emphasized earlier, include materials, equipment, space, time, technology, and access to new ideas and expertise (Fullan, Rolheiser, Mascall, & Edge, 2001, p. 8).

Figures 5.9 and 5.10 illustrate the scale and evidences for Domain 5, Element 5.

Figure 5.9. Scale for Domain 5, Element 5

Scale Value	Description
Innovating (4)	The school leader actively seeks and procures extra resources to enhance instruction and the achievement of all students.
Applying (3)	The school leader manages the fiscal, operational, and technological resources necessary to support effective teaching AND monitors the extent to which the resources and efficiencies enhance instruction and the achievement of all students.
Developing (2)	The school leader manages the fiscal, operational, and technological resources necessary to support effective teaching.
Beginning (1)	The school leader attempts to manage the fiscal, operational, and technological resources necessary to support effective teaching but does not complete the task or does so partially.
Not Using (0)	The school leader does not attempt to manage the fiscal, operational, and technological resources necessary to support effective teaching.

Figure 5.10. Sample evidences for Domain 5, Element 5

Sample Evidences for Domain 5, Element 5
• Materials and resources for specific classes and courses meet the state or district specifications for those classes and courses.
• Detailed budgets are developed, submitted, and implemented.
• The school leader successfully accesses and leverages a variety of resources (e.g., grants and local, state, and federal funds).
• Data are available to show that resources and expenditures produce results (i.e., curriculum programs improve student learning).
• The school leader manages time effectively to maximize focus on instruction.
• The school leader appropriately directs the use of technology to improve teaching and learning.
• Adequate training is provided for the instructional technology teachers are expected to use.
• When asked, faculty and staff report they have adequate materials to teach effectively.
• When asked, faculty and staff report they have adequate time to teach effectively.

Key Questions

1. How do you develop your budget to ensure that teachers have adequate resources for teaching?

2. How often do you evaluate your instructional technology to determine if it is up to date, and teachers are actually using the technology that is available to them?

Go to www.learningsciences.com/bookresources to download figures and tables.

3. What are your procedures for getting feedback from teachers and students about the availability of resources and any specific needs they may have for particular resources?

4. Can you cite examples of ways you have secured funds outside of your local funding sources (e.g., community grants, state grants, or federal grants)?

5. Do you have a contingency plan in place, in the event of a financial, technological, or teacher resource emergency?

6. How do you monitor the effect of your resource allocation on student learning?

Scenario

The principal of Carter Heights High School has oversight of her school budget and takes pride that she has singlehandedly increased the number of computers available to the students in her school. There is almost a one-to-one ratio of computers to students. However, a recent survey of students at the school revealed accessibility to computers was limited. The school's leadership team sent a report to the school district's information technology department asking for assistance in securing additional bandwidth and updating the school's infrastructure to allow live streaming and downloading. The team reported multiple examples of internal system crashes and their frustration with having so many computers without the structure to be able to utilize these resources.

Explanation and Feedback

The supervisor of this principal would give feedback at the *Beginning* level. The desired result of this element is that students and teachers have the resources they need to increase achievement. For the principal to move to the *Developing* level, she must provide evidence demonstrating that *she manages the fiscal, operational, and technological resources of the school in a way that focuses on effective instruction and the achievement of all students*. In this scenario, that would include planning for the infrastructure required for teachers and students to have access to the computers. The supervisor may coach the principal to seek assistance from technical experts to help her develop a plan for correcting the immediate issues and to involve a committee to help her determine how to best use the resources available to the school.

Acknowledging Successes (Domain 5, Element 6)

The school leader acknowledges the success of the whole school, as well as the individuals within the school.

Individuals who feel secure and purposeful as a result of these connections, identities, and commitments are, in turn, less susceptible to the mind-set of fatalism and disempowerment.
—The Wallace Foundation (Leithwood et al., 2004, p. 54)

Element 6 focuses on ways to cultivate that collective sense of belonging, specifically by planning and implementing ways to celebrate success of both the school as a whole and individuals within it.

There's a reason why 6,000 schools have received National Blue Ribbon awards since the awards were created three decades ago. The secretary of education recognizes the value of celebrating success in keeping educators motivated and providing models for other schools to emulate. Effective leaders set goals and plan celebrations to mark their accomplishment.

In their 2004 report from the Wallace Foundation, *How Leadership Influences Student Learning*, authors Kenneth Leithwood, Karen Seashore-Louis, Stephen Anderson, and Kyla Wahlstrom discuss the relationship between what they called "affective bonds" and the sense of school community:

> The affective bonds between students and teachers associated with a sense of community are crucial in engaging and motivating students to learn in schools of any type. A widely shared sense of community is also important as an antidote to the unstable, sometimes threatening and often insecure world inhabited by a significant proportion of the families and children by especially challenging schools. (p. 53)

Figure 5.11 illustrates the scale for Domain 5, Element 6.

Figure 5.11. Scale for Domain 5, Element 6

Scale Value	Description
Innovating (4)	The school leader actively seeks a variety of methods for acknowledging individual and school-wide success that meets the unique needs of faculty and staff.
Applying (3)	The school leader, at the appropriate time, acknowledges and celebrates the accomplishments of the school as a whole and the accomplishments of individuals within the school AND monitors the extent to which people feel honored for their contributions.
Developing (2)	The school leader, at the appropriate time, acknowledges and celebrates the accomplishments of the school as a whole and the accomplishments of individuals within the school.
Beginning (1)	The school leader attempts to acknowledge and celebrate the accomplishments of the school as a whole and the accomplishments of individuals within the school but does not complete the task or does so partially.
Not Using (0)	The school leader does not attempt to acknowledge and celebrate the accomplishments of the school as a whole or the accomplishments of individuals within the school.

Go to www.learningsciences.com/bookresources to download figures and tables.

What kind of data might the school leader gather as evidence of success with Element 6? For one thing, the school leader might gather evidence of student, teacher, and parent participation in a variety of activities; that is, school events, open houses, course curriculum nights, award ceremonies, sports activities, and other events that draw family, students, faculty, and community together. Within the building, the school leader might also help set up grade-level teams to articulate goals and celebrate accomplishments. The leader might encourage cross-grade-level initiatives and cross-curricular academic games and document and celebrate quarterly and yearly grade-level achievement gains. Whole school assemblies, newsletters, and other forms of communication can also be used to celebrate success.

Other useful data might include college acceptance rates and data related to teacher compliance with school initiatives such as reading programs. It's important to note that in Figure 5.11, at the *Applying* level, the school leader is not only celebrating success but monitoring the extent to which faculty and students feel that they have been honored and celebrated. One way to look at the desired effect for Element 6 is that students (and their parents) actively desire to attend the school. Figure 5.12 illustrates evidences for Domain 5, Element 6.

Figure 5.12. Sample evidences for Domain 5, Element 6

Sample Evidences for Domain 5, Element 6
• The accomplishments of individual teachers, teams of teachers, and the whole school are celebrated in a variety of ways (e.g., faculty celebrations, newsletters to parents, announcements, websites, social media).
• The incremental successes of students and teachers are routinely recognized.
• The successes of the diverse school community are celebrated.
• When asked, faculty and staff report that accomplishments of the school and their individual accomplishments have been adequately acknowledged and celebrated.
• When asked, students, parents, and community report their accomplishments are adequately acknowledged and celebrated.

It's important to note that there are ways to celebrate success beyond awards ceremonies and public announcements. A 30-year teaching veteran recently related a touching story about the ways her school leaders had celebrated her success over the years—and ways she found to celebrate her own successes in moments of doubt!

At a recent retirement party, a retiring teacher related that she had saved every note any principal had ever written her. As she cleaned out her office, she sat back and reflected on those notes. There were times, she said, when she worked under principals who did not leave her any notes at all: "Sometimes

I'd need a little inspiration, and I'd go back and get the notes that gave me some very specific praise or feedback about things I was either doing with my students, or things that have been noticed in my classroom. Those notes often inspired me to keep going when times got tough."

This may not be a typical example of celebration. But sometimes it is just those very subtle celebrations and acknowledgments that have profound outcomes. In thinking about celebrating school success, we need to remember that celebrations can include anything from public "employee of the year" celebrations for teachers or noninstructional staff all the way down to notes left on teacher or staff member desks acknowledging hard work.

Celebration plays a major role in how the school feels about itself. Do we have a school where we recognize members not just for major accomplishments but the many contributions they make to the school's successful functioning?

A school leader who takes the time to recognize and celebrate many different forms of accomplishment will go a long way to building trust and support from school staff and community. For this reason, Element 6 of Domain 5 truly is the culminating element—it reflects all the elements in all the domains that have gone before. We must celebrate and give nourishment to the people in our organizations, or they will not continue to grow, produce productive students, or be productive themselves.

School personnel who go without recognition are like flowers that wither on the vine. Celebration is the water that allows the school garden to flourish.

Key Questions

1. How do you celebrate the accomplishments of individuals within the school as well as individuals outside the school?

2. Cite multiple ways that you celebrate and recognize success.

3. How do you measure whether the celebration activities that you plan are actually achieving the desired effect (i.e., people are inspired to work at the school or are motivated to be a part of the school)?

4. Can you cite examples of people within the school or community who can attest that the celebrations inspire them to higher levels of performance or to keep achieving higher levels of performance?

5. How do you recognize students not only for major accomplishments but also for the progress that they have made?

6. How do you make the community aware of positive things happening in your school?

Conclusion

A school that has a positive climate rooted in clear expectations, and supported with recognition and respect, leads to students and staff making decisions that are in the best interest of not only the school but also themselves.
—Patchin (2012a)

Preliminary research conducted by Justin W. Patchin (2012b) for the Cyber Bullying Research Center tested the hypothesis that positive school climate could serve a protective function in "reducing cyber bullying, sexting, and other high-tech misbehaviors that largely occur *away from school*." In a random sample of approximately 4,400 middle and high school students from 33 schools in a large US school district, the research found that the better the climate of the school, the less likely students were to report experiencing either cyberbullying or sexting incidents. The Cyberbullying Research Center also suggests that there is greater efficacy in improving school climate than merely banning technological devices such as cell phones and laptops outright. This is yet another example of how school climate has profound influences that radiate far beyond the school walls.

Our final chapter discusses implementation of the Marzano School Leader Evaluation Model, scoring, and evaluation rubrics: what district leaders, school leaders, and evaluators of school leaders can expect, and methods for achieving the best possible results.

CHAPTER 6

Implementation and Scoring

Most schools and districts implementing the Marzano School Leader Evaluation Model will be moving from a summative evaluation system for school leaders into a formative mode of evaluation. In the past, many districts may have used evaluation systems that were far less focused on school leader growth and far more focused on compliance with district and state initiatives. So in many senses, this model will be a new experience for both leaders being evaluated and the supervisors conducting evaluations. Growth and developing expertise should be the primary goal of implementing this evaluation system.

A formative model requires that the evaluator have regular consultations with the school leader so that formative data is collected along the way. Such ongoing consultation allows both the school leader and evaluator to monitor progress, provide and receive feedback, and identify areas for improvement. As we have seen, this evaluation model also requires a constant feedback loop from many sources of data—teacher surveys; student assessments; communications with parents, students, and community; feedback from supervisors; and other sources. What this means is that both school leaders and their supervisors will have access to a steady stream of information about how the leader and the school as a whole are doing.

Planning the Process of Implementation

Schools planning implementation of the school leader evaluation model have to take one important preliminary step: achieve consensus on the need to move to an evaluation system focused on growth rather than merely compliance. Districts that have previously implemented growth-based *teacher* evaluation systems will often perceive the clear need to move their leader evaluation system toward a growth-based model. But the focus on continuous leader professional growth must be clearly communicated and understood throughout the district.

Typically, once a district has made the decision to use the Marzano School Leader Evaluation Model, Learning Sciences International will begin professional development to introduce the framework and deepen understanding of the model's domains, its elements, and the specific bodies of evidence applicable to the individual district. As part of this introduction to the model, personnel who supervise principals need to be active participants along with principals and assistant principals.

Schools may choose to implement all twenty-four elements in their first year, or the implementation team may identify specific domains to focus on in Year 1 and Year 2. We often recommend that schools use a phase-in process, where they identify one or two domains in which school leaders will be evaluated in Year 1. Based on our experience, if a district uses the phase-in approach, we recommend phasing in Domain 1 and 2 in Year 1, and Domains 3 through 5 in Year 2. After Year 2, as we have noted, all twenty-four elements should be rated every year.

A second, equally effective option is that the committee selects a few elements from each of the five domains to focus on in Year 1 and adds in the remaining elements in Year 2.

Finding a Champion

We have found that for implementation to be effective, obtaining buy-in from school leaders is a requisite first step. Having a champion at the district level who shares this vision for a growth model ensures not only clear communication about the rationale for the model but also that training and planning for implementation is successful. Open, honest communication about the evaluation system should include everyone who will be impacted.

One such champion of the Marzano School Leader Evaluation Model is Assistant Superintendent of Human Resources Dr. April Grace, of Putnam City, Oklahoma, schools. Dr. Grace shared with us how important gathering and analyzing feedback around implementation can be. The process may be painful at times, but it can also result in enormous shifts in practice that spur professional growth.

Working with Learning Sciences Marzano Center to implement the model in 2012, Dr. Grace's team decided to focus on Domain 5 (School Climate), Elements 1 and 2 (*recognition of leadership* and *trust of faculty and staff*) in their first year. Early in the year, administrators sent a survey to faculty and staff asking them to describe the effectiveness of their school leader. Dr. Grace recounts the initial shockwaves, and the subsequent breakthroughs, this way:

> Probably the greatest growth we experienced from using the model last year resulted in a focus on Domain 5 Elements 1 and 2. Each administrator sent out a survey to all staff that related the "faculty and staff describe the school leader as" statements in the evidences. The results were sent to their supervisors, and the teachers did not have to identify themselves. Some of the data from the survey was a huge blow to principals and even the executive director. It caused them to completely reflect on their practice in a manner that produced tremen-

dous personal growth, and eventually a more collaborative approach to working with staff. I personally saw two complete turnarounds as a result of a focus on these two elements in Domain 5. (Personal communication)

Grace notes that her district chose to begin implementation with a few elements of the model that were nonnegotiable, items from each domain that they felt were critical for the principals and assistant principals to master. She adds,

> The leader model provided us with a laser-like focus, with more specificity for conversation about the principal's work. It provided more direction for principals and increased the depth of conversation between the district-level evaluator and the building-level leader, as well as between the building-level leader and the assistant principal. With regard to building-level leaders, this forced specific leader-focused conversation with their assistant principals, where previously the conversation may have been more management-focused. Now we are seeing conversations that led to the further development of each assistant principal and the role they played in school improvement and climate. This made all stakeholders more accountable for the improvement efforts. There was more focus, and a clearer base-line for conversation.
>
> One of the greatest benefits has been the reflective pieces that the model offers to principals. This model asks them to examine goals, perceptions, feedback, and data from staff members through a variety of methods. We have seen leaders transformed by the feedback they received from their staff related to the work they were doing in their schools. (Personal communication)

With this evaluation model, the objective is for the school leader's supervisor to collect formative pieces of evidence so that, by year's end, the supervisor can compile formative evidence and data for an end-of-year summative evaluation score. We believe the great benefit of this system is that *school leaders are empowered to make adjustments and refine their actions throughout the course of the year*, effectively taking control of their professional development as they increase their expertise.

Planning Support for Implementation

In planning for implementation, it is critical that both supervisors and school leaders understand that each element in the model has a desired result. During implementation, the district implementation team will begin the work of constituting the body of evidence to demonstrate that the school leader is achieving desired results for each element. Creating this body of evidence is a developmental process, requiring a concerted effort from the implementation team and clear communication to school leaders. The sample evidences provided in the Marzano School Leader Evaluation Model are written in generic terms and can be customized to meet the expectations of individual districts.

In the absence of agreed-upon bodies of evidence, the implementation will most likely remain at the compliance level. However, when the team, with the buy-in of school leaders, moves into identifying specific evidence of desired effects, the model becomes a true growth model for development of expertise.

Five Steps of the Evaluation Cycle

As Figure 6.1 indicates, supervisors should plan to meet with each school leader during at least five designated points within the evaluation cycle. Before the initial meeting, it's recommended that school leaders conduct self-assessments on each element in the model. (If the district uses the iObservation platform, there is a self-assessment form available to expedite this process. We discuss iObservation later in this chapter.)

Five designated meeting points are indicated in Figure 6.1.

Figure 6.1. The Evaluation Cycle

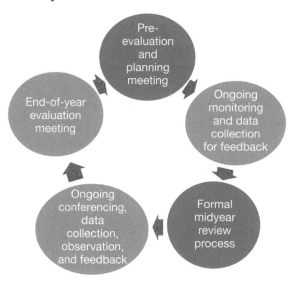

Step 1 in the evaluation cycle is the *pre-evaluation and planning meeting* between the supervisor and school leader or between the school leader and his assistant principal. This meeting provides an opportunity for the leader who is being evaluated to share his goals and vision for the year and identify potential growth areas. This meeting is also a good time for the supervisor to outline his own potential goals for the school leader. We recommend that one result of this meeting should be that the school leader not only formulates goals but also develops a growth plan for the year (an annual growth plan form is also available in iObservation).

Go to www.learningsciences.com/bookresources to download figures and tables.

Step 2 of the cycle is a focus on *ongoing monitoring and data collection* so that the supervisor can provide feedback regarding the leader's growth plan. Such monitoring typically includes face-to-face visits with the school leader in the school building to discuss performance data, test data, surveys, and so on, and should be a dynamic, ongoing process. These regular meetings, which provide a space for mentoring, collaboration, and feedback, are an important component of a growth model.

By midyear, in Step 3, the supervisor will want to conduct the first *formal review* to ensure that the leader is on track for obtaining desired results.

We stress that supervisors and school leaders can and will prioritize certain elements to work on and discuss during each meeting in Year 1 and Year 2 of implementation. It is not necessary to cover all twenty-four elements of the model in every meeting, or even all elements during the entire first year. The elements under discussion at the beginning of the year will likely differ from the elements focused on at the end. How the school leader and supervisor choose to prioritize the elements will depend on many factors: the specific needs of the school during different times of year, the growth areas of most concern to the leader and supervisor, and so on.

The evaluation cycle continues to Step 4, which is about *ongoing conferencing, monitoring, and feedback.* Typically, observations of principal behavior include not only formal and informal school visits but other opportunities where the supervisor can witness the principal in action—town hall meetings and community forums, conference presentations, school board meetings, school celebrations, and so on.

The final step in the cycle is for the supervisor to conduct an *end-of-year evaluation meeting* to take all the formative pieces collected throughout the year and aggregate them to produce the summative school leadership score (scoring will be discussed in detail later in the chapter).

Deliberate Practice as an Added Measure

Many districts provide a deliberate practice score as an optional measure. As we note in Chapter 2, deliberate practice is a mindful, systematic, highly structured effort to continuously seek solutions to clearly defined problems. School leaders use deliberate practice to grow expertise in clearly identified areas through a series of planned activities, reflection, and collaboration. A leader including a deliberate practice growth plan will be scored and given feedback as she deliberately practices to improve. Growth from the beginning of the school year in selected elements is credited toward the final evaluation. The purpose is to align and incentivize growth, professional development, and evaluation into a single initiative.

Scoring

The Marzano leader evaluation model uses, in effect, a standards-based scoring system. Each *element* functions as the standard, and leaders are scored on their competency relating to each element. It is also important to note that formative scores are not "averaged." A leader may well start the year at the *Beginning* level in any one element, move to *Developing* during the year, and finish the year at *Innovating*—the leader's end score reflects his or her competency in the element and becomes the final score. The leader's final summative score is based on how well she meets the standard. Because formative assessment is focused on growth, we do not recommend that school leaders be penalized in their early stages of progress.

After Years 1 and 2, the school leader should expect to be rated on all twenty-four elements during any given year, as these elements are a research-based measure of school leader effectiveness and competency. In other words, each of the twenty-four elements is critical to developing effective leadership.

Figure 6.2 shows how each domain in the model is weighted for the final score. You will note that Domains 1 and 2 carry significantly more weight than Domains 4 and 5. These percentages reflect that the Marzano School Leader Evaluation Model was designed for an essential focus on instructional leadership. But districts may make decisions about how to weight individual domains based on the needs and goals of the individual district. Figure 6.3 illustrates comparison of scores to scales to achieve the final practice rating.

Growth Cycle Is a Process

The Marzano School Leader Evaluation Model was designed so that school leaders are expected to complete a growth cycle in one academic year. Leader evaluation should be an ongoing, collaborative process.

Districts simultaneously using the Marzano Teacher Evaluation Model with the leader model will note that the scoring weights and process between the two models differ. The two models do share similarities in scoring, however: both draw on both formative and summative assessments, they draw on multiple uses of data, and scoring is focused on behaviors that research says effective leaders (or teachers) should implement. This close alignment furthers the goal of a shared, school-wide understanding of instruction and evaluation procedures. Because the leader evaluation process mirrors teacher evaluation, teachers and leaders feel that they "are in this together" and they share the same challenges, goals, and successes. In this way, aligned models help foster collegiality and collaboration, strengthening the focus of Domain 4.

Figure 6.2. Weighting and scoring the Marzano School Leader Evaluation Model

Element	Weight	Weighted Score
Domain 1	20%	
Element 1	5%	0.135
Element 2	4%	0.166
Element 3	3%	0.093
Element 4	3%	0.072
Element 5	5%	0.150
Domain 2	40%	
Element 1	10%	0.290
Element 2	9%	0.279
Element 3	8%	0.248
Element 4	4%	0.108
Element 5	4%	0.096
Element 6	5%	0.140
Domain 3	20%	
Element 1	8%	0.192
Element 2	4%	0.108
Element 3	4%	0.108
Element 4	4%	0.104
Domain 4	10%	
Element 1	3%	0.099
Element 2	2%	0.060
Element 3	2%	0.056
Element 4	2%	0.056
Element 5	1%	0.010
Domain 5	10%	
Element 1	2%	0.056
Element 2	2%	0.050
Element 3	2%	0.060
Element 4	2%	0.062
Element 5	1%	0.024
Element 6	1%	0.022
	TOTAL:	2.844

Figure 6.3. Computing the final annual score for leadership practice

Compare score to scale
for final leadership practice
status rating

Level	Rule
Highly Effective	>= 3.5
Effective	<3.5 and >= 2.5
Needs Improvement	<2.5 and >= 1.5
Unsatisfactory	<1.5

Overall Leadership Practice Status Score:	2.844
Overall Leadership Practice Status:	Effective

Establishing Inter-Rater Reliability

If a district has more than one supervisor who provides input for a school leader's evaluation, those supervisors must establish a degree of inter-rater reliability. Inter-rater reliability is achieved if multiple people observing the same body of evidence give the same or similar feedback based on the evidence. In a best-case scenario, they will score the leader identically on the element in question. Beyond this, there is also a district-wide aspect to inter-rater reliability: All school leaders in the district are held to the same measures for desired results. If the district establishes, first, a clear body of evidence to measure whether school leaders have achieved desired results, evaluations are more likely to be objective, and will be perceived as such. Common evidence-based measures help ensure objectivity, reliability, accuracy, and fairness, which are requirements of all effective evaluation systems (U.S. Department of Education, 2009b). Although each school has unique needs, the Marzano leader model is a standards- and evidence-based model that requires a consistent body of evidence.

If the district has multiple raters, we recommend that raters either achieve consensus or average their endpoint scores. Depending on their roles, supervisors may be evaluated through different lenses when rating school leaders (e.g., special education directors, curriculum directors). Ideally, all evaluators should demonstrate rater proficiency and understand best practices for analyzing data.

Data Management and Feedback Systems With the Marzano Models

In *Teacher Evaluation That Makes a Difference*, Marzano and Toth (2013) discuss technology platforms that foster cooperation and sharing, optimize data management, and play a role in the feedback loop necessary for deliberate practice. The Marzano School Leader Evaluation Model is available exclusively with the

Go to www.learningsciences.com/bookresources to download figures and tables.

iObservation technology platform developed by Learning Sciences International. The platform allows school leaders and their evaluators to engage in private conferences, participate in discussions with other school leaders and professionals, view and share resources, and communicate best practices both within schools and across the district so that all school leaders within the district share a common language and common goals and can collaborate toward those ends. The system saves time, ensures consistency of implementation across schools and between school leaders, and offers useful virtual tools to extend and enrich professional growth. Evaluators may use the system to compile formative evidence throughout the year, review data and supporting evidence before meetings or conferences, and provide virtual monitoring and mentoring. Additionally, school leaders have access to resources and libraries that can help them build the necessary skills to succeed.

In the screen shot in Figure 6.4, the school leader is using iObservation to review recommendations from his evaluator before the final evaluation. The discussion includes reference resources the school leader may use to guide professional development. Coaching from a supervisor can occur in real time, taking advantage of the resources embedded in the platform. The platform also facilitates virtual coaching and may help foster virtual learning communities of school leaders who are geographically remote. iObservation facilitates uploading and sharing of materials: school leaders may upload and send bodies of evidence directly to their supervisors using the forms provided by the system.

Figure 6.4. Using iObservation to provide feedback and resources to school leaders during the evaluation cycle.

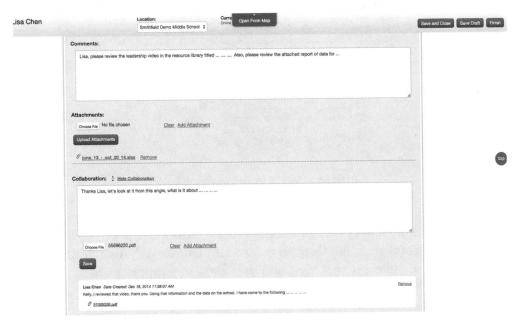

About Hierarchical Evaluation

Research has established the interdependent relationships between teachers, instructional support members, school leaders, and district leaders (Leithwood, Seashore-Louis, Anderson, & Wahlstrom, 2004). Increasingly, researchers and policy makers understand that the classroom behaviors of teachers, behavior of instructional support members, vision and daily practices of principals and assistant principals, and priorities of central office constitute a dynamic body of influence. The Marzano hierarchical evaluation systems recognize that the role of district leaders is to support school leaders, the role of school leaders is to support teachers, and the role of teachers is to support their students. A misaligned system—one without mutual goals, clear focus, and a common language of instruction—may struggle to meet high standards for student performance.

Figure 6.5. Cascading domains of influence in the Marzano Hierarchical Evaluation System

Cascading Domains of Influence

Achievement	Instruction	Curriculum	Cooperation and Collaboration	Climate	Resources
District Domain 1 Nonnegotiable goals to support student learning	**District Domain 2** Support for continuous improvement of instruction	**District Domain 3** Continuous support for a guaranteed and viable curriculum	**District Domain 4** Cooperation and collaboration	**District Domain 5** District climate	**District Domain 6** Resource Allocation
School Domain 1 A data-driven focus on student learning	**School Domain 2** Continuous improvement of instruction	**School Domain 3** Guaranteed and viable curriculum	**School Domain 4** Cooperation and collaboration	**School Domain 5** School climate	

Teacher Domain 4
Collegiality and professionalism

Teacher Domain 3
Reflecting on teaching

Teacher Domain 2
Planning and preparing

Teacher Domain 1
Classroom strategies and behaviors

Achievement of Individual Students

In Figure 6.5, we see how the aligned Marzano evaluation models for district leaders, school leaders, and teachers work to support and enhance one another and keep stakeholders focused on student learning. A district leader, for example, is evaluated on how well she uses data to support student learning; the processes in place to support continuous improvement of instruction, to promote cooperation and collaboration; and so on. These six district leader do-

Go to www.learningsciences.com/bookresources to download figures and tables.

mains directly impact the domains of the school leader model, which in turn impact the domains of the teacher model. All models foster a collaborative, collegial culture in which effective instruction and a common language to speak about effective instruction is a nonnegotiable goal.

It seems most districts understand the benefits of a common language of instruction, even if they have not yet implemented a system that encourages it. A common language of instruction allows district leadership to focus on improving instruction and student achievement. Visionary district leadership will use implementation of a common language of instruction as a measure and criterion for all district-level decisions, recognizing that teacher behavior and strategies are a leading indicator in predicting student achievement (Gates Foundation, 2013; Marzano & Toth, 2013; U.S. Department of Education, 2011). Along these lines, Shannon and Bylsma (2004) write, "Effective leadership that focuses on all students learning is at the core of improved school districts. Leadership is committed, persistent, proactive, and distributed through the system. . . . And district vision and strategies must be sustained by educational leaders for significant change to occur" (p. 13). As such, district-level focus "cascades down" to principals and school leaders, who ought to receive the support they need to drive instructional improvement both for themselves, and their teachers and instructional support members (or licensed nonclassroom personnel).

Before entire districts can achieve alignment, however, some longstanding issues must be addressed. As we have outlined in this book, school leaders must build the instructional expertise to conduct more extensive, frequent, and rigorous teacher observations to help teachers develop their classroom practice. The National Association of Elementary School Principals (NAESP) found in a 2008 report, for example, that the average percentage of school time allocated to professional development by principals was just 2 percent (as quoted in Schachter, 2013). Ensuring that school leaders are able to build the instructional expertise they need to effectively mentor their teachers, then, should be a top priority.

Teachers facing more rigorous evaluations, too, want principals who are qualified instructional leaders. MetLife (2012) reports in the twenty-ninth annual *MetLife Survey of the American Teacher* that teachers rated experience as a classroom teacher as the most critical attribute for principals.

Common Language and Common Goals

An understanding of a common language and common goals, from district and central office to teachers and support personnel, allows for clear communication across the system, both vertically (from district leader to school leader to teacher) and horizontally (between teachers and instructional support members and between teachers across the district). One powerful way to ensure that the components of the entire system are aligned is to employ *hierarchical evaluation* (Marzano & Toth, 2013). With hierarchical evaluation, district leaders are evaluated on the extent to which they produce specific results in the actions of school leaders; school leaders are evaluated on the extent to which they produce specific results in the actions of teachers; and teachers and instructional support members are evaluated on the extent to which they produce specific results in students. By definition, hierarchical evaluation produces a fully aligned system. The four aligned Marzano evaluation models for district leaders, school leaders, teachers, and instructional support personnel are an example of one such aligned system focused on a common language of instruction and set of common goals that span classrooms, schools, and district (for further discussion of the alignment of the four Marzano Center models, see Marzano & Toth, 2013, *Teacher Evaluation That Makes a Difference*).

Conclusion

As we have noted in previous chapters, many elements in the Marzano School Leader Evaluation Model are interrelated: We do not recommend a checklist approach to professional development and evaluation. Evidences supplied for elements of Domain 3 may also provide evidence for elements in Domain 2, as we have seen in previous chapters. A school leader who presents evidence for hiring and retaining the best teachers may, in some circumstances, provide that same evidence for ensuring a guaranteed and viable curriculum. Further, a school leader who has hired the best teachers to teach a guaranteed and viable curriculum may use evidence from those domains to show progress in Domain 5 regarding how teachers help create a safe and orderly environment. In sum, elements and evidences should never be considered in total isolation. This interconnected model facilitates the use of evidences in multiple elements and domains.

In *Teacher Evaluation That Makes a Difference*, Marzano and Toth (2013) outline a plan for implementing a teacher evaluation model that applies equally well to implementation of the Marzano School Leader Evaluation Model. Implementation is broken into five phases:

1. Planning
2. Initial Implementation
3. Fidelity
4. Efficacy
5. Sustainability and a Human Capital Continuum

If planning is done well, succeeding phases of implementation should progress smoothly, given good communication, regular reporting, effective delegation of responsibilities, and recognition of best practices as they begin to emerge.

With faithful implementation and sustained effort and focus, even schools and districts in early phases of implementation may experience dramatic results. Drew Eichelberger, executive director of Elementary Education Putnam City Schools, describes his partnership with Learning Sciences Marzano Center to implement the model this way:

> The Marzano Leader Evaluation Model has provided focus to our district leadership team. We have seen significant professional growth in our elementary principals as a result of use of the evaluation tool. The example evidences provided for each element have spurred valuable conversation, which has challenged our principals to operate outside their comfort zone.
>
> We saw academic achievement growth in all eighteen elementary schools with significant growth in fifteen of the eighteen schools. We believe the Marzano Leader Evaluation tool has been instrumental in this growth.
>
> Principal feedback on the evaluation instrument has been positive. Principals feel the model is not only fair, but provides the necessary information to document yearly leadership growth. (Personal communication)

The actions of the school leader serve as the leading indicator for teacher improvement within the school. But such large second-order changes take time. Successful improvement in leadership capacity must be carefully planned and monitored, and the commitment to improvement must be sustained over many years. In *How Leadership Influences Student Learning*, Leithwood et al. (2004) put it this way:

> The contribution of effective leadership is largest when it is needed the most: There are virtually no documented instances of troubled schools being turned around in the absence of intervention by talented leaders . . . leadership is the catalyst. (p. 17)

Good schools need good leaders. We have developed this model, and written this book, to help every leader become the catalyst for her school's success.

Resource A: Resources for the Marzano School Leader Evaluation Model

Videos and Webinars

Dr. Marzano discusses the Leadership Model
https://www.youtube.com/watch?v=QYUr7lor3qc

Michael Toth and Robert Marzano discuss Hierarchical Evaluation
https://www.youtube.com/watch?v=R7GFHVz9Mjo

White Papers

The Marzano School Leader Evaluation Model

http://www.marzanocenter.com/Leadership-Evaluation/Leadership
-Support/

Teaching for Rigor: A Call for a Critical Instructional Shift

Early reports reveal that student scores are dropping on assessments aligned to rigorous state standards. Experts worry that the achievement gap may be widening. And data analyzed by Learning Sciences Marzano Center indicates that teachers are spending less than 6 percent of classroom lessons teaching the cognitively complex skills students need to succeed.

http://www.marzanocenter.com/essentials/

Teaching for Rigor: Three Challenges for School Leaders

The Marzano Center Essentials for Achieving Rigor instructional model provides school leaders with resources, support, and the confidence they need to succeed.

http://www.marzanocenter.com/Teacher-Evaluation-Resources/#ES

Common Language, Common Goals: How an Aligned Evaluation and Growth System for District Leaders, School Leaders, Teachers, and Support Personnel Drives Student Achievement

An understanding of a common language and of common goals allows for clear communication across the system, both vertically (from district leader to school leader to teacher) and horizontally (between teachers and instructional support members and between teachers across the district).

http://www.marzanocenter.com/files/MarzanoCenter-Hierarchical -Evaluation-20130529.pdf

Learning Sciences International Trainings in Leadership

School Leader Evaluation Model Domain Map

http://www.marzanocenter.com/files/Leadership-Model-Map-20120417.pdf

Marzano School Leader Evaluation Model Domains 1–5

http://www.marzanocenter.com/files/ProdSheet_D1-5.pdf

Training for Monitoring the Progress of Leader Evaluation

http://www.marzanocenter.com/files/ProdSheet_Monitoring-Progress.pdf

End of Year Monitoring

http://www.marzanocenter.com/files/ProdSheet_Year-End.pdf

Blogs, Books, and Articles
Articles

"The Principal's Role in Hierarchical Evaluation"

http://www.ascd.org/publications/educational-leadership/apr13/vol70/num07/ The-Principal%27s-Role-in-Hierarchical-Evaluation.aspx

Blogs

On Hierarchical Evaluation

http://www.marzanocenter.com/blog/article/hierarchical-evaluation -growth-system-common-language-common-goals/

On School Leader Impact

http://www.marzanocenter.com/blog/article/principals-impact-on-student -learning-the-marzano-school-leader-evaluation-/

On School Leaders and Reflective Conversations

http://www.marzanocenter.com/blog/article/school-leaders-and-reflective -conversations-questions-that-promote-meaningf/

On School Leaders Creating a Vision of Instruction

http://www.marzanocenter.com/blog/article/school-leaders-creating-a-vision-of-instructiontelling-is-not-enough/

Books and DVDs

School Leadership Evaluation Model DVD

http://education-store.learningsciences.com/product_p/dv000-ml-001.htm

Marzano Essentials for Achieving Rigor Series

http://education-store.learningsciences.com/product_p/bpp140001.htm

Teacher Evaluation That Makes a Difference by Robert J. Marzano and Michael D. Toth

Teacher Evaluation That Makes a Difference describes next-generation teacher evaluation instruments and aligned evaluation systems for school leaders, district leaders, and noninstructional support personnel, which are grounded in research and designed to help educators develop expertise with the ultimate goal of improved student achievement.

http://education-store.learningsciences.com/product_p/978-1416615736mc.htm

Video discussion of *Teacher Evaluation That Makes a Difference*

https://www.youtube.com/watch?v=-GhL1Pv2Brg

Leaders of Learning: How District, School, and Classroom Leaders Improve Student Achievement

Page 30 of the catalog (978-1-935542667)

Book by Richard DuFour and Robert Marzano

For many years, the authors traveled around, helping educators improve their schools. Their first coauthored book focuses on district leadership, principal leadership, and team leadership, and addresses how individual teachers can be most effective in leading students—by learning with colleagues how to implement the most promising pedagogy in their classrooms.

http://education-store.learningsciences.com/product_p/978-1935542667mc.htm

School Leadership That Works: From Research to Results

Page 30 of the catalog (978-1-416602-27-9)

Book by Robert J. Marzano, Timothy Waters, and Brian A. McNulty

What can school leaders really do to increase student achievement, and which leadership practices have the biggest impact on school effectiveness? For the first time in the history of leadership research in the United States, here's a book that answers these questions definitively and gives a list of research-based leadership competencies.

http://education-store.learningsciences.com/product_p/978-1-416602-27-9
.htm

Other Helpful Resources

Summary and Links to the Research upon which the School Leader Model Is Based

http://www.marzanocenter.com/Leadership-Evaluation/leadership
-evaluation-research/

School Leader Evaluation and the Marzano Teacher Evalution Model

http://www.marzanocenter.com/Leadership-Evaluation/integrated
-approach/

Summary of How the School Leader Evaluation Model Connects to Student Achievement

http://www.marzanocenter.com/Leadership-Evaluation/Student
-Achievement/

Summary of School Leader Domains

http://www.marzanocenter.com/Leadership-Evaluation/Leadership-Model
-Domains/

Summary of School Leader Evaluation Model Scales and Evidences

http://www.marzanocenter.com/Leadership-Evaluation/Scales-and
-Evidences/#Evidences

Resource B: The Research Base for the Marzano School Leader Model

Four primary research efforts formed the basis for the Marzano School Leader Evaluation Model:

The Marzano Study of School Effectiveness

The original basis of the Marzano School Leader Evaluation Model was a synthesis of the research on effective schooling published in the book *What Works in Schools* (Marzano, 2003). Although this study was reported as a review of the literature on school reform, it did so with an eye toward school leadership. The study was a synthesis of a number of previous syntheses of the research (Bosker, 1992; Bosker & Witziers, 1995, 1996; Edmonds, 1979a, 1979b, 1979c, 1981a, 1981b; Levine & Lezotte, 1990; Marzano, 2000; Sammons, 1999; Sammons, Hillman, & Mortimore, 1995; Scheerens, 1992; Scheerens & Bosker, 1997). The study identified five school-level factors (as well as six other teacher- and student-level factors) that were well-established correlates of effective schools. Those five school-level correlates formed the basis of early versions of the Marzano School Leader Model. In order of their correlation with student achievement at the school level, these elements were a guaranteed and viable curriculum, challenging goals and effective feedback, parent and community involvement, a safe and orderly environment, and collegiality and professionalism.

A sixty-eight-item survey was constructed for the model, and the Association for Supervision and Curriculum Development distributed it. An initial reliability and validity study was conducted in 2004 (Marzano, 2004). Using a sample of more than 2,400 teachers who were asked to rate their principals' behaviors relative to the elements of the model, alpha coefficients were computed that ranged from .56 to .75, along with a split-half reliability of .91 for the entire instrument. To establish construct validity, a factor analysis was conducted indicating support for the various factors in the model.

In 2007, the Marzano School Leader Model was adapted specifically for the Michigan Coalition of Educational Leadership to give feedback to principals (Shen et al., 2007). This effort might be considered the first third-party application and study of the model as a tool for feedback to school leaders and was a joint effort of the Michigan Department of Education, Western Michigan University, the Michigan Association of School Administrators, the Michigan Association of School Boards, the Michigan Association of Secondary School Principals, and the Michigan Elementary and Middle School Principals Association. The effort was funded in part by the Wallace Foundation. Based on a sample of 258 principals, the researchers concluded that "data indicate the instrument has a high level of reliability for all the subscales as well as for the whole instrument" (p. 2). The researchers also concluded that "confirmatory factor analyses through structural equation modeling indicate that the instrument has a high level of validity" (p. 2).

Since that study, the original sixty-eight-item survey has been administered to more than 66,000 teachers and administrators.

Marzano, Waters, and McNulty Meta-Analysis of School Leadership

To add perspective to the evaluation model, the original Marzano framework was cross-referenced with the research on general characteristics of effective school leaders. Specifically, a meta-analysis of school leadership research was published in the book *School Leadership That Works* (Marzano, Waters, & McNulty, 2005). The purpose of the study was to examine the research literature from 1978 to 2001 on those general school leadership factors that have a statistically significant relationship with student achievement. More than 300 studies were examined and sixty-nine met the criteria for inclusion, one of which was that student achievement data were correlated with school administrator characteristics, or correlations could be computed from the data available. In all, 2,802 K–12 schools were involved in the studies synthesized, with an estimated 14,000 teachers and 1.4 million students. The overall finding was that the characteristics of school leaders have a statistically significant relationship with student achievement. Additionally, twenty-one specific types of school leader characteristics (referred to as "responsibilities") were found to correlate with student achievement.

The twenty-four elements of the Marzano School Leader Evaluation Model integrate quite well with the twenty-one responsibilities from the school leader research articulated in the literature between 1978 and 2001, and the elements of the model add detail to many of the twenty-one responsibilities.

Based on the cross-referencing with the twenty-one responsibilities from the Marzano et al. (2005) study, adaptations were made to the Marzano School Leader Evaluation Model to better incorporate the research on general school leadership characteristics.

The Wallace Study

A final cross-referencing was conducted on the Marzano School Leader Evaluation Model using the findings from a study The Wallace Foundation funded and was cooperatively conducted by the Center for Applied Research and Educational Improvement (CAREI) at the University of Minnesota and the Ontario Institute for Studies in Education at the University of Toronto (Louis, Leithwood, Wahlstrom, & Anderson, 2010). This multiyear study, *Investigating the Links to Improved Student Learning*, is perhaps the most current and comprehensive study on the relationship between school administrator behaviors and actions and student academic achievement. The study involved survey data from 8,391 teachers and 471 school administrators; interview data from 581 teachers and administrators, 304 district-level educators, and 124 state personnel; and observational data from 312 classrooms. Student achievement data for literacy and mathematics in elementary and secondary schools were also obtained using scores on state tests designed to measure Adequate Yearly Progress as mandated by the No Child Left Behind Act of 2001. The findings of this study as they relate specifically to school leadership were summarized in the report *The School Principal as Leader: Guiding Schools to Better Teaching and Learning (The Wallace Foundation, 2012)*. The report identified five key functions of school leaders: shaping a vision of academic success for all students; creating a climate hospitable to education; cultivating leadership in others; improving instruction; and managing people, data, and processes to foster school improvement.

As with the twenty-one responsibilities from the Marzano et al. (2005) study, the Marzano School Leader Evaluation Model was cross-referenced with the findings of the Wallace study. Table B.1 provides a very general cross-referencing of the Wallace 2012 report and Marzano School Leader Evaluation Model.

Table B.1. Cross-Referencing of the Marzano School Leader Evaluation Model With the Wallace Study

The Wallace Perspective: The five key functions that effective principals perform well	The Marzano School Leader Evaluation Model: Domains and Elements
1. Shaping a vision of academic success for all students	1(1), 1(2), 1(3), 1(4), 3(3), 4(3), 5(1), 5(2)
2. Creating a climate hospitable to education	2(1), 4(1), 5(3), 5(4)
3. Cultivating leadership in others	4(1), 4(2), 4(3), 4(4), 4(5)
4. Improving instruction	1(5), 2(2), 2(3), 2(4), 2(5), 4(3)
5. Managing people, data, and processes to foster school improvement	1(5), 2(4), 5(5)

Go to www.learningsciences.com/bookresources to download figures and tables.

Based on a more specific analysis of the findings in an earlier, 2010 technical report from The Wallace Foundation (Louis et al., 2010), minor adaptations were made to the Marzano School Leader Evaluation Model in an attempt to keep the model as current as possible.

What Works in Oklahoma Schools

The final research effort (to date) that underpins the Marzano School Leader Evaluation Model was a study of what works in Oklahoma schools that was conducted by Marzano Research Laboratory for the Oklahoma State Department of Education (OSDE) over the 2009–2010 and 2010–2011 school years (Marzano Research Laboratory, 2011). This study was conducted to determine those elements that are related to being classified as an improvement school (i.e., a school that needs improvement) as opposed to a school that is not classified as needing improvement (i.e., schools not on improvement status). Fifty-nine matched elementary, middle, and high schools were involved in the study. Of those fifty-nine schools, thirty-two were classified as needing improvement and twenty-seven were not. Survey data from teachers, administrators, students, and parents were used in the study along with on-site observations of teachers, interviews with administrators, and videotapes of classroom activities. State test data in mathematics and the English language arts were the primary dependent measures when examining the effects of specific elements. From the fifty-nine matched schools, 1,117 teachers, 13,373 students, and 516 parents were involved.

The first phase of the study (see Marzano Research Laboratory, 2011) examined the relationship between nine general factors (referred to as the nine essential elements by the Oklahoma State Department of Education) and average student achievement in schools:

1. Curriculum
2. Classroom Evaluation/Assessment
3. Instruction
4. School Culture
5. Student, Family, and Community Support
6. Professional Growth, Development, and Evaluation
7. Leadership
8. Organizational Structure and Resources
9. Comprehensive and Effective Planning

For each of these nine elements, surveys were constructed of teachers and administrators using the twenty-four elements of the Marzano School Leader Evaluation Model to provide specificity. In effect, while the nine categories the Oklahoma State Department of Education specified were not derived from the evaluation model, the items used in the surveys pertaining to those categories were either directly taken or adapted from the evaluation model. Survey results were then analyzed in terms of how well they discriminated between schools that were classified as needing improvement or not.

For the teacher surveys, average scores for schools that were not classified as needing improvement were higher than average for schools needing improvement. All differences were statistically significant. For the administrator surveys, average scores for schools that were not classified as needing improvement were again higher than average for schools needing improvement, and six out of nine differences were statistically significant.

Average scores for each school were also correlated with average student achievement on the state's mathematics and reading tests. For the teacher survey, all correlations were positive and ranged from .08 to .39 in mathematics and .12 to .53 in reading. For the administrator survey, all correlations were positive and ranged from .28 to .58 in mathematics and .16 to .54 in reading.

Conclusion

The Marzano School Leader Evaluation Model has a rather long developmental history that began using Robert Marzano's meta-analytic syntheses of research as far back as 2000. Since then the model has been continually updated and cross-referenced with the most current research to keep it as current as possible for school leader feedback. A third-party developer has also adapted and examined it in terms of its reliability and validity. Research and development on the model continues to date, and adaptations will be made as new research dictates.

References

Bosker, R. J. (1992). *The stability and consistency of school effects in primary education*. Enschede, The Netherlands: University of Twente.

Bosker, R. J., & Witziers, B. (1995). *School effects, problems, solutions, and a meta-analysis*. Paper presented at the International Congress for School Effectiveness and School Improvement, Leeuwarden, The Netherlands.

Bosker, R. J., & Witziers, B. (1996). *The magnitude of school effects. or: Does it really matter which school a student attends?* Paper presented at the annual meeting of the American Educational Research Association, New York.

Edmonds, R. R. (1979a). *A discussion of the literature and issues related to effective schooling*. Cambridge, MA: Center for Urban Studies, Harvard Graduate School of Education.

Edmonds, R. R. (1979b, October). Effective schools for the urban poor. *Educational Leadership, 37*, 15–27.

Edmonds, R. R. (1979c). Some schools work and more can. *Social Policy, 9*, 28–32.

Edmonds, R. R. (1981a). Making public schools effective. *Social Policy, 12*(2), 56–60.

Edmonds, R. R. (1981b). *A report on the research project, "Search for effective schools . . ." and certain of the designs for school improvement that are associated with the project.* Unpublished report prepared for NIE. East Lansing, MI: The Institute for Research on Teaching, College of Education, Michigan State University.

Levine, D. U., & Lezotte, L. W. (1990). *Unusually effective schools: A review and analysis of research and practice.* Madison, WI: National Center for Effective Schools Research and Development.

Louis, K. S., Leithwood, K., Wahlstrom, K. L., & Anderson, S. E. (2010). *Investigating the links to improved student learning: Final report of research findings.* New York, NY: The Wallace Foundation.

Marzano, R. J. (2000). *A new era of school reform: Going where the research takes us.* Denver, CO: McREL.

Marzano, R. J. (2003). *What works in schools: Translating research into action.* Alexandria, VA: ASCD.

Marzano, R. J. (2004). *Validity and reliability report for the snapshot survey of school effectiveness factors.* Englewood, CO: Marzano and Associates.

Marzano, R. J. (2007). Leadership and school reform factors. In T. Townsend (Ed.), *International handbook of school effectiveness and improvement: Review, reflection, and reframing* (pp. 597–614). Dordrecht, The Netherlands: Springer International.

Marzano, R. J., Waters, T., & McNulty, B. A. (2005). *School leadership that works: From research to results.* Alexandria, VA: ASCD.

Marzano Research Laboratory. (2011). *What works in Oklahoma schools: Phase I state report.* Englewood, CO: Author.

Sammons, P. (1999). *School effectiveness: Coming of age in the twenty-first century.* Lisse, The Netherlands: Swets and Zeitlinger.

Sammons, P., Hillman, J., & Mortimore, P. (1995). *Key characteristics of effective schools: A review of school effectiveness research.* London, England: Office of Standards in Education and Institute of Education.

Scheerens, J. (1992). *Effective schooling: Research, theory, and practice.* London, England: Cassell.

Scheerens, J., & Bosker, R. (1997). *The foundations of educational effectiveness.* New York, NY: Elsevier.

Shen, J., Cooley, V., Ma, X., Reeves, P., Burt, W., Rainey, M., & Wen, Y. (2007). *Data-informed decision-making on high-impact strategies: A measurement tool for school principals.* Kalamazoo, MI: Michigan Coalition of Educational Leadership.

The Wallace Foundation (2012). *The school principal as leader: Guiding schools to better teaching and learning.* New York, NY: Author.

Resource C: Learning Map for the Marzano School Leader Evaluation Model

Domain 1
A Data-Driven Focus on Student Achievement

Element 1:
The school leader ensures clear and measurable goals are established and focused on critical needs regarding improving overall student achievement at the school level.

Element 2:
The school leader ensures clear and measurable goals are established and focused on critical needs regarding improving achievement of individual students within the school.

Element 3:
The school leader ensures that data are analyzed, interpreted, and used to regularly monitor progress toward school achievement goals.

Element 4:
The school leader ensures that data are analyzed, interpreted, and used to regularly monitor progress toward achievement goals for individual students.

Element 5:
The school leader ensures that appropriate school-level and class-room-level programs and practices are in place to help all students meet individual achievement goals when data indicate interventions are needed.

Domain 2
Continuous Improvement of Instruction

Element 1:
The school leader provides a clear vision as to how instruction should be addressed in the school.

Element 2:
The school leader effectively supports and retains teachers who continually enhance their pedagogical skills through reflection and professional growth plans.

Element 3:
The school leader is aware of predominant instructional practices throughout the school.

Element 4:
The school leader ensures that teachers are provided with clear, ongoing evaluations of their pedagogical strengths and weaknesses that are based on multiple sources of data and are consistent with student achievement data.

Element 5:
The school leader ensures that teachers are provided with job-embedded professional development that is directly related to their instructional growth goals.

Domain 3
A Guaranteed and Viable Curriculum

Element 1:
The school leader ensures that the school curriculum and accompanying assessments adhere to state and district standards.

Element 2:
The school leader ensures that the school curriculum is focused enough that it can be adequately addressed in the time available to teachers.

Element 3:
The school leader ensures that all students have the opportunity to learn the critical content of the curriculum.

Domain 4
Cooperation and Collaboration

Element 1:
The school leader ensures that teachers have opportunities to observe and discuss effective teaching.

Element 2:
The school leader ensures that teachers have formal roles in the decision-making process regarding school initiatives.

Element 3:
The school leader ensures that teacher teams and collaborative groups regularly interact to address common issues regarding curriculum, assessment, instruction, and the achievement of all students.

Element 4:
The school leader ensures that teachers and staff have formal ways to provide input regarding the optimal functioning of the school and delegates responsibilities appropriately.

Element 5:
The school leader ensures that students, parents, and community have formal ways to provide input regarding the optimal functioning of the school.

Domain 5
School Climate

Element 1:
The school leader is recognized as the leader of the school who continually improves his or her professional practice.

Element 2:
The school leader has the trust of the faculty and staff that his or her actions are guided by what is best for all student populations.

Element 3:
The school leader ensures that faculty and staff perceive the school environment as safe and orderly.

Element 4:
The school leader ensures that students, parents, and the community perceive the school environment as safe and orderly.

Element 5:
The school leader manages the fiscal, operational, and technological resources of the school in a way that focuses on effective instruction and the achievement of all students.

Element 6:
The school leader acknowledges the success of the whole school, as well as individuals within the school.

Go to www.learningsciences.com/bookresources to download this page.   171

School Leadership for Results © 2015 Learning Sciences International

Resource D: Full Scales and Evidences for the Marzano School Leader Evaluation Model

Domain 1: A Data-Driven Focus on Student Achievement

1(1): The school leader ensures clear and measurable goals are established and focused on critical needs regarding improving overall student achievement at the school level.

Scale Value	Description
Innovating (4)	The school leader ensures adjustments are made, or new methods are utilized so that all stakeholders sufficiently understand the goals.
Applying (3)	The school leader ensures clear, measurable goals with specific timelines focused on critical needs regarding improving student achievement are established at the school level AND regularly monitors that everyone has understanding of the goals.
Developing (2)	The school leader ensures clear, measurable goals with specific timelines focused on critical needs regarding improving student achievement are established at the school level.
Beginning (1)	The school leader attempts to ensure clear, measurable goals with specific timelines focused on critical needs regarding improving student achievement are established at the school level but does not complete the task or does so partially.
Not Using (0)	The school leader does not attempt to ensure clear, measurable goals with specific timelines focused on critical needs regarding improving student achievement are established at the school level.

Sample Evidences for Domain 1, Element 1
• Written goals are established as a percentage of students who will score at a proficient or higher level on state assessments or benchmark assessments.
• School-wide achievement goals are posted and discussed regularly at faculty and staff gatherings.
• Written goals are established for eliminating the achievement gap for all students.
• Written goals address the most critical and severe achievement deficiencies.
• Written timelines contain specific benchmarks for each goal including individual(s) responsible for the goal.
• Scales are in place to chart student and school progress toward meeting the standards.
• When asked, faculty and staff can explain how goals eliminate differences in achievement for students of differing ethnicities.
• When asked, faculty and staff can explain how goals eliminate differences in achievement for students at different socioeconomic levels, English language learners, and students with disabilities.
• When asked, faculty and staff can describe the school-wide achievement goals.
• When asked, faculty and staff can identify the school's most critical needs goals.

1(2): The school leader ensures clear and measurable goals are established and focused on critical needs regarding improving achievement of individual students within the school.

Scale Value	Description
Innovating (4)	The school leader ensures adjustments are made, or new methods are utilized so that all faculty and students sufficiently understand the goals.
Applying (3)	The school leader ensures each student has written achievement goals that are clear, measurable, and focused on appropriate needs AND regularly monitors that teachers and students have understanding of individual student goals.
Developing (2)	The school leader ensures each student has written achievement goals that are clear, measurable, and focused on appropriate needs.
Beginning (1)	The school leader attempts to ensure that written achievement goals that are clear, measurable, and focused are established for each student but does not complete the task or does so partially.
Not Using (0)	The school leader does not attempt to ensure that written achievement goals that are clear, measurable, and focused are established for each student.

Sample Evidences for Domain 1, Element 2
• Written goals are established for each student in terms of his/her performance on state/district assessments, benchmark assessments, or common assessments.
• Written goals accompanied by proficiency scales are established for each student in terms of his/her knowledge gain.
• Students keep data notebooks regarding their individual goals.
• Student-led conferences focus on the individual student's goals.
• Parent-teacher conferences focus on the individual student's goals.
• When asked, teachers can explain the learning goals of their students.
• When asked, students perceive that their individual goals are academically challenging.
• When asked, students are aware of their status on the achievement goals specific to them.
• When asked, parents are aware of their child's achievement goals.

1(3): The school leader ensures that data are analyzed, interpreted, and used to regularly monitor progress toward school achievement goals.

Scale Value	Description
Innovating (4)	The school leader ensures that data are analyzed in a variety of ways to provide the most useful information and refines achievement goals or the tracking process as achievement data accrue.
Applying (3)	The school leader ensures that data are available for tracking overall student achievement AND monitors the extent to which student data are used to track progress toward goal.
Developing (2)	The school leader ensures that data are available for tracking overall student achievement.
Beginning (1)	The school leader attempts to ensure that data are available for tracking overall student achievement but does not complete the task or does so partially.
Not Using (0)	The school leader does not attempt to ensure that data are available for tracking overall student achievement.

Sample Evidences for Domain 1, Element 3
• Reports, graphs, and charts are available for overall student achievement.
• Student achievement is examined from the perspective of value-added results.
• Results from multiple types of assessments are regularly reported and used (e.g., benchmark, common assessments).
• Reports, graphs, and charts are regularly updated to track growth in student achievement.
• Achievement data for student subgroups within the school are routinely analyzed.
• School leadership teams regularly analyze school growth data.
• Data briefings are conducted at faculty meetings.
• When asked, faculty and staff can describe the different types of reports available to them.
• When asked, faculty and staff can explain how data are used to track growth in student achievement.

1(4): The school leader ensures that data are analyzed, interpreted, and used to regularly monitor progress toward achievement goals for individual students.

Scale Value	Description
Innovating (4)	The school leader ensures that data are analyzed in a variety of ways to provide the most useful information and refines individual achievement goals or the tracking process as achievement data accrue.
Applying (3)	The school leader ensures that data are available for individual student achievement AND monitors the extent to which data are used to track progress toward individual student goals.
Developing (2)	The school leader ensures that data are available for individual student achievement.
Beginning (1)	The school leader attempts to ensure that data are available for individual student achievement but does not complete the task or does so partially.
Not Using (0)	The school leader does not attempt to ensure that data are available for individual student achievement.

Sample Evidences for Domain 1, Element 4
• Reports, charts, and graphs are available for individual students depicting their status and growth.
• Individual student achievement is examined from the perspective of value-added results.
• Individual student results from multiple types of assessments are regularly reported and used (e.g., benchmark, common assessments).
• Individual student reports, graphs, and charts are regularly updated to track growth in student achievement.
• Teachers regularly analyze school growth data for individual students.
• School leadership teams regularly analyze individual student performance.
• When asked, individual students and their parents can describe the student's achievement status and growth.
• When asked, faculty can describe the different types of individual student reports available to them.
• When asked, faculty and staff can analyze data of their individual students, including all subgroups.

1(5): The school leader ensures that appropriate school-level and classroom-level programs and practices are in place to help all students meet individual achievement goals when data indicate interventions are needed.

Scale Value	Description
Innovating (4)	The school leader continually examines and expands the options for individual students to make adequate progress.
Applying (3)	The school leader ensures that programs and practices are in place for individual students who are not making adequate progress AND monitors whether interventions are helping students meet their achievement goals.
Developing (2)	The school leader ensures that programs and practices are in place for individual students who are not making adequate progress.
Beginning (1)	The school leader attempts to ensure that programs and practices are in place for individual students who are not making adequate progress but does not complete the task or does so partially.
Not Using (0)	The school leader does not attempt to ensure that programs and practices are in place for individual students who are not making adequate progress.

Sample Evidences for Domain 1, Element 5
• Extended school-day, -week, or -year programs are in place.
• Tutorial programs are in place (during the school day and/or after school).
• Individual student completion of programs designed to enhance their academic achievement is monitored (e.g., gifted and talented, advanced placement, STEM).
• Response to intervention measures is in place.
• Enrichment programs are in place.
• Data are collected and available to monitor student progress and achievement as a result of enrollment in intervention or enrichment programs.
• When asked, teachers can explain how interventions in place help individual students meet their goals.
• When asked, student and/or parents can identify interventions in place to meet the student's goals.
• When asked, students report their school has programs in place to help them meet their achievement goals.

Domain 2: Continuous Improvement of Instruction

2(1): The school leader provides a clear vision as to how instruction should be addressed in the school.

Scale Value	Description
Innovating (4)	The school leader continually examines and makes adjustments so that all faculty and staff understand the nuances of the instructional model and integrates new instructional initiatives into the school instructional model.
Applying (3)	The school leader ensures that a school-wide language or model of instruction is in place AND monitors the extent to which the faculty and staff understand the instructional model.
Developing (2)	The school leader ensures that a school-wide language or model of instruction is in place.
Beginning (1)	The school leader attempts to ensure that a school-wide language or model of instruction is in place but does not complete the task or does so partially.
Not Using (0)	The school leader does not attempt to ensure that a school-wide language or model of instruction is in place.

Sample Evidences for Domain 2, Element 1
• A written document articulating the school-wide model of instruction is in place.
• The school-wide language of instruction is used regularly by faculty in their professional learning communities and faculty and/or department meetings.
• Professional development opportunities are provided for new teachers regarding the school-wide model of instruction.
• Professional development opportunities are provided for all teachers regarding the school-wide model of instruction.
• New initiatives are prioritized and limited in number to support the instructional model.
• The school-wide language of instruction is used regularly by faculty in their informal conversations.
• When asked, teachers can describe the major components of the school-wide model of instruction.
• When asked, teachers can explain how strategies in the instructional framework promote learning for the school's diverse population.

2(2): The school leader effectively supports and retains teachers who continually enhance their pedagogical skills through reflection and professional growth plans.

Scale Value	Description
Innovating (4)	The school leader regularly intervenes with and supports teachers who are not meeting their growth goals or adequately enhancing the achievement of their students.
Applying (3)	The school leader ensures that teachers establish growth goals regarding their pedagogical skills and track their individual progress AND monitors the extent to which teachers achieve their growth goals.
Developing (2)	The school leader ensures that teachers establish growth goals regarding their pedagogical skills and track their individual progress.
Beginning (1)	The school leader attempts to ensure that teachers establish growth goals regarding their pedagogical skills and track their individual progress but does not complete the task or does so partially.
Not Using (0)	The school leader does not attempt to ensure that teachers establish growth goals regarding their pedagogical skills and track their individual progress.

Sample Evidences for Domain 2, Element 2
• Individual teachers have written pedagogical growth goals.
• Individual teachers keep track of their progress on their pedagogical growth goals.
• Evaluation results, growth plans, and interventions for struggling teachers are available.
• Meetings are regularly scheduled with teachers regarding their growth goals and tracking of their progress.
• A system is in place to effectively evaluate and revise the school's new teacher induction program.
• The school leader has demonstrated a track record of hiring effective teachers.
• The school leader has a track record of retaining effective teachers.
• When asked, teachers can describe their progress on their pedagogical growth goals.
• When asked, teachers can share documented examples of how reflection has improved their instructional practice.

2(3): The school leader is aware of predominant instructional practices throughout the school.

Scale Value	Description
Innovating (4)	The school leader regularly intervenes to ensure that ineffective instructional practices are corrected and effective instructional practices are proliferating.
Applying (3)	The school leader ensures that information about predominant instructional strategies in the school is collected, regularly interacts with teachers about the effectiveness of these strategies, AND monitors the extent to which the information is used to identify effective and ineffective practices.
Developing (2)	The school leader ensures that information about predominant instructional strategies in the school is collected and regularly interacts with teachers about the effectiveness of these strategies.
Beginning (1)	The school leader attempts to ensure that information about predominant instructional strategies in the school is collected and regularly interacts with teachers about the effectiveness of these strategies but does not complete the task or does so partially.
Not Using (0)	The school leader does not attempt to ensure that information about predominant instructional strategies in the school is collected.

Sample Evidences for Domain 2, Element 3
• Walk-through or other informal observation data are aggregated in such a way as to disclose predominant instructional practices in the school.
• Forthright feedback is provided to teachers regarding their instructional practices.
• Systems are in place to monitor the effect of the predominant instructional practices for all subgroups in the school.
• Data are available to document the predominant instructional practices in the school.
• The school leader can describe effective practices and problems of practice.
• When asked, teachers can describe the predominant instructional practices used in the school.

2(4): The school leader ensures that teachers are provided with clear, ongoing evaluations of their pedagogical strengths and weaknesses that are based on multiple sources of data and are consistent with student achievement data.

Scale Value	Description
Innovating (4)	The school leader ensures that teacher evaluation processes are updated regularly to ensure the results are consistent with student achievement data.
Applying (3)	The school leader ensures that specific evaluation data are collected on each teacher regarding his/her pedagogical strengths and weaknesses and that these data are gathered from multiple sources AND monitors the extent to which teacher evaluations are consistent with student achievement data.
Developing (2)	The school leader ensures that specific evaluation data are collected on each teacher regarding his/her pedagogical strengths and weaknesses, and that these data are gathered from multiple sources.
Beginning (1)	The school leader attempts to ensure that specific evaluation data are collected on each teacher regarding his/her pedagogical strengths and weaknesses and that these data are gathered from multiple sources, but does not complete the task or does so partially.
Not Using (0)	The school leader does not attempt to ensure that specific evaluation data are collected on each teacher regarding his/her pedagogical strengths and weaknesses, and that these data are gathered from multiple sources.

Sample Evidences for Domain 2, Element 4
• Highly specific scales are in place to provide teachers accurate feedback on their pedagogical strengths and weaknesses.
• Teacher feedback and evaluation data are based on multiple sources of information including but not limited to: direct observation, teacher self-report, analysis of teacher performance as captured on video, student reports on teacher effectiveness, and peer feedback to teachers.
• Teacher evaluation data are regularly used as the subject of conversation between school leaders and teachers.
• Data show the school leader provides frequent observations and meaningful feedback to teachers.
• Ongoing data are available to support that teacher evaluations are consistent with student achievement data.
• When asked, teachers can describe their instructional strategies that have the strongest and weakest relationships to student achievement.

2(5): The school leader ensures that teachers are provided with job-embedded professional development that is directly related to their instructional growth goals.

Scale Value	Description
Innovating (4)	The school leader continually reevaluates the professional development program to ensure that it remains job-embedded and focused on instructional growth goals, and intervenes with teachers who are not making sufficient progress toward achieving growth goals.
Applying (3)	The school leader ensures that job-embedded professional development that is directly related to their instructional growth goals is provided to teachers AND monitors the extent to which teachers improve their instructional practices.
Developing (2)	The school leader ensures that job-embedded professional development that is directly related to their instructional growth goals is provided to teachers.
Beginning (1)	The school leader attempts to ensure that job-embedded professional development that is directly related to their instructional growth goals is provided to teachers but does not complete the task or does so partially.
Not Using (0)	The school leader does not attempt to ensure that job-embedded professional development that is directly related to their instructional growth goals is provided to teachers.

Sample Evidences for Domain 2, Element 5
• Online professional development courses and resources are available to teachers regarding their instructional growth goals.
• The school leader tracks teacher participation in professional development activities.
• Teacher-led professional development is available to teachers regarding their instructional growth goals.
• Instructional coaching is available to teachers regarding their instructional growth goals.
• Data are collected linking the effectiveness of professional development to the improvement of teacher practices.
• Data are available supporting deliberate practice in improving teacher performance.
• When asked, teachers can describe how the professional development supports their attainment of instructional growth goals.

Domain 3: A Guaranteed and Viable Curriculum

3(1): The school leader ensures that the school curriculum and accompanying assessments adhere to state and district standards.

Scale Value	Description
Innovating (4)	The school leader ensures that the assessment and reporting system focuses on state and district standards, and intervenes with teachers who do not follow state and district standards.
Applying (3)	The school leader ensures that both the written curriculum and accompanying assessments adhere to state and district standards, AND monitors the extent to which the curriculum is delivered and the assessments measure the curriculum.
Developing (2)	The school leader ensures that both the written curriculum and accompanying assessments adhere to state and district standards.
Beginning (1)	The school leader attempts to ensure that both the written curriculum and accompanying assessments adhere to state and district standards but does not complete the task or does so partially.
Not Using (0)	The school leader does not attempt to ensure that both the written curriculum and accompanying assessments adhere to state and district standards.

Sample Evidences for Domain 3, Element 1
• Curriculum documents are in place that correlate the written curriculum to state and district standards.
• Rubrics or proficiency scales are in place that clearly delineate student levels of performance on essential elements of the state and district standards.
• Information is available correlating what is taught in the classroom (i.e., the taught curriculum) and the written curriculum.
• Information is available examining the extent to which assessments accurately measure the written and taught curriculums.
• School teams regularly analyze the relationship between the written curriculum, taught curriculum, and assessments.
• Evidence is available demonstrating the assessments are accurately measuring the state and district standards.
• When asked, teachers can describe the essential content and standards for their subject area(s) or grade level(s).
• When asked, teachers demonstrate understanding of how the curriculum and assessments are aligned.

3(2): The school leader ensures that the school curriculum is focused enough that it can be adequately addressed in the time available to teachers.

Scale Value	Description
Innovating (4)	The school leader ensures that essential elements of the curriculum are regularly examined and revised with an eye toward making instruction more focused and efficient.
Applying (3)	The school leader ensures that the written curriculum has been unpacked in such a manner that essential elements have been identified AND monitors the extent to which the essential elements are few enough to allow adequate time for students to learn them.
Developing (2)	The school leader ensures that the written curriculum has been unpacked in such a manner that essential elements have been identified.
Beginning (1)	The school leader attempts to ensure that the written curriculum has been unpacked in such a manner that essential elements have been identified but does not complete the task or does so partially.
Not Using (0)	The school leader does not attempt to ensure that the written curriculum has been unpacked in such a manner that essential elements have been identified.

Sample Evidences for Domain 3, Element 2
• A written list of essential elements is in place.
• A curriculum audit has been conducted that delineates how much time it would take to adequately address the essential elements.
• Teams regularly meet to discuss the progression and viability of documents that articulate essential content and timing of delivery (e.g., pacing guides, curriculum maps).
• Time available for specific classes and courses meets the state or district specifications for those classes and courses.
• Data are available to show that students are ready to be contributing members of society and participate in a global community.
• Data are available to show that students are college and career ready.
• A plan is in place to monitor that the curriculum is taught in the time available to teachers.
• When asked, teachers can describe which elements are essential and can be taught in the scheduled time.
• When asked, students report they have time to learn the essential curriculum.

3(3): The school leader ensures that all students have the opportunity to learn the critical content of the curriculum.

Scale Value	Description
Innovating (4)	The school leader intervenes with teachers whose students do not have adequate access to essential elements and instructional strategies that most strongly increase their chances of learning the essential elements.
Applying (3)	The school leader ensures that all students have access to the courses and classes that directly address the essential elements of the curriculum AND monitors the extent to which those courses and classes utilize instructional strategies that most strongly increase their chances of learning the essential elements.
Developing (2)	The school leader ensures that all students have access to the courses and classes that directly address the essential elements of the curriculum.
Beginning (1)	The school leader attempts to ensure that all students have access to the courses and classes that directly address the essential elements of the curriculum but does not complete the task or does so partially.
Not Using (0)	The school leader does not attempt to ensure that all students have access to the courses and classes that directly address the essential elements of the curriculum.

Sample Evidences for Domain 3, Element 3
• Tracking systems are in place that examine each student's access to the essential elements of the curriculum.
• Parents are aware of their child's current access to the essential elements of the curriculum.
• All students have access to advanced placement or other rigorous courses.
• All students have a prescribed program of study that documents access to courses.
• Data are available to show teachers have completed appropriate content area training in their subject area courses.
• Data are available to verify student achievement in critical content and standards.
• When asked, teachers can describe the content strategies that result in the highest student learning for specific courses and topics.
• When asked, students report they have the opportunity to learn the critical content of the curriculum.

Domain 4: Cooperation and Collaboration

4(1): The school leader ensures that teachers have opportunities to observe and discuss effective teaching.

Scale Value	Description
Innovating (4)	The school leader intervenes and supports teachers who do not actively participate in opportunities to interact regarding effective instructional practices.
Applying (3)	The school leader ensures that teachers have regular opportunities to interact regarding effective instructional practices and observe specific examples of effective teaching virtually or in person AND monitors the extent to which teachers who actively participate in these opportunities improve their pedagogy.
Developing (2)	The school leader ensures that teachers have regular opportunities to interact regarding effective instructional practices and observe specific examples of effective teaching virtually or in person.
Beginning (1)	The school leader attempts to ensure that teachers have regular opportunities to interact regarding effective instructional practices and observe specific examples of effective teaching virtually or in person but does not complete the task or does so partially.
Not Using (0)	The school leader does not attempt to ensure that teachers have regular opportunities to interact regarding effective instructional practices and observe specific examples of effective teaching virtually or in person.

Sample Evidences for Domain 4, Element 1
• Teachers have opportunities to engage in instructional rounds.
• Teachers have opportunities to view and discuss video-based examples of exemplary teaching.
• Teachers have regular times to meet and discuss effective instructional practices (e.g., lesson study, professional learning communities).
• Teachers have opportunities to interact about effective teaching via technology.
• Instructional practices are regularly discussed at faculty and department meetings.
• Video segments of instructional practices are regularly viewed and discussed at faculty and department meetings.
• Procedures are in place for scheduling teachers to observe and discuss effective instructional practices.
• Data are available to document that teachers who participate in observational rounds improve their pedagogy.
• When asked, teachers report their participation in observing other teachers results in individual self-reflection and pedagogical growth.

4(2): The school leader ensures that teachers have formal roles in the decision-making process regarding school initiatives.

Scale Value	Description
Innovating (4)	The school leader continually seeks new venues for teacher input regarding important decisions.
Applying (3)	For specific types of decisions, the school leader ensures that formal processes are in place to collect data from all teachers regarding their preferences AND monitors the extent to which those data are used to make decisions and the transparency of those decisions.
Developing (2)	For specific types of decisions, the school leader ensures that formal processes are in place to collect data from all teachers regarding their preferences.
Beginning (1)	The school leader attempts to ensure that formal processes are in place to collect data from all teachers regarding their preferences on specific decisions but does not complete the task or does so partially.
Not Using (0)	The school leader does not attempt to ensure that formal processes are in place to collect data from all teachers regarding their preferences on specific decisions.

Sample Evidences for Domain 4, Element 2
• Teachers are advised of the specific types of decisions in which they will have direct input.
• Data-gathering techniques are in place to collect information from teachers.
• Notes and reports are in place that describe how teacher input was used when making specific decisions.
• Electronic tools are utilized to collect and report teacher opinions regarding specific decisions (e.g., online surveys).
• Groups of teachers are selected and utilized to provide input regarding specific decisions.
• Teacher leaders are enabled to proactively initiate, plan, implement, and monitor projects.
• The school leadership team has critical roles in facilitating school initiatives.
• Data are available to show input is used by the school leader.
• When asked, teachers report they feel their input is valued and used by the school leader.

4(3): The school leader ensures that teacher teams and collaborative groups regularly interact to address common issues regarding curriculum, assessment, instruction, and the achievement of all students.

Scale Value	Description
Innovating (4)	The school leader ensures that group goals relative to curriculum, assessment, and instruction are regularly revised to reflect the changes in student achievement data and intervenes and supports teacher teams whose goals do not adequately address the achievement of all students.
Applying (3)	The school leader ensures that formal teams or collaborative groups of teachers and other relevant staff meet regularly and have specific goals relative to curriculum, assessment, and instruction AND monitors the extent to which these goals are designed to enhance the achievement of all students.
Developing (2)	The school leader ensures that formal teams or collaborative groups of teachers and other relevant staff meet regularly and have specific goals relative to curriculum, assessment, and instruction.
Beginning (1)	The school leader attempts to ensure that formal teams or collaborative groups of teachers and other relevant staff meet regularly and have specific goals relative to curriculum, assessment, and instruction but does not complete the task or does so partially.
Not Using (0)	The school leader does not attempt to ensure that formal teams or collaborative groups of teachers and other relevant staff meet regularly and have specific goals relative to curriculum, assessment, and instruction.

Sample Evidences for Domain 4, Element 3
• Professional learning communities (PLCs) are in place and meet regularly.
• PLCs have written goals.
• The school leader regularly examines the PLCs' progress toward goals.
• Common assessments are created by PLCs.
• Student achievement and growth are analyzed by PLCs.
• Data teams are in place and have written goals.
• The progress of each data team toward reaching its goals is regularly examined.
• To maintain a focus on student achievement, the school leader collects and reviews minutes, notes, and goals from meetings.
• When asked, teachers can explain how being a member of a PLC has helped them grow their pedagogy.
• When asked, teachers can explain how PLCs analyze data to identify appropriate instructional practices.

4(4): The school leader ensures that teachers and staff have formal ways to provide input regarding the optimal functioning of the school and delegates responsibilities appropriately.

Scale Value	Description
Innovating (4)	The school leader intervenes and provides support when delegation of authority and teacher input is not working to optimize the function of the school.
Applying (3)	The school leader ensures that input is regularly collected from teachers and staff, appropriately delegates responsibilities, AND monitors the extent to which the inputs and delegations are contributing to the optimal functioning of the school.
Developing (2)	The school leader ensures that input is regularly collected from teachers and staff and appropriately delegates responsibilities.
Beginning (1)	The school leader attempts to ensure that input is regularly collected from teachers and staff and appropriately delegates responsibilities but does not complete the task or does so partially.
Not Using (0)	The school leader does not attempt to ensure that input is regularly collected from teachers and staff and does not appropriately delegate responsibilities.

Sample Evidences for Domain 4, Element 4
• Data collection systems are in place to collect opinion data from teachers and staff regarding the optimal functioning of the school.
• Data are archived and reports regularly generated regarding these data.
• The manner in which data are used is made transparent.
• The school improvement team provides input to the leader regarding the school improvement plan.
• Appropriate faculty and staff are identified and mentored for succession planning and provided appropriate growth opportunities.
• Faculty and staff are assisted with career planning and continuing educational opportunities.
• Teacher leaders and other faculty are empowered to share in the leadership of the school.
• Potential leaders are identified and guided in career development.
• The school leader can cite examples of where teacher input has resulted in effective change at the school.
• The school leader demonstrates ongoing mentoring of teacher leaders.
• When asked, teachers explain formal ways they have to give input regarding optimal functioning of the school.
• When asked, teachers can identify examples of when their input has resulted in effective change at the school.

4(5): The school leader ensures that students, parents, and community have formal ways to provide input regarding the optimal functioning of the school.

Scale Value	Description
Innovating (4)	The school leader intervenes and provides support when student, parent, and community input is not working to optimize the function of the school.
Applying (3)	The school leader ensures that input is regularly collected from students, parents, and community AND monitors the extent to which the inputs are contributing to the optimal functioning of the school.
Developing (2)	The school leader ensures that input is regularly collected from students, parents, and community.
Beginning (1)	The school leader attempts to ensure that input is regularly collected from students, parents, and community but does not complete the task or does so partially.
Not Using (0)	The school leader does not attempt to ensure that input is regularly collected from students, parents, and community.

Sample Evidences for Domain 4, Element 5
• Data collection systems are in place to collect opinion data from students, parents, and community regarding the optimal functioning of the school.
• Data are archived and reports regularly generated regarding these data.
• The manner in which these data are used is made transparent.
• Data are available to show that input from the school's diverse population is valued and used.
• An interactive website is provided for students, parents, and community to provide input.
• Appropriate social networking technologies (e.g., Twitter, Facebook) are utilized to involve students, parents, and community.
• Focus group meetings with students and parents are routinely scheduled.
• The school leader hosts or speaks at community/business luncheons.
• The school leader can explain how the use of input from the school community has resulted in improved functioning of the school.
• The school leader can demonstrate how data gathered from subpopulations at the school are incorporated in school planning.
• When asked, students, parents, and community members report their input is valued and used by the school leader to better the functioning of the school.

Domain 5: Positive School Climate

5(1): The school leader is recognized as the leader of the school who continually improves his or her professional practice.

Scale Value	Description
Innovating (4)	The school leader actively seeks expertise/mentors for validation and feedback to confirm or improve leadership skills.
Applying (3)	The school leader demonstrates leadership skills and continually engages in activities to improve his/her professional practices AND monitors the extent to which these activities enhance personal leadership skills and the staff's confidence about his/her ability to lead.
Developing (2)	The school leader demonstrates leadership skills and continually engages in activities to improve his/her professional practices.
Beginning (1)	The school leader attempts to demonstrate leadership skills and engage in activities to improve his/her professional practices but does not complete the task or does so partially.
Not Using (0)	The school leader does not attempt to demonstrate leadership skills and does not engage in activities to improve his/her professional practices.

Sample Evidences for Domain 5, Element 1
• A written annual growth plan is in place to address how the school leader will address strengths and weaknesses.
• Professional development activities consistent with the leader's growth plan have been identified.
• Evidence of leadership initiatives is available.
• Adherence to district and state policies and procedures is evident.
• The school leader has demonstrated the ability to be a problem solver.
• The school leader has identified mentors and regularly interacts with them.
• When asked, faculty and staff identify the school administrator as the leader of the school.
• When asked, faculty and staff describe the school leader as uncompromising in regard to raising student achievement.
• When asked, faculty and staff describe the school leader as effectively communicating those nonnegotiable factors that have an impact on student achievement.
• When asked, faculty and staff generally agree as to the vision provided by the school leader.

5(2): The school leader has the trust of the faculty and staff that his/her actions are guided by what is best for all student populations.

Scale Value	Description
Innovating (4)	The school leader actively seeks expertise/mentors for validation and feedback to confirm or improve how he/she performs or is perceived.
Applying (3)	The school leader performs with integrity and in the best interest of all students AND monitors the extent to which faculty and staff perceive him/her as an individual who will follow through with initiatives and whose actions are guided by the desire to help all students learn.
Developing (2)	The school leader performs with integrity and in the best interest of all students.
Beginning (1)	The school leader attempts to perform with integrity and in the best interest of all students but does so sporadically or inconsistently.
Not Using (0)	The school leader does not attempt to perform with integrity and in the best interest of all students.

Sample Evidences for Domain 5, Element 2
• The school leader is recognized by the school community as one who is willing to "take on tough issues"
• The school leader acknowledges when school goals have not been met or initiatives have failed and revises the plan for success
• When asked, faculty and staff describe the school leader as an individual whose actions are guided by a desire to help all students learn.
• When asked, faculty and staff describe the school leader as an individual who will follow through with his/her initiatives.
• When asked, faculty and staff describe the school leader as one whose actions support his/ her talk and expectations.
• When asked, faculty and staff describe the school leader as one who speaks with candor and "takes on tough issues."

5(3): The school leader ensures that faculty and staff perceive the school environment as safe and orderly.

Scale Value	Description
Innovating (4)	The school leader ensures that rules and procedures are reviewed and updated as necessary to ensure a safe and orderly school environment and the perception of such by school faculty and staff.
Applying (3)	The school leader ensures that well-defined routines and procedures that lead to safe and orderly conduct are in place AND monitors the extent to which faculty and staff share the perception that the school environment is safe and orderly.
Developing (2)	The school leader ensures that well-defined routines and procedures that lead to orderly conduct are in place.
Beginning (1)	The school leader attempts to ensure that well-defined routines and procedures that lead to orderly conduct are in place but does not complete the task or does so partially.
Not Using (0)	The school leader does not attempt to ensure that well-defined routines and procedures that lead to safe and orderly conduct are in place.

Sample Evidences for Domain 5, Element 3
• Clear and specific rules and procedures are in place for the running of the school.
• Faculty and staff are provided the means to communicate about the safety of the school.
• Faculty and staff know emergency management procedures and how to implement them for specific incidents.
• Evidence of practicing emergency management procedures for specific incidents is available.
• Evidence of updates to the emergency management plans, and communication of those plans to the faculty and staff, is available.
• When asked, faculty and staff describe the school as a safe and orderly place.
• When asked, the faculty and staff describe the school leader as highly visible and accessible.
• When asked, faculty and staff describe the school as a place focused on learning.

5(4): The school leader ensures that students, parents, and community perceive the school environment as safe and orderly.

Scale Value	Description
Innovating (4)	The school leader ensures that rules and procedures are reviewed and updated as necessary to ensure a safe and orderly school environment and the perception of such by students, parents, and community.
Applying (3)	The school leader ensures that well-defined routines and procedures that lead to orderly conduct are in place AND monitors the extent to which students, parents, and community share the perception that the school environment is safe and orderly.
Developing (2)	The school leader ensures that well-defined routines and procedures that lead to orderly conduct are in place.
Beginning (1)	The school leader attempts to ensure that well-defined routines and procedures that lead to orderly conduct are in place but does not complete the task or does so partially.
Not Using (0)	The school leader does not attempt to ensure that well-defined routines and procedures that lead to orderly conduct are in place.

Sample Evidences for Domain 5, Element 4
• Clear and specific rules and procedures are in place for the running of the school.
• Social media is utilized so that students may anonymously report potential incidents.
• A system is in place for mass communicating to parents about issues regarding school safety (e.g., a callout system).
• Coordination with local law enforcement agencies regarding school safety issues is a routine event.
• Parents and community are engaged to give input regarding issues of school safety.
• When asked, parents and students describe the school as a safe place.
• When asked, parents and students describe the school as an orderly place.
• When asked, community members perceive the school as safe and orderly.
• When asked, parents, students, and community members describe the school leader as highly visible and accessible.

5(5): The school leader manages the fiscal, operational, and technological resources of the school in a way that focuses on effective instruction and the achievement of all students.

Scale Value	Description
Innovating (4)	The school leader actively seeks and procures extra resources to enhance instruction and the achievement of all students.
Applying (3)	The school leader manages the fiscal, operational, and technological resources necessary to support effective teaching AND monitors the extent to which the resources and efficiencies enhance instruction and the achievement of all students.
Developing (2)	The school leader manages the fiscal, operational, and technological resources necessary to support effective teaching.
Beginning (1)	The school leader attempts to manage the fiscal, operational, and technological resources necessary to support effective teaching but does not complete the task or does so partially.
Not Using (0)	The school leader does not attempt to manage the fiscal, operational, and technological resources necessary to support effective teaching.

Sample Evidences for Domain 5, Element 5
• Materials and resources for specific classes and courses meet the state or district specifications for those classes and courses.
• Detailed budgets are developed, submitted, and implemented.
• The school leader successfully accesses and leverages a variety of resources (e.g., grants and local, state, and federal funds).
• Data are available to show that resources and expenditures produce results (i.e., curriculum programs improve student learning).
• The school leader manages time effectively to maximize focus on instruction.
• The school leader appropriately directs the use of technology to improve teaching and learning.
• Adequate training is provided for the instructional technology teachers are expected to use.
• When asked, faculty and staff report they have adequate materials to teach effectively.
• When asked, faculty and staff report they have adequate time to teach effectively.

5(6): The school leader acknowledges the success of the whole school, as well as individuals within the school.

Scale Value	Description
Innovating (4)	The school leader actively seeks a variety of methods for acknowledging individual and school-wide success that meets the unique needs of faculty and staff.
Applying (3)	The school leader, at the appropriate time, acknowledges and celebrates the accomplishments of the school as a whole and the accomplishments of individuals within the school AND monitors the extent to which people feel honored for their contributions.
Developing (2)	The school leader, at the appropriate time, acknowledges and celebrates the accomplishments of the school as a whole and the accomplishments of individuals within the school.
Beginning (1)	The school leader attempts to acknowledge and celebrate the accomplishments of the school as a whole and the accomplishments of individuals within the school but does not complete the task or does so partially.
Not Using (0)	The school leader does not attempt to acknowledge and celebrate the accomplishments of the school as a whole or the accomplishments of individuals within the school.

Sample Evidences for Domain 5, Element 6
• The accomplishments of individual teachers, teams of teachers, and the whole school are celebrated in a variety of ways (e.g., faculty celebrations, newsletters to parents, announcements, websites, social media).
• The incremental successes of students and teachers are routinely recognized.
• The successes of the diverse school community are celebrated.
• When asked, faculty and staff report that accomplishments of the school and their individual accomplishments have been adequately acknowledged and celebrated.
• When asked, students, parents, and community report their accomplishments are adequately acknowledged and celebrated.

Endnote

1. No measurement expert says that a single score should be used as the indicator of student learning. Experts have agreed, for example, that value-added tests are useful at the state level, but that because of inherent sampling error in any measurement system, a system incorporating multiple measures is a much more reliable way to get an accurate picture of where an individual student is succeeding or failing.

   Given the technical issues that surround growth measures computed using state assessments, multiple measures seem to be an absolute necessity if we are to accurately measure the effect of teachers on students. Braun, Chudowsky, and Koenig (2010) note that this was the ultimate conclusion of the measurement experts convened by the National Research Council: "Many workshop presenters favored using value-added models in combination with other measures, particularly when high stakes are attached to results" (p. 61).

   We recommend that school leaders draw on at least five types of student growth scores to make accurate determinations. These include state VAM scores, end-of-year course or benchmark VAMs, common assessments at the unit level, student surveys, and student learning objectives (SLO) (Marzano & Toth, 2013).

References

Abrams, L. M. (2007). Implications of high stakes testing for the use of formative classroom assessment. In J. H. McMillan (Ed.), *Formative classroom assessment: Theory into practice* (pp. 79–98). New York, NY: Teachers College Press.

Alexander, K., & Entwisle, D. (1996). Schools and children at risk. In A. Booth & J. Dunn (Eds.), *Family-school links: How do they affect educational outcomes?* (pp. 67–88). Mahwah, NJ: Erlbaum.

Alonzo, R., Delgado, A., Flores, G., Garza, J., Hanson, M. Mejia, M., . . . Brown, J. (2007). *California collaborative on district reform policy briefs on California education finance and governance.* Retrieved from http://www.cacollaborative.org/sites/default/files/CA_Collaborative_CA_Education_Finance_and_Governance.pdf

Ancess, J. (2003). *Beating the odds: High schools as communities of commitment.* New York, NY: Teachers College Press.

Andrews, R., & Soder, R. (1987). *Principal leadership and student achievement. Educational Leadership, 44*(6), 9–11.

Antunez, B. (2000). When everyone is involved: Parents and communities in school reform. In *Framing effective practice.* Washington, DC: National Clearinghouse for Bilingual Education.

ASCD. (n.d.). School culture and climate. *A Lexicon of Learning.* Retrieved from http://www.ascd.org/research-a-topic/school-culture-and-climate-resources.aspx.

Astuto, T. A., Clark, D. L., Read, A-M., McGree, K., & Fernandez, L. (1993). *Challenges to dominant assumptions controlling educational reform.* Andover, MA: Regional Laboratory for the Educational Improvement of the Northeast and Islands.

Auguste, B., Kihn, P., & Miller M. (2010). *Closing the talent gap: Attracting and retaining top-third graduates to careers in teaching.* Retrieved from http://mckinseyonsociety.com/downloads/reports/Education/Closing_the_talent_gap.pdf

Baglieri, S., & Knopf, J. H. (2004). Normalizing difference in inclusive teaching. *Journal of Learning Disabilities, 37*(6), 525–529.

Barnes, V. A., Bauza, L. B., & Treiber, F. A. (2003). Impact of stress reduction on negative school behavior in adolescents. *Health and Quality of Life Outcomes, 1*(1), 10–17.

Barth, R. S. (1990). *Improving schools from within: Teachers, parents, and principals can make the difference.* San Francisco, CA: Jossey-Bass.

Bass, B. (1985). *Leadership and performance beyond expectations.* New York, NY: The Free Press.

Bass, B., & Avolio, B. (1994). *Improving organizational effectiveness through transformational leadership.* Thousand Oaks, CA: Sage.

Berry, B., Johnson, D., & Montgomery, D. (2005). The power of teacher leadership. *Educational Leadership, 62*(5), 56.

Black, P. J., & Wiliam, D. (1998a). Assessment and classroom learning. *Assessment in Education, 5*(1), 7–74.

Black, P. J., & Wiliam, D. (1998b). *Inside the black box: Raising standards through classroom assessment.* London, England: GL Assessment Limited.

Blase, J., & Blase, J. (2004). *Handbook of instructional leadership: How successful principals promote teaching and learning* (2nd ed.). Thousand Oaks, CA: Corwin Press.

Block, P. (2003). *The answer to how is yes: Acting on what matters.* San Francisco, CA: Berrett-Koehler.

Bolman, L, & Deal, T. (2003). *Reframing organizations: Artistry, choice, and leadership* (3rd ed.). San Francisco, CA: Jossey-Bass

Bosker, R. J. (1992). *The stability and consistency of school effects in primary education.* Enschede, The Netherlands: University of Twente.

Bosker, R. J., & Witziers, B. (1995). *School effects, problems, solutions, and a meta-analysis.* Paper presented at the International Congress for School Effectiveness and School Improvement, Leeuwarden, The Netherlands.

Bosker, R. J., & Witziers, B. (1996). *The magnitude of school effects. Or: Does it really matter which school a student attends?* Paper presented at the annual meeting of the American Educational Research Association, New York, NY.

Branch, G. F., Hanushek, E. A., & Rivkin, S. G. (2009). *Estimating principal effects.* Retrieved from http://www.urban.org/uploadedpdf/1001439-Estimating-Principal-Effectiveness.pdf

Branch, G. F., Hanushek, E. A., & Rivkin, S. G. (2012). *Estimating the effect of leaders on public sector productivity: The case of school principals.* Center for Analysis of Longitudinal Data in Education Research. Retrieved from http://www.caldercenter.org/upload/Hanushek_Estimating-the-Effect-of-Leaders.pdf

Braun, H., Chudowski, N., & Koenig, J. (2010). *Getting value out of value-added: Report of a workshop.* Washington, DC: National Academies Press.

Brewer, D. J., & Stacz, C. (1996). *Enhancing opportunity to learn measures in NCES data.* Santa Monica, CA: RAND.

Brookhart, S. (2010). *How to assess higher-order thinking skills in your classroom.* Alexandria, VA: ASCD.

Brown, J. S., Collins, A., & Duguid, P. (1989). Situated cognition and the culture of learning. *Educational Researcher, 18*(1) 32–42.

Bryk, A. S., Easton, J. Q., Rollow, S. G., & Sebring, P. A. (1994). The state of Chicago school reform. *Phi Delta Kappan, 76*(1), 74–78.

Burns, J. M. (1978). *Leadership.* New York, NY: Harper & Row.

Cantrell, S., & Kane, J. (2013). *Ensuring fair and reliable measures of effective teaching.* Seattle, WA: Bill and Melinda Gates Foundation. Retrieved from http://www.metproject.org/downloads/MET_Ensuring_Fair_and_Reliable_Measures_Practitioner_Brief.pdf.

Carroll, T. (2009). The next generation of learning teams. *Phi Delta Kappa, 91*(2), 8–13.

Chase, G., & Kane, M. (1983). *The principal as instructional leader: How much more time before we act?* Denver, CO: Education Commission of the States.

Christle, C. A., Jolivette, K., & Nelson, C. M. (2005). Breaking the school to prison pipeline: Identifying school risk and protective factors for youth delinquency. *Exceptionality, 13*(2), 69–88.

Chubb, J. E., & Moe, T. M. (1990). *Politics, markets and America's schools.* Washington, DC: The Brookings Institution.

City, E. A., Elmore, R. F., Fiarman, S. E., & Teitel, L. (2009). *Instructional rounds in education: A network approach to improving teaching and learning.* Cambridge, MA: Harvard Education Press.

Cizek, G. J. (2007). Formative classroom and large-scale assessment: Implications for future research and development. In J. H. McMillan (Ed.), *Formative classroom assessment: Theory into practice* (pp. 99–115). New York, NY: Teachers College Press.

Clark, D., Martorell, P., & Rockoff, J. (2009). *School principals and school performance.* Working paper 38. Washington, DC: The Urban Institute.

Clifford, M., Menon, R., Gangi, T., Condon, C., & Hornung, K. (2012). *Measuring school climate for gauging principal performance: A review of the validity and reliability of publicly accessible measures.* Washington, DC: American Institutes for Research.

Clifford, M., & Ross, S. (2011). *Designing principal evaluation: Research to guide decision-making.* Washington, DC: National Association of Elementary School Principals.

Clifford, M., & Ross, S. (2012). *Rethinking principal evaluation: A new paradigm informed by research and practice.* Retrieved from https://www.naesp.org/sites/default/files/PrincipalEvaluationReport.pdf

Condon, C., & Clifford, M. (2010). *Measuring principal performance: How rigorous are commonly used principal performance assessment instruments?* Naperville, IL: Learning Point Associates.

Conzemius, A., & O'Neill, J. (2001). *Building shared responsibility for student learning.* Alexandria, VA: ASCD.

Crosnoe, R. (2011). *Fitting in, standing out: Navigating the social challenges of high school to get an education.* Cambridge, MA: Cambridge University Press.

Darling-Hammond, L. (1994). *The current status of teaching and teacher development in the United States.* New York, NY: Teachers College, Columbia University.

Darling-Hammond, L. (1996). The quiet revolution: Rethinking teacher development. *Educational Leadership, 53*(6), 4–10.

Davis, S., Kearney, K., Sanders, N., Thomas, C., & Leon, R. (2011). *The policies and practices of principal evaluation: A review of the literature.* San Francisco, CA: WestEd.

Deering, A., Dilts, R., & Russell, J. (2003). Leadership cults and cultures. *Leader to Leader Institute, 28*, 31–38.

Del Prete, T. A. (2013). *Teacher rounds: A guide to collaborative learning in and from practice.* Thousand Oaks, CA: Corwin Press.

Demaray, M. K., & Malecki, C. K. (2002). Critical levels of perceived social support associated with student adjustment. *School Psychology Quarterly, 17*(3), 213–214.

DeVita, M. C., Colvin, R. L., Darling-Hammond, L. & Haycock, K. (2007). *Education leadership: A bridge to school reform.* New York, NY: The Wallace Foundation.

DuFour, R. (2004). What is a professional learning community? *Educational Leadership, 61*(8), 6–11.

DuFour, R., DuFour, R., Eaker, T., & Many, T. (2010). *Learning by doing: A handbook for professional communities at work.* Bloomington, IN: Solution Tree Press.

DuFour, R., & Marzano, R. J. (2011). *Leaders of learning: How district, school and classroom leaders improve student achievement.* Bloomington, IN: Solution Tree Press.

Edmonds, R. R. (1979a). *A discussion of the literature and issues related to effective schooling.* Cambridge, MA: Center for Urban Studies, Harvard Graduate School of Education.

Edmonds, R. R. (1979b, October). Effective schools for the urban poor. *Educational Leadership, 37*, 15–27.

Edmonds, R. R. (1979c). Some schools work and more can. *Social Policy, 9*, 28–32.

Edmonds, R. R. (1981a). Making public schools effective. *Social Policy, 12*(2), 56–60.

Edmonds, R. R. (1981b). A report on the research project, *"Search for effective schools . . ." and certain of the designs for school improvement that are associated with the project.* Unpublished report prepared for NIE. East Lansing, MI: The Institute for Research on Teaching, College of Education, Michigan State University.

Educational Leadership Constituencies Council. (2002). *Standards for educational leaders.* Arlington, VA: National Policy Board for Educational Administration.

Elementary and Secondary Education Act of 1965, Public Law 89-10 (1965).

Elmore, R. F. (2000). *Building a new structure for school leadership.* Washington, DC: Albert Shanker Institute.

Elmore, R. (2003).The limits of change. In Milli Pierce & Deborah Stapleton (Eds.), *The 21st-century principal: Current issues in leadership and policy* (pp. 9–17). Cambridge, MA: Harvard Education Press. Retrieved from http://files.eric.ed.gov/fulltext/ED479054.pdf

Ericsson, K. A., Krampe, R. T., & Tesch-Romer, C. (1993). The role of deliberate practice in the acquisition of expert performance. *Psychological Review, 100*(3), 363–406.

Fullan, M. (1993). *Change forces: Probing the depths of educational reform.* London, England: Falmer Press.

Fullan, M. (2000). The three stories of education reform. *Phi Delta Kappan, 81*(8), 581–584.

Fullan, M. (2007). *Leading in a culture of change.* San Francisco, CA: Jossey-Bass.

Fullan, M. (2010). *All systems go: The change imperative for whole system reform.* Thousand Oaks, CA: Corwin Press.

Fullan, M., Rolheiser, C., Mascall, B., & Edge, K. (2001). *Accomplishing large scale reform: A tri-level proposition.* Toronto, Canada: University of Toronto. Retrieved from www.michaelfullan.ca/media/13396045990.pdf

Garmezy, N. (1991). Resiliency and vulnerability to adverse developmental outcomes associated with poverty. *American Behavioral Scientist, (34)*4, 416–430.

Gastic, B. (2007). The back-to-school discount on student safety. *Teachers College Record.* Retrieved from http://www.tcrecord.org/content.asp?contentid=14581

Gates Foundation. (2013). *Ensuring fair and reliable measures of effective teaching.* Seattle, WA: Author. Retrieved from http://www.edweek.org/media/17teach-met1.pdf

Gawande, A. (2011, October 3). Personal best. *The New Yorker.* Retrieved from http://www.newyorker.com/reporting/2011/10/03/111003fa_fact_gawande

Gehrke, N. J., Knapp, M. S., & Sirotnik, K. A. (1992). In search of the school curriculum. *Review of Research in Education, 18*, 51–110.

Glanz, J. (2009). Decisions you can live with. *Principal Leadership, 10*(2), 24–28.

Goals 2000: Educate America Act, H.R. 1804,103rd Congress (1993–1994).

Goddard, R. D. (2003). Relational networks, social trust, and norms: A social capital perspective on students' chances of academic success. *Educational Evaluation and Policy Analysis, 25*(1), 59–74.

Goldring, E., Cravens, X. C., Murphy, J., Elliot, S. N., & Carson, B. (2009). The evaluation of principals: What and how do states and urban districts assess leadership? *Elementary School Journal, 110*(1), 19–39.

Goldring, E., Porter, A. C., Murphy, J., Elliott, S. N., & Cravens, X. (2007). *Assessing learning-centered leadership: Connections to research, professional standards, and current practices*. Nashville, TN: Vanderbilt University.

Graham-Clay, S. (2005). Communicating with parents: Strategies for teachers. *School Community Journal, 16*(1), 117–129.

Hallinger, P., & Heck, R. (1998). Exploring the principal's contribution to school effectiveness: 1980–1995. *School Effectiveness and School Improvement, 9*(2), 157–191.

Hattie, J. (2012). Know thy impact. *Educational Leadership, 70*(1), 18–23.

Heck, R. H., & Marcoulides, G. A. (1996). School culture and performance: Testing the invariance of an organizational model. *School Effectiveness and School Improvement, 7*(1), 76–95.

Henderson, A. T., & Berla, N. (1994). *A new generation of evidence: The family is critical to student achievement*. Washington, DC: National Committee for Citizens in Education.

Herman, J. L., Klein, D. C., & Abedi, J. (2000). Assessing students' opportunity to learn: Teacher and student perspectives. *Educational Measurement: Issues and Practice, 19*(4), 16–24.

Hirsch, L., & Lowen, C. (Producers). (2011). *Bully* [Documentary]. New York, NY: Weinstein Company & Where We Live Films.

Hollins, E. R., McIntyre, L. R., DeBose, C., Hollins, K. S., & Towner, A. (2004). Promoting a self-sustaining learning community: Investigating an internal model for teacher development. *International Journal of Qualitative Studies in Education, 17*(2), 247–264.

Hord, S. M. (1997). *Professional learning communities: Communities of continuous inquiry and improvement*. Austin, TX: Southwest Educational Development Laboratory.

Interstate School Leaders Licensure Consortium. (1996). *Standards for school leaders*. Washington, DC: Council of Chief State School Officers.

Interstate School Leaders Licensure Consortium. (2014). *2014 ISLLC Standards*. Washington, DC: Council of Chief State School Officers. Retrieved from http://blogs .edweek.org/edweek/District_Dossier/Draft%202014%20ISLLC%20Standards %2009102014.pdf

Jensen, E. (2009). *Teaching with poverty in mind: What being poor does to kids' brains and what schools can do about it*. Alexandria, VA: ASCD.

Johnson, S. M. (2010). How best to add value? Strike a balance between the individual and the organization in school reform. *Voices in Urban Education*, no. 27. Retrieved from http://www.epi.org/publication/bp249/

Kolata, G. (2007, January 3). A surprising secret to a long life: Stay in school. *The New York Times*. Retrieved from http://www.nytimes.com/2007/01/03/health/03aging .html?pagewanted=all&_r=0

Kotter, J. (2012). *The 8-step process for leading change*. Retrieved from http://www .kotterinternational.com/our-principles/changesteps/step-4

Kruse, S., Seashore-Louis, K., & Bryk, A. (1995). *Building professional learning community in schools*. Madison, WI: Center for School Organization and Restructuring.

Leana, C. (2011). The missing link in school reform. *Stanford Social Innovation Review*. Retrieved from http://www.ssireview.org/articles/entry/the_missing_link_in_ school_reform

Leithwood, K. & Riehl, C. (2003). *What do we already know about successful school leadership?* Washington, DC: AERA Division A Task Force on Developing Research in Educational Leadership.

Leithwood, K., Seashore-Louis, K., Anderson, S., & Wahlstrom, K. (2004). *Review of research: How leadership influences student learning*. Retrieved from http://www .sisd.net/cms/lib/TX01001452/Centricity/Domain/33/ReviewofResearch -LearningFromLeadership.pdf

Levine, D. U., & Lezotte, L. W. (1990). *Unusually effective schools: A review and analysis of research and practice*. Madison, WI: National Center for Effective Schools Research and Development.

Levine, D., & Lezotte, L. (1995). Effective schools research. In J. A. Banks & C. A. M. Banks (Eds.), *Handbook of research on multicultural education* (pp. 525–547). New York, NY: Macmillan.

Lieberman, A., & Mace, P. (2010). Making practice public: Teacher learning in the 21st century. *Journal of Teacher Education, 61*(12), 77–88.

Little, J. T. (2006). *Professional community and professional development in the learning-centered school*. Washington, DC: National Education Association. Retrieved from http://www.nea.org/assets/docs/HE/mf_pdreport.pdf

Loeb, S., Kalogrides, D., & Horng, E. (2010). Principal preferences and the uneven distribution of principals across schools. *Educational Evaluation and Policy Analysis, 32*(2), 205–229.

Lortie, D. C. (1975). *Schoolteacher: A sociological study*. Chicago, IL: University of Chicago Press.

Louis, K. S., Leithwood, K., Wahlstrom, K. L., & Anderson, S. E. (2010). *Investigating the links to improved student learning: Final report of research findings*. New York, NY: The Wallace Foundation.

McCauley, C., & Van Velsor, E. (2003). *The Center for Creative Leadership handbook of leadership development*. San Francisco, CA: Jossey-Bass.

Makiewicz, M. K. (2011). *An investigation of teacher trust in the principal* (Doctoral Dissertation). Retrieved from UMI Dissertations. (Order No. 3465350).

Marzano, R. J. (2000). *A new era of school reform: Going where the research takes us*. Denver, CO: McREL.

Marzano, R. J. (2003). *What works in schools: Translating research into action*. Alexandria, VA: ASCD.

Marzano, R. J. (2004). *Validity and reliability report for the snapshot survey of school effectiveness factors*. Englewood, CO: Marzano and Associates.

Marzano, R. J. (2011). Art and science of teaching: What teachers gain from deliberate practice. *Educational Leadership, 68*(4), 82–85.

Marzano, R. J. (2012). The two purposes of teacher evaluation. *Educational Leadership, 70*(3), 14–19.

Marzano, R. J. (2013). *Becoming a high reliability school: The next step in school reform.* Centennial, CO: Marzano Research Laboratory.

Marzano, R. J., & Toth, M. D. (2013). *Teacher evaluation that makes a difference: A new model for teacher growth and student achievement.* Alexandria, VA: ASCD.

Marzano, R. J., & Waters, T. (2009). *District leadership that works: Striking the right balance.* Bloomington, IN: Solution Tree Press.

Marzano, R. J., Waters, T., & McNulty, B. A. (2005). *School leadership that works: From research to results.* Alexandria, VA: ASCD.

Marzano Research Laboratory. (2011). *What works in Oklahoma schools: Phase I state report.* Englewood, CO: Author.

Mayer, D. P., Mullins, J. F., Moore, M. T., & Ralph, J. (2000). *Monitoring school quality: Staff satisfaction with administration. An indicators report.* Washington, DC: U.S. Department of Education, Office of Education Research and Improvement, National Center on Education Statistics, 2000-030.

MetLife. (2009). *The MetLife Survey of the American Teacher: Collaborating for Student Success.* Retrieved from http://www.eric.ed.gov/PDFS/ED509650.pdf

MetLife. (2012). *The MetLife survey of the American teacher.* Retrieved from https://www.metlife.com/assets/cao/foundation/MetLife-Teacher-Survey-2012.pdf

Michigan State University. (2004, December). School climate and learning. *Best Practice Briefs.* Retrieved from http://outreach.msu.edu/bpbriefs/issues/brief31.pdf

Mishook, J. (2011). *Supporting the collective practice of teachers. Annenberg Institute for School Reform.* Retrieved from http://annenberginstitute.org/commentary/2011/06/supporting-collective-practice-teachers

Moorman, R. H., & Grover, S. (2009). Why does leader integrity matter to followers? An uncertainty management-based explanation. *International Journal of Leadership Studies, 5*(2), 102–114.

Murphy, J. (2014). *2014 ISLLC Standards for school leaders.* Manuscript in preparation.

Murphy, J., Beck, L. G., Crawford, M., Hodges, A., & McGaughy, C. L. (2001). The productive high school: Creating personalized academic communities. Thousand Oaks, CA: Corwin Press.

Murphy, J., & Torre, D. (2014). *Creating productive cultures in schools: For students, teachers, and parents.* Corwin Press. Thousand Oaks, CA.

National School Climate Center, the Center for Social and Emotional Education, & the National Center for Learning and Citizenship at the Education Commission of the States. (2007). *The school climate challenge: Narrowing the gap between school climate research and school climate policy, practice guidelines and teacher education policy.* Retrieved from http://www.ecs.org/html/projectspartners/nclc/docs/school-climate-challenge-web.pdf

Newmann, F., & Wehlage, G. (1995). *Success school restructuring: A report to the public and educators by the Center for Restructuring Schools.* Madison: University of Wisconsin.

Nye, K., Capelluti, J. & (2003). Old stories for new leaders: The ABCs of decision making. *Principal Leadership, 3*(9), 8–9.

No Child Left Behind Act, Public Law 107-110, §7801[37] (2001).

Oakes, J. (1989). What educational indicators? The case for assessing the school context. *Educational Evaluation and Policy Analysis, 11*(2), 181–199.

Office of Innovation and Improvement—United States Department of Education. (2007). *Choosing a school for your child.* Retrieved from https://www2.ed.gov/ parents/schools/find/choose/choosing.pdf

Office of Superintendent of Public Instruction, Olympia, Washington. (2004). *Characteristics of improved school districts: Themes from research.* Retrieved from http://www.k12.wa.us/research/pubdocs/districtimprovementreport.pdf

Partnership for 21st Century Skills. (2002). *Learning for the 21st century: A report and mile guide for 21st century skills.* Retrieved from http://www.p21.org/storage/ documents/P21_Report.pdf

Patchin, J. W. (2012a). *A positive school climate makes everything possible.* Cyberbullying Research Center. Retrieved from http://cyberbullying.us/a-positive-school -climate-makes-everything-possible/

Patchin, J. W. (2012b). *School climate and cyberbullying: An empirical link.* Cyberbullying Research Center. Retrieved from http://cyberbullying.us/school-climate-and -cyberbullying-an-empirical-link/

Phillips, J. (2003). Powerful learning: Creating learning communities in urban school reform. *Journal of Curriculum and Supervision, 18*(3), 240–258.

Pierce, P. R. (1935). *The origin and development of the public school principalship.* Chicago, IL: University of Chicago Press.

Pittman, K. J. (2010). College and career readiness. *The School Administrator, 6*(67), 10–14.

Portin, B. S., Feldman, S., & Knapp, M. S. (2006). *Purposes, uses, and practices of leadership assessment in education.* Seattle: Center for the Study of Teaching and Policy, University of Washington.

Preuss, P. G. (2003). *School leader's guide to root cause analysis: Using data to dissolve problems.* Larchmont, NY: Eye on Education.

Programme for International Student Assessment. (2012). *PISA 2012 results in focus: What 15-year-olds know and what they can do with what they know.* Retrieved from www.oecd.org/pisa/keyfindings/pisa-2012-results-overview.pdf

Reeves, D. B. (2009). *Leading change in your school: How to conquer myths, build commitment, and get results.* Alexandria, VA: ASCD.

Resmovits, J. (2014, January 10). How the Common Core became education's biggest bogeyman. *Huff Post Political.* Retrieved from http://www.huffingtonpost .com/2014/01/10/common-core_n_4537284.html

Ripley, A. (2013). *The smartest kids in the world: And how they got that way.* New York, NY: Simon & Schuster.

Robitaille, D. (Ed.). (1993). *Curriculum frameworks for mathematics and science.* Vancouver, Canada: Pacific Educational Press.

Rumberger, R. W. (2011). *Dropping out: Why students drop out of high school and what can be done about it.* Cambridge, MA: Harvard University Press.

Sammons, P. (1999). *School effectiveness: Coming of age in the twenty-first century.* Lisse, The Netherlands: Swets and Zeitlinger.

Sammons, P., Hillman, J., & Mortimore, P. (1995). *Key characteristics of effective schools: A review of school effectiveness research.* London, England: Office of Standards in Education and Institute of Education.

Schachter, R. (2013, January 11). Priming principal pipelines. *District Administration.* Retrieved from www.districtadministration.com/article/priming-principal -pipelines

Scheerens, J. (1992). *Effective schooling: Research, theory, and practice.* London, England: Cassell.

Scheerens, J., & Bosker, R. (1997). *The foundations of educational effectiveness.* New York, NY: Elsevier.

Scherer, M. (2001). How and why standards can improve student achievement: A conversation with Robert J. Marzano. *Educational Leadership, 59*(1), 14–18.

Schlechty, P. (2009). *Leading for learning: How to transform schools into learning organizations.* San Francisco, CA: Jossey-Bass.

Scholastic & the Gates Foundation. (2012). *Primary sources: 2012.* Retrieved from http://www.scholastic.com/primarysources/pdfs/Gates2012_full.pdf

Seashore-Louis, K., Leithwood, K., Wahlstrom, K., & Anderson, S. (2010). *Learning from leadership: Investigating the links to improved student learning.* Retrieved from http://www.wallacefoundation.org/knowledge-center/school-leadership/ key-research/Pages/Investigating-the-Links-to-Improved-Student-Learning .aspx

Senechal, D. (2011, February 9). The NYS teaching standards: Too many, too broad? (Web log). *Chalkbeat New York.* Retrieved from http://ny.chalkbeat.org/2011/ 02/09/the-nys-teaching-standards-too-many-too-broad/#.VHqEQcnzuu8

Senge, P. (1990). *The fifth discipline: The art and practice of the learning organization.* New York, NY: Doubleday.

Sergiovanni, T. J. (2004). Building a community of hope. *Educational Leadership, 61*(8), 33–37.

Shannon, G. S., & Bylsma, P. (2004). *Characteristics of improved school districts: Themes from research.* Olympia, WA: OSPI.

Shen, J., Cooley, V., Ma, X., Reeves, P., Burt, W., Rainey, M., & Wen Y. (2007). *Data-informed decision-making on high-impact strategies: A measurement tool for school principals.* Kalamazoo, MI: Michigan Coalition of Educational Leadership.

Showers, B., Murphy, C., & Joyce, B. (1996). The River City program: Staff development becomes school improvement. In B. Joyce & E. Calhoun (Eds.), *Learning experiences in school renewal: An exploration of five successful programs* (pp. 13–51). Eugene, OR: ERIC Clearinghouse on Educational Management. (ERIC Document Reproduction Service No. ED 401 600).

Silins, H. C., Mulford, W. R., & Zarins, S. (2002). Organizational learning and school change. *Educational Administration Quarterly, 38*(5), 613–642.

Southern Regional Education Board. (2010). *The three essentials: Improving schools requires district vision, district and state support, and principal leadership.* Atlanta, GA: Author. Retrieved from http://publications.sreb.org/2010/10V16_Three_ Essentials.pdf

Sparks, D. (2004). Broader purpose calls for higher understanding: An interview with Andy Hargreaves. *Journal of Staff Development, 25*(2), 46–50.

Stallworth, J. T., & Williams, D. L. (1982). *A survey of parents regarding parent involvement in schools.* Austin, TX: Southwest Education Development Laboratory.

Stiggins, R. J. (1996). *Student-centered classroom assessment.* New York, NY: Macmillan College.

Strahan, D. (2003). Promoting a collaborative professional culture in three elementary schools that have beaten the odds. *The Elementary School Journal, 104*(2), 127–146.

Supovitz, J. A. (2002). Developing communities of instructional practice. *Teachers College Record, 104*(8), 1591–1626.

Supovitz, J. A. (2008). Instructional influence in American high schools. In M. M. Mangin & S. Stoelinga (Eds.), *Effective teacher leadership: Using research to inform and reform* (pp. 144–162). New York, NY: Teachers College Press.

Supovitz, J. A., & Christman, J. B. (2003). *Developing communities of instructional practice: Lessons for Cincinnati and Philadelphia.* (CPRE Policy Briefs). Philadelphia: University of Pennsylvania, Graduate School of Education.

Tangri, S., & Moles, O. (1987). Parents and the community. In V. Richardson-Koehler (Ed.), *Educators' handbook: A research perspective* (2nd ed., pp. 519–550). New York, NY: Longman.

Thomas, D. W., Holdaway, E., & Ward, K. (2000). Policies and practices involved in the evaluation of school principals. *Journal of Personnel Evaluation in Education, 14*(3), 215–240.

Toch, T., & Rothman, R. (2008). *Rush to judgment: Teacher evaluation in public education.* Washington, DC: Education Sector.

The New Teacher Project. (2010). *Teacher evaluation 2.0.* Retrieved from http://tntp .org/assets/documents/Teacher-Evaluation-Oct10F.pdf?files/Teacher -Evaluation-Oct10F.pdf

The New Teacher Project. (2013). *Perspectives of irreplaceable teachers: What America's best teachers think about teaching.* Retrieved from http://tntp.org/assets/documents/ TNTP_Perspectives_2013.pdf

Ujifusa, A. (2014, January 7). State lawmakers face tough choices on Common Core. *Education Week.* Retrieved from http://www.edweek.org/ew/articles/2014/ 01/08/15sessions_ep.h33.html?qs=270+unique+bills

University of California–Irvine. (2008, March 13). Short-term stress can affect learning and memory. *Science Daily.* Retrieved from www.sciencedaily.com/releases/ 2008/03/080311182434.htm

U.S. Department of Education. (2009a). *Mapping state proficiency standards onto NAEP scales: 2005–2007.* Retrieved from http://nces.ed.gov/nationsreportcard/pdf/ studies/2010456.pdf

U.S. Department of Education. (2009b). *Race to the Top program: Executive summary.* Washington, DC: Author.

U.S. Department of Education. (2011). *Great teachers and great leaders: A blueprint for reform.* Retrieved from http://www2.ed.gov/policy/elsec/leg/blueprint/ publication_pg5.html

Van Driel, J. H., & De Jong, O. (2001). *Investigating the development of preservice teachers' pedagogical content knowledge.* Paper presented at the 2001 Annual Meeting of the National Association for Research and Science Teaching, St. Louis, MO. Retrieved from http://course.zjnu.cn/kcjx/uploadfile/200812322335739.pdf

The Wallace Foundation (2012). *The school principal as leader: Guiding schools to better teaching and learning.* New York, NY: Author.

Waters, J. T., & Marzano, R. J. (2006). *School leadership that works: The effect of superintendent leadership on student achievement.* Denver, CO: Mid-continent Research for Education and Learning.

Waters, J. T., Marzano, R. J., & McNulty, B. A. (2003). *Balanced leadership: What 30 years of research tells us about the effect of leadership on student achievement.* Aurora, CO: Mid-continent Research for Education and Learning.

Weisberg, D., Sexton, S., Mulhern, J., & Keeling, D. (2009). *The widget effect: Our national failure to acknowledge and act on differences in teacher effectiveness.* Brooklyn, NY: The New Teacher Project. Retrieved from http://widgeteffect.org/downloads/The WidgetEffect.pdf

Wellisch, J., MacQueen, A. H., Carriere, R. A., & Duck, G. A. (1978). School management and organization in successful schools. *Sociology of Education, 51*(3), 211–226.

Wiliam, D., & Leahy, S. (2007). A theoretical foundation for formative assessment. In J. H. McMillan (Ed.), *Formative classroom assessment: Theory into practice* (pp. 29–42). New York, NY: Teachers College Press.

Wiliam, D. (2012, November 2). *Embedding formative assessment with teacher learning communities.* Paterson Stadium, Subiaco, Australia. Assessment Institute Workshop.

Young, J., Sheets, J., & Knight, D. (2005). *Mentoring principals: Frameworks, agendas, tips, and case stories for mentors and mentees.* Thousand Oaks, CA: Corwin Press.

Index